THE BEST IN TENT CAMPING

MONTANA

Other titles in the series:

The Best in Tent Camping: The Carolinas
The Best in Tent Camping: Colorado
The Best in Tent Camping: Florida
The Best in Tent Camping: Georgia
The Best in Tent Camping: Minnesota
The Best in Tent Camping: Missouri and the Ozarks
The Best in Tent Camping: New England
The Best in Tent Camping: New Jersey
The Best in Tent Camping: Northern California
The Best in Tent Camping: Oregon
The Best in Tent Camping: The Southern Appalachian and Smoky Mountains
The Best in Tent Camping: Southern California
The Best in Tent Camping: Tennessee and Kentucky
The Best in Tent Camping: Virginia
The Best in Tent Camping: Washington
The Best in Tent Camping: West Virginia
The Best in Tent Camping: Wisconsin

THE BEST IN TENT CAMPING

A GUIDE FOR CAR CAMPERS WHO HATE RVs, CONCRETE SLABS, AND LOUD PORTABLE STEREOS

MONTANA

KEN AND VICKY SODERBERG

MENASHA RIDGE PRESS
BIRMINGHAM, ALABAMA

To Tyler, who traveled with us from Ekalaka to Yaak:
thank you for your love, your patience, your laughter,
and for reminding us to have fun (and ice cream) along the way.

Printed in the United States of America
Published by Menasha Ridge Press
Distributed by the Globe Pequot Press
First edition, first printing

Library of Congress Cataloging in Publication
Soderberg, Vicky.
The best in tent camping, Montana : a guide for campers who hate RVs, concrete slabs, and loud portable stereos / by Vicky Soderberg and Ken Soderberg.—1st ed.
p.cm.
Includes bibliographical references (p.) and index
ISBN 0-89732-598-2
1. Campsites, facilities, etc.—Montana—Guidebooks. 2. Camping—Montana—Guidebooks.
3 Montana—Guidebooks. I. Soderberg, Ken. II. Title.
GV191.42M9S63 2005
917.86'068—dc22

2005041662

Cover and text design by Ian Szymkowiak, Palace Press International, Inc.
Cover photo by Robert Harding Picture Library Ltd./Alamy
Maps by Jennie Zehmer
Indexing by Galen Schroeder

Menasha Ridge Press
P.O. Box 43673
Birmingham, Alabama 35243
www.menasharidge.com

TABLE OF CONTENTS

SOUTH CENTRAL MONTANA

SOUTHWEST MONTANA

APPENDIXES

MONTANA MAPS KEY

NORTHWEST MONTANA

1 BAD MEDICINE CAMPGROUND
2 BIG ARM STATE PARK CAMPGROUND
3 BIG CREEK CAMPGROUND
4 BIG THERRIAULT CAMPGROUND
5 CUTBANK CAMPGROUND
6 FISH CREEK CAMPGROUND
7 HOLLAND LAKE CAMPGROUND
8 KINTLA LAKE CAMPGROUND
9 LAKE ALVA CAMPGROUND
10 PETE CREEK CAMPGROUND
11 PETERS CREEK CAMPGROUND
12 SPRAGUE CREEK CAMPGROUND
13 THOMPSON FALLS STATE PARK CAMPGROUND

NORTH CENTRAL MONTANA

14 CAVE MOUNTAIN CAMPGROUND
15 HOME GULCH CAMPGROUND
16 INDIAN HILL CAMPGROUND
17 KADING CAMPGROUND
18 LOGGING CREEK CAMPGROUND
19 MANY PINES CAMPGROUND
20 PARK LAKE CAMPGROUND
21 THAIN CREEK CAMPGROUND
22 WOOD LAKE CAMPGROUND

EASTERN MONTANA

23 BEAVER CREEK COUNTY PARK CAMPGROUND
24 CAMP CREEK CAMPGROUND
25 CRYSTAL LAKE CAMPGROUND
26 MAKOSHIKA STATE PARK CAMPGROUNDS
27 SAGE CREEK CAMPGROUND

SOUTH CENTRAL MONTANA

28 BEAVER CREEK CAMPGROUNDS
29 FALLS CREEK CAMPGROUND
30 GREENOUGH LAKE CAMPGROUND
31 HALFMOON CAMPGROUND
32 HOOD CREEK CAMPGROUND
33 POTOSI CAMPGROUND
34 SHERIDAN CAMPGROUND
35 SWAN CREEK CAMPGROUND
36 TOM MINER CAMPGROUND
37 WADE LAKE AREA CAMPGROUND
38 WEST FORK MADISON DISPERSED SITES

SOUTHWEST MONTANA

39 BANNACK STATE PARK CAMPGROUND
40 CHARLES WATERS CAMPGROUND
41 DALLES CAMPGROUND
42 GRASSHOPPER CAMPGROUND
43 LOST CREEK STATE PARK CAMPGROUND
44 MARTIN CREEK CAMPGROUND
45 MINER LAKE CAMPGROUND
46 PHILIPSBURG BAY CAMPGROUND
47 RESERVOIR LAKE CAMPGROUND
48 ROCK CREEK DISPERSED SITES
49 TWIN LAKES CAMPGROUND
50 UPPER LAKE COMO CAMPGROUND

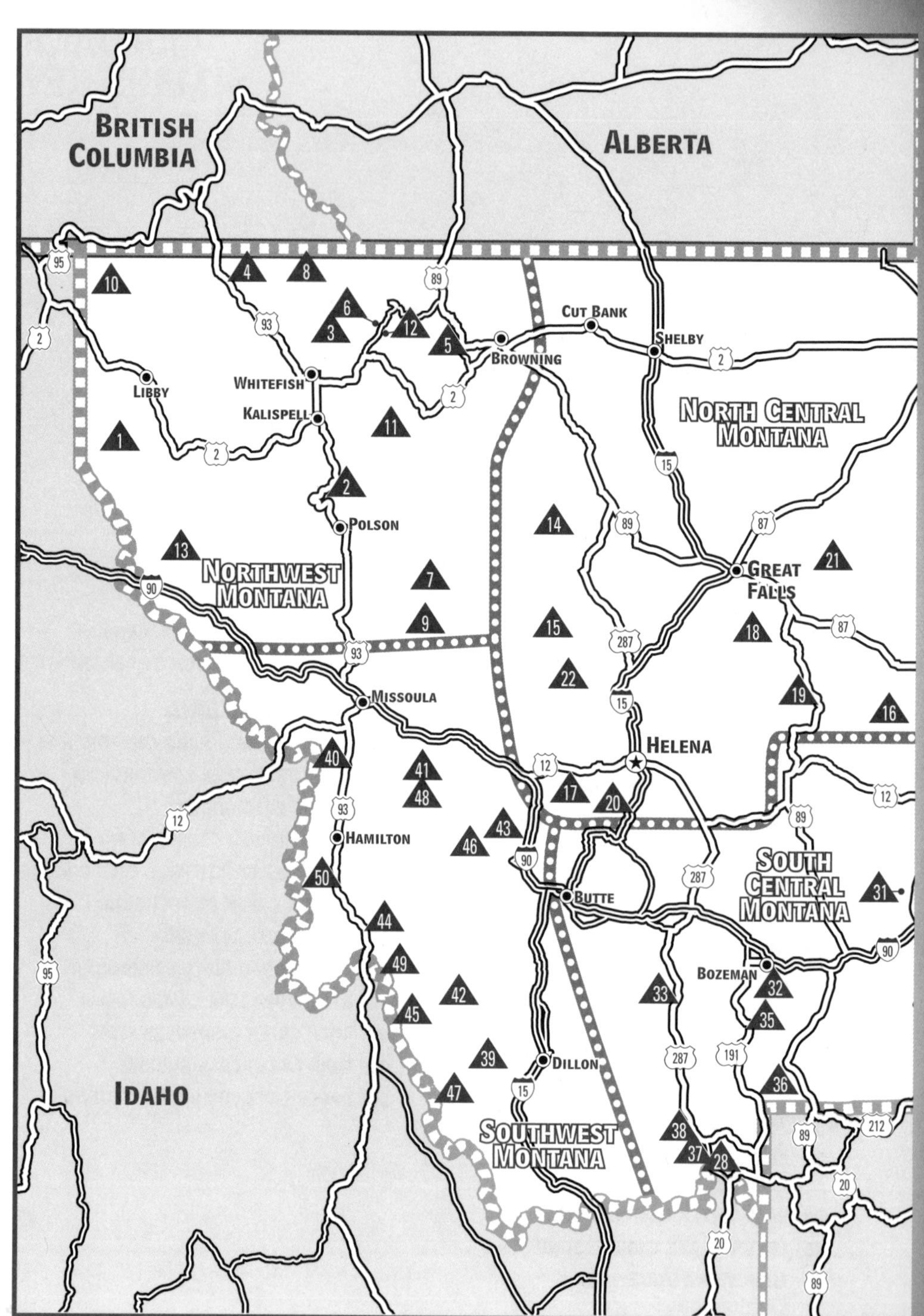
BRITISH COLUMBIA
ALBERTA
IDAHO
NORTHWEST MONTANA
NORTH CENTRAL MONTANA
SOUTH CENTRAL MONTANA
SOUTHWEST MONTANA
LIBBY
WHITEFISH
KALISPELL
POLSON
MISSOULA
HAMILTON
CUT BANK
SHELBY
BROWNING
GREAT FALLS
HELENA
BUTTE
BOZEMAN
DILLON

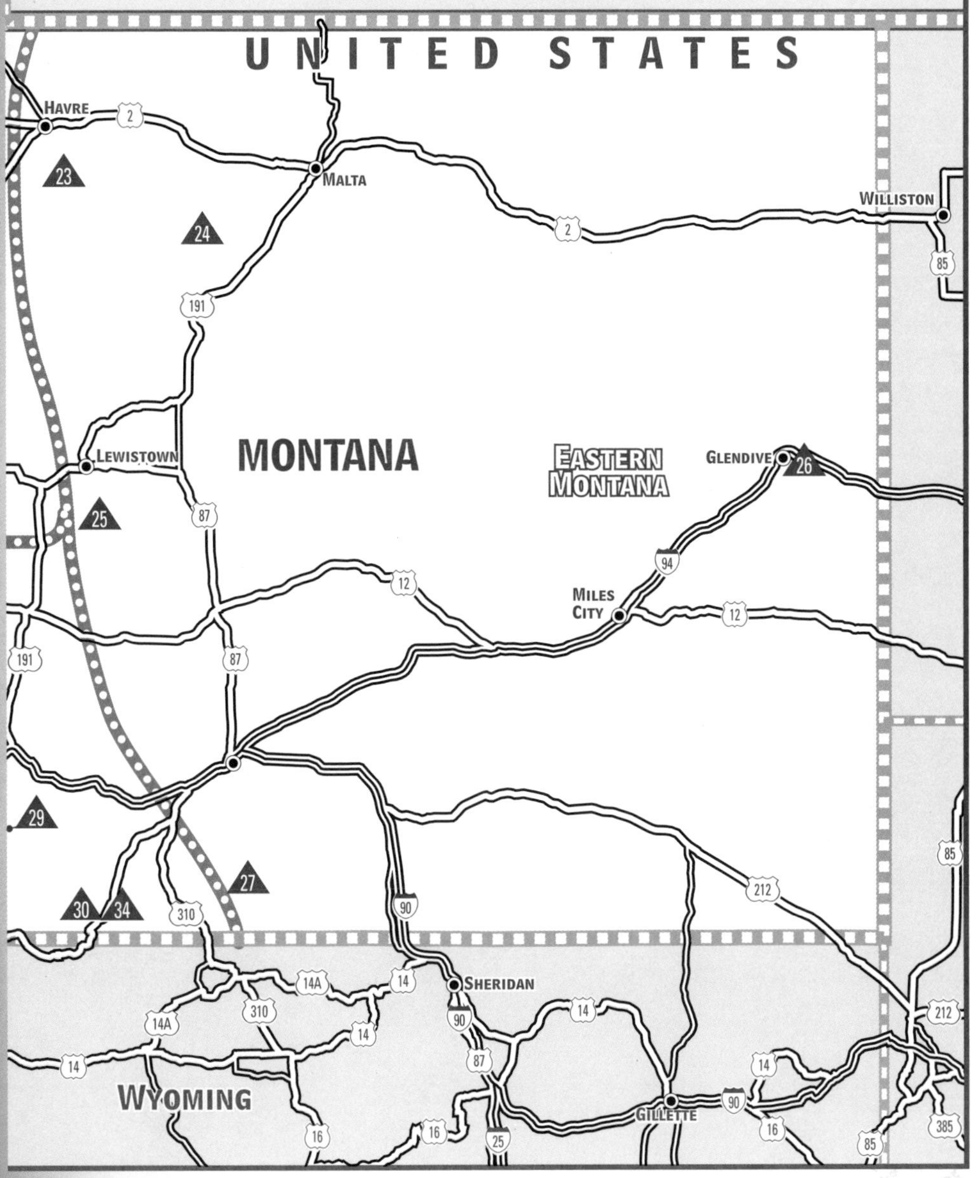

MONTANA CAMPGROUND LOCATOR
SASKATCHEWAN
CANADA
UNITED STATES
HAVRE
MALTA
WILLISTON
LEWISTOWN
MONTANA
EASTERN MONTANA
GLENDIVE
MILES CITY
SHERIDAN
WYOMING
GILLETTE

MAP LEGEND

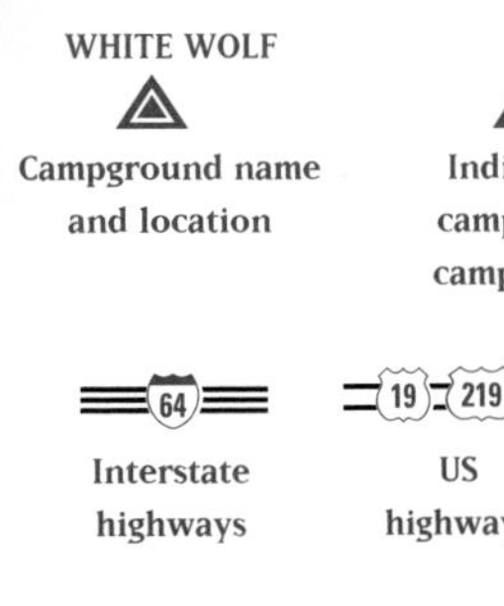
WHITE WOLF
Campground name and location
Interstate highways
64

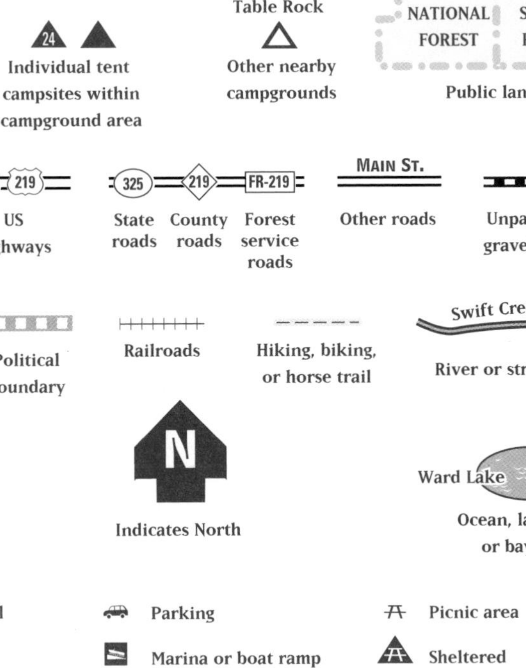
24
Individual tent campsites within campground area
Table Rock
Other nearby campgrounds
NATIONAL FOREST
STATE PARK
Public lands
19
219
US highways
325
State roads
219
County roads
FR-219
Forest service roads
MAIN ST.
Other roads
Unpaved or gravel roads
Political boundary
Railroads
Hiking, biking, or horse trail
Swift Creek
River or stream
Asheville
City or town
N
Indicates North
Ward Lake
Ocean, lake, or bay

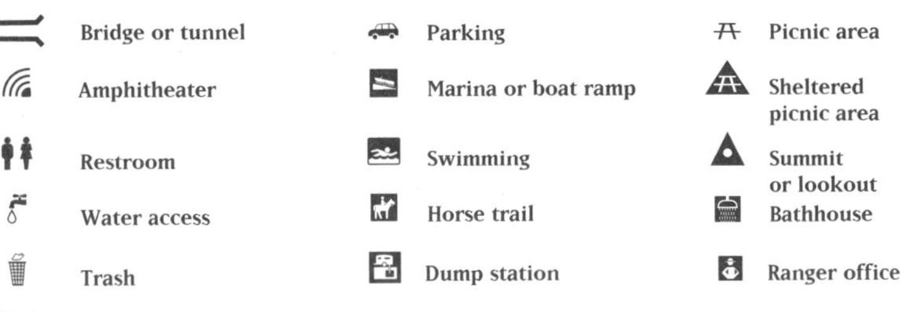
Bridge or tunnel
Amphitheater
Restroom
Water access
Trash
Wheelchair accessible
Parking
Marina or boat ramp
Swimming
Horse trail
Dump station
Picnic area
Sheltered picnic area
Summit or lookout
Bathhouse
Ranger office

ACKNOWLEDGMENTS

THANK YOU TO:

- The dedicated state and federal employees who took time to answer questions, dig up information and maps, and review our final product
- The campground hosts who shared their enthusiasm with us and often invited us in for a cup of coffee
- Russell Helms, Christina Crowe, and the crew at Menasha Ridge for their patience and professionalism
- The 4th Day boys—Bill, Chuck, Tripp, and Tom—for their suggestions and encouragement
- Our parents, Ken and Hanne Soderberg and Paul and Carol Schwan, for nurturing our love of road trips
- Our beautiful daughters, Betsy and Ellen, for their love and support and for not being jealous that since they are all grown up they had to spend the summer working while Tyler had all the fun

PREFACE

WHEN WE WERE GROWING UP our family's vacations were quite different. Ken's family loaded up five kids in the station wagon and headed out for the annual two-week vacation equipped with Coleman sleeping bags, gas lantern and stove, a canvas tent, and a popup trailer. They camped across North America, touring the mountains, shorelines, and National Parks.

Vicky's vacations included only four kids in the station wagon, and her family never packed sleeping bags or tents. They visited historic sites, amusement parks, and museums, and attended as many Cubs games as possible. Vicky did go to Girl Scouts camp, but her wilderness experience was pretty limited.

We got married while Ken was in college, and for graduation he received a family-sized tent from Vicky's family (go figure!). That tent housed our brood of three—Betsy, Ellen, and Tyler—in some of the most beautiful places on Earth. Nearly 25 years later, we're still tenting it. We enjoy waking to the subtle morning sounds and the burst of sunlight that awaits when the door zips open to reveal a new day.

But the world around us keeps changing. RVs continue to get more luxurious and people are willing to drag and drive them to more remote places, often squeezing them into very tiny sites. As we found while researching this book, it's getting tough to find campgrounds that aren't overrun with RVs.

For Ken, camping means leaving the car miles behind and hiking to a setting near a creek or lake to pitch a tent and soak in the view. For Vicky, it includes the creek or lake but it also means meeting some basic necessities—a clean outhouse, a picnic table, and a fire beside which to read. We chose places reachable by car that came close to meeting both our requirements. At most of these campgrounds you will probably have a few RVs for neighbors, but each site offers something unique, outweighing any negatives.

There are at least a few, previously excellent campgrounds that are not listed either because they were closed due to recent fire damage or for renovation. We'll have to catch them in the next edition.

Throughout the national forests there are also thousands of acres open to dispersed camping. Seek out one of these (many are along forest roads) and try spending at least one night where it's just you and the wilderness, and maybe you're a bit outside your comfort level. Be sure you know how to protect yourself, your food, and your belongings from the local wildlife and PLEASE take any fire restrictions seriously.

To say the 50 campgrounds listed here are definitively the best in the state would be inaccurate. This is a subjective list of many of the best based upon our travels to more than 300 public campgrounds throughout Montana. We know you'll discover personal favorites and we hope that you'll share your discoveries with us.

Montana is a vast, dynamic wonderland with a special place just waiting for you. Enjoy the adventure!

THE BEST IN TENT CAMPING

A GUIDE FOR CAR CAMPERS WHO HATE RVs, CONCRETE SLABS, AND LOUD PORTABLE STEREOS

MONTANA

INTRODUCTION

A Word about This Book and Montana Tent Camping

MONTANA IS A BIG STATE. Don't be fooled by its comparable size in an atlas. The reality is that 53 of the 56 counties are individually bigger than Rhode Island, and it's farther from Yaak to Alzada than it is from Washington, D.C., to Chicago or Jacksonville, Florida. Travel in Montana is an exhilarating adventure. We've experienced flat tires, blown engines, and closed roads, as well as unexpected sightings of bighorn sheep, moose, and bears. We've followed roads on the highway map that were nothing more than tire ruts and awakened to six inches of snow in August, subfreezing temperatures in July, and seemingly endless days of sunshine. We can also confirm that when a tree falls in the woods (or in our case, just up the hill from our campsite) it does make a sound.

Montana is also a landscape of breathtaking diversity. We've stood atop the Continental Divide and hiked trails in the Crazies, the Big Belts, the Bridgers, the Tobacco Roots, and the Missions. Each has its own unique characteristics. We never tire of spring wildflowers or watching waterfalls created by the icy cold spring runoff. We welcome summer-afternoon thunderstorms that roll across the sky, drench us, and leave behind spectacular rainbows. We marvel at cool fall days with their splashes of yellows and oranges set against the deep blue sky, and we can even appreciate those winter weekends where the temperature swings from 30 above on Friday to 30 below by Saturday afternoon.

Yes, Montana is a land of extremes. Summers are typically warm and dry, but you should be prepared for any kind of weather. Snow in July at higher elevations is not uncommon, and sudden rainstorms can make roads dangerous and impassable. The same type of hailstorms that menaced the Lewis and Clark expedition may pummel your outing. It's nothing to worry about if you are prepared and take proper precautions.

Being prepared is a constant challenge, since being totally prepared for every possibility would involve more gear than any vehicle can hold. Planning ahead and getting current information is key. Check the weather report and contact local agencies (remembering that most are only open on weekdays). State road conditions are available 24 hours a day by calling 511 from any phone.

Cell phone coverage is spotty to nonexistent in many areas of Montana. Once you get off the interstates and away from the bigger cities, you can't depend on service, and many providers don't offer service in Montana at all. Carry a phone card as backup, since pay phones are usually available even in the tiniest of crossroad towns.

One of our most recent challenges occurred while driving south through a burn area on the Inside North Fork Road in Glacier National Park. A storm was moving in, and as we rounded a curve, we found the road blocked by a large tree with another car already stopped ahead of us. Turning around wasn't much of an option since the high winds made the odds of meeting the same type of obstacle pretty high.

There we were: four adults, a 13-year-old, a rental car, and our 1987 four-wheel-drive station wagon versus a 30-foot tree with not an ax, hatchet, rope, or chainsaw between us. The wind blew, the rain came, and we worked together, removing brush on the hillside, levering, brainstorming, and laughing. A third vehicle pulled up and let us know we really were trapped: another tree was down a few miles in the other direction. Adding two more adults helped some; we now had more brains and a little more brawn but still no equipment.

We found a hammock and some rope in our gear, and by attaching it to the wagon, around a standing tree, and then to the downed tree, and with everyone else working with levers we managed to move the tree about three inches. We regrouped, reattached, and inch-by-inch pivoted the trunk across the road. It was a great exercise in perseverance, resourcefulness, and teamwork among strangers. Thanks to Bill and Martina Owens and Jim and Caroline Cochran for being part of our adventure.

THE RATING SYSTEM

Each of the campground descriptions includes a rating system for beauty, site privacy, site spaciousness, quiet, security, and cleanliness, and each attribute is ranked with one to five stars with five being the best. We know these are subjective, but we've tried to select campgrounds that offer something for everyone.

BEAUTY

Exceptional scenery is practically a given throughout Montana, but the five-star sites will provide excellent views, and you will know you're in a special place. The campground will be oriented to blend with and complement the natural surroundings, with the sounds and smells of nature rounding out the experience.

SITE PRIVACY

Ideally, trees, shrubs, and boulders or other natural features will be left in place or incorporated into the site development to offer privacy and barriers between adjacent sites. The best campgrounds have well-spaced sites with little visual contact between neighbors and a sense of solitude due to the campground's distance from the nearest roads and towns.

SITE SPACIOUSNESS

Spacious to us means plenty of room for two tents to be set back from the parking area and away from the fire ring. There should also be space for separate areas to cook, eat, and just kick back without being on top of your neighbors.

QUIET

Our top rating for quiet means little or no overhead or road noise, minimal social noise, an aura of solitude, and quiet hours enforced by staff (if there is any). It was a plus if we could hear the water from a nearby river or stream, birds singing, or the wind through the trees. Quiet is a difficult attribute to quantify since we all know it can change quickly, depending on your neighbor.

SECURITY

Many sites have no on-site host, but those that do and those where there is cell phone coverage (or a pay phone) received higher ratings. We also looked for the absence of vandalism.

CLEANLINESS

Everyone wants to see restrooms, fire pits, and picnic tables that are clean and a campground free of ground litter. If the site was well maintained—signs in good repair and up-to-date, buildings in good repair, and roads maintained—the campground received high marks. Signs of noxious weeds that were out of control resulted in a lower rating.

HELPFUL HINTS

Be sure you are equipped with a state highway map, and if you're venturing off the main roads, a copy of DeLorme's *Montana Atlas & Gazetteer* is a must, along with Forest Service travel-plan maps.

Rain may come at any time, but keep in mind that weather patterns are most likely to change in the late afternoon when warm and cool air begin to mix. Winds may kick up with little warning, so stay alert if you're floating on lakes or rivers. Summer afternoons often bring intense but short rainstorms with lightning and hail followed by spectacular rainbows and interesting, low cloud formations. Know what to do and how to seek safe shelter when these storms hit.

The weather is part of what makes Montana such a wonderful, magical place. Watching ominous thunderheads roll across the undulating landscape and transform into early evening skies filled with glowing clouds of pink, blue, and orange against a mountain backdrop takes your breath away. Waking on a cool, damp morning to see a snowcapped mountaintop peeking out above the low-lying fog intensifies feelings of solitude and peacefulness. Don't let the weather's unpredictability frighten you off; just pay attention to the changes and be prepared. Along with your shorts and camera, throw in some warm clothing and good raingear.

With a good map, plenty of water, decent tires (including a spare filled with air), and a full gas tank, you should be able to tackle the route to any campground in this book. Be sure to bring your own firewood and check locally or with the agency managing your campground for fire restrictions. During the summer fire season, restrictions may be enacted ranging from no open campfires tototal restrictions and closures of areas.

During particularly dry periods, we've seen the fire-danger level go from moderate to high to extreme in a single afternoon, and orange and red restriction signs can appear on outhouse doors overnight. At a minimum, always keep a full water bucket nearby and pack a small shovel. Campfires must be built in a ring or other designated fire enclosure and should never be left unattended. Cigarettes should always be extinguished and disposed of in an appropriate container. Don't experience your 15 minutes of fame as the person whose carelessness started a fire that destroyed thousands of acres, homes, and lives.

NORTHWEST **MONTANA**

BAD MEDICINE CAMPGROUND

Troy

DRIVING THE DENSELY FORESTED access road to this campground provides a strong contrast to the dramatic peaks you see to the east along MT 56. Part of the 94,000-acre Cabinet Mountain Wilderness, these mountains top out at under 7,000 feet but seem to tower over the landscape. It's not an optical illusion. The fact that their base elevations are so low provides 4,000 feet of visible mountainside, making them just as impressive as the 10,000-foot peaks around Red Lodge.

Nearby Ross Creek Cedars is as close as Montana gets to a rain forest.

In this peaceful setting on the southwest corner of Bull Lake, you'll find a variety of options under the conifer canopy. The well-spaced sites are level, and tents definitely rule the upper bluff-top loop. The sites there are plentiful and spacious, and it's easy to orient your camp to create privacy. Sites 3, 4, and 12 through 15 are best for tenters, especially family groups.

That rapping noise you may hear is probably a pileated woodpecker. *Dryocopus pileatus* for all you Woody Woodpecker fans, this bird is the original upon which the cartoon character was based. If you look for these birds, try the large, old trees where they typically nest in jackhammered holes or snags formed in the treetops. Large, downed logs produce a feast of carpenter ants and beetle larvae important to the woodpecker's diet.

Watch for other birds and wildlife, including red crossbill, pine siskin, and Steller's jay in the early morning, along with deer and an occasional elk. Coyote may be heard at night, but they tend to stay away from the campground area.

With 7 miles of lake beckoning, a canoe or boat might be a great addition to your gear, especially if you want to pursue the kokanee found in the deeper waters. However, if you don't have a boat you can fish from shore and try landing a largemouth bass or brook

RATINGS

Beauty: ★ ★ ★ ★
Privacy: ★ ★ ★ ★
Spaciousness: ★ ★ ★ ★ ★
Quiet: ★ ★ ★ ★ ★
Security: ★ ★ ★ ★ ★
Cleanliness: ★ ★ ★ ★ ★

KEY INFORMATION

ADDRESS: Three Rivers Ranger District
1437 North US 2
Troy, MT 59935
OPERATED BY: Kootenai National Forest
INFORMATION: (406) 295-4693; www.fs.fed.us/r1/kootenai
OPEN: April–November; full services mid-May–early September
SITES: 16
EACH SITE HAS: Picnic table, fire grate
ASSIGNMENT: First come, first served; no reservations
REGISTRATION: On-site self-registration
FACILITIES: Water spigots, vault toilets, boat ramp, beach, picnic area
PARKING: At campsites
FEE: $8
ELEVATION: 2,350 feet
RESTRICTIONS: Pets: On leash only
Fires: In fire rings only
Alcohol: Permitted
Vehicles: 32-foot length limit
Other: 14-day stay limit; bear country food storage restrictions; campground host

or rainbow trout. If the fish aren't biting, take a refreshing swim or relax on the shore. In general, this is a peaceful site, although on busy weekends there may be a bit too much boat noise during the day. But don't let that scare you away; this is still a wonderful campground.

Four miles away at Ross Creek Cedars is a unique cluster of old-growth timber spared from the loggers' saws. Views of the Cabinet Mountain Wilderness to the east are an extra delight on the narrow, winding road to the picnic area and parking lot of Ross Creek Cedars. You should make time to explore this Forest Service–designated scenic area. A mile-long loop trail with a wealth of interpretive signs winds along the base of massive, 175-foot-tall western red cedars. These ancient mammoths, up to 12 feet in diameter, dwarf the mature western hemlock, western white pine, western larch, mountain maples, and lodgepoles that round out the forest.

The humid forest floor of the Cedars, with its babbling streams, lush ferns, and variety of wildflowers, is as close as Montana gets to a rain forest. The cathedral hush is calming, and the minimal bugs (due to the altitude) are a pleasant surprise. Try finding some of the burned stumps throughout the forest. They are remnants of the August 1910 fire, during which a virtual hurricane of flames swept across the region, burning more than 3 million acres in Idaho and western Montana.

Ross Creek Cedars offers additional hiking options. Ross Creek Trail #142 is a 9-mile out-and-back hike to Sawtooth Mountain that follows the creek beneath a shelter of cedars and hemlocks. For those seeking a bit more exertion, Spar Peak Trail #324 is a 6.5-mile out-and-back from Spar Lake. With a 3,000-foot altitude gain from the lake to Spar Peak, the view is worth it for those who can handle the trek.

You'll find a different view of the forest 10 miles south of the campground off MT 56 at the historic 1908 Bull River Ranger Station. From MT 56, take Forest Service Road 407 east for 2 miles to FR 2278, then drive another mile to the parking area. This section of forest was impacted by the 1910 firestorm, so this provides an opportunity to see what a century of

MAP

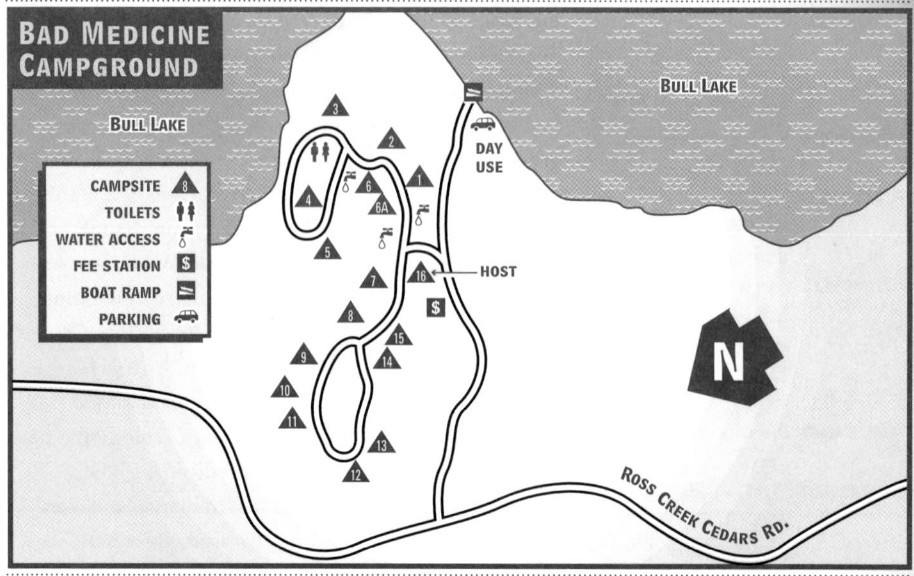

ecosystem regeneration looks like. The self-guided nature trail is well marked, and the brochure details the surrounding flora along with local geology and weather history. The Ranger Station itself has been converted into a nature center offering a full schedule of classes and informational programs throughout the year.

GETTING THERE

From Troy, take US 2 south 3 miles to the junction with MT 56. Turn right and go 21 miles south on MT 56 to Ross Creek Cedars Road. Turn right and follow signs for 2 miles to the campground.

From Trout Creek, take MT 200 north for 18 miles to MT 56. Turn right and go 15 miles north on MT 56 to Ross Creek Cedars Road. Turn left and follow signs for 2 miles to the campground.

BIG ARM STATE PARK CAMPGROUND

These are the best tent sites on spectacular Flathead Lake.

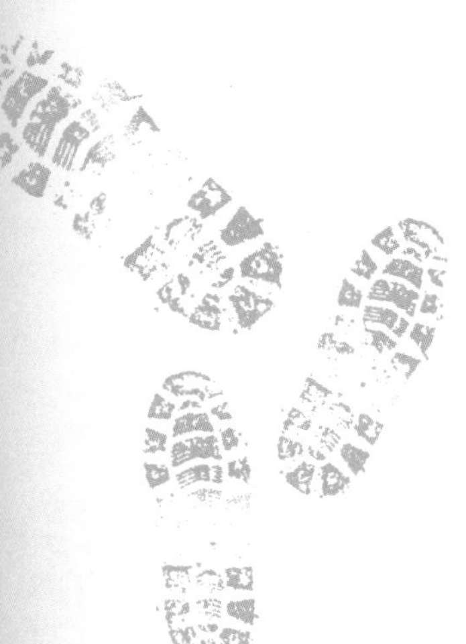

RATINGS

Beauty: ☆ ☆ ☆ ☆
Privacy: ☆ ☆ ☆ ☆
Spaciousness: ☆ ☆ ☆ ☆
Quiet: ☆ ☆ ☆
Security: ☆ ☆ ☆ ☆
Cleanliness: ☆ ☆ ☆ ☆

SET BETWEEN THE SWAN and Mission ranges to the east and the Salish Mountains to the west, Flathead Lake is a sparkling northwestern Montana jewel carved thousands of years ago by receding glaciers. At 28 miles long, it's the largest freshwater lake west of the Mississippi and draws 80 percent of its water from a watershed larger than the states of Delaware and Rhode Island combined.

No wonder so many people drive up to "the Flathead," stopping at the highway stands selling Flathead cherries (be sure to check one out–you won't be sorry). These prized cherries thrive on the microenvironment created by the lake. But visitors don't stop for long; they're on their way to a recreational heaven for boaters, anglers, swimmers, and just plain loafers.

However, a century ago things were not as bucolic–the timber industry was a strong presence, and the Flathead Indian Reservation was just being carved out. Back then it took three to four hours for steamboats to make the trip from north to south, and it could take longer depending on the weather. We're not sure which was more unpredictable, the weather or the Flathead Lake Monster.

The what? Yup, that's right, the Flathead Lake Monster was first seen by a group aboard a steamboat in 1889 who claimed they observed a 20-foot-long creature in the water. They weren't the only ones. Reported sightings have occurred in every decade since then. In 1955, someone claimed to have caught the monster. What they caught was actually a 181-pound white sturgeon now displayed in the museum in Polson. Here's the question: If the monster was caught, what do people keep seeing in the lake? In any case, it's a good sales pitch for everything from hamburgers to T-shirts. But for some, the monster's legend is not all in jest. He (or she) still has some very serious believers.

There are six individual state parks located around Flathead Lake with Big Arm and Wild Horse Island being the two largest. Of the 21 campsites at Big Arm, the prime ones are the six reserved for tents. These sites, A10 through A15, are spacious and right on the water. They may be a bit too close together, but claiming your own piece of Flathead Lake frontage outweighs a need for privacy. If these sites aren't available, sites A3 through A8 are lakefront but not on the shore, as are sites B9 through B13. Site B2 is large, with plenty of room to spread out. It's near the loop intersection but is set off nicely from the surrounding sites. As a heads-up, this is the only campground in the book with hot showers available (don't forget your quarters).

For a somewhat different tenting experience, consider renting the yurt at Big Arm. The yurt as a dwelling dates back at least 1,000 years, when it was used as a traditional home for Central Asian nomads, and its simple design is a masterpiece of geometric engineering. A round lattice frame forms the round wall, with roof beams leading to a smaller diameter roof ring to allow for light and ventilation. The one for rent at Big Arm sleeps six and is complete with beds and tables.

Fishing from shore or boat is productive for whitefish or lake trout, while yellow perch is found only at the southern end of the lake near Big Arm. This end of the lake is on the Flathead Indian Reservation, so you need both a state fishing license and a tribal fishing permit. Regulations, licenses, charter trips, and boat rentals are available in Big Arm and Polson.

This campground is also one of the best locations from which to launch an exploration of Wild Horse Island. Accessible only by boat, this island fills 2,163 acres of Flathead Lake. You'll find a magnificent and diverse collection of wildlife and native plants here. Along with the small namesake herd of wild horses, you may encounter bighorn sheep, eagles, osprey, mule deer, songbirds, geese, owls, and a variety of small mammals. Bring plenty of water, since there is no drinking water available. The closest restrooms are back at the campground.

If you're seeking a little more challenge, try the Flathead Lake marine trail. This "trail" is actually a

KEY INFORMATION

ADDRESS: FWP Region 1 Headquarters 490 North Meridian Road Kalispell, MT 59901

OPERATED BY: Montana Fish, Wildlife & Parks

INFORMATION: (406) 752-5501; www.fwp.state.mt.us

OPEN: May–September

SITES: 21

EACH SITE HAS: Picnic table, fire ring

ASSIGNMENT: First come, first served; no reservations

REGISTRATION: On-site self-registration

FACILITIES: Hot showers, water spigots, flush toilets, pay phone, boat ramp, yurt

PARKING: At campsites

FEE: $14

ELEVATION: 2,967 feet

RESTRICTIONS: **Pets:** On leash only
Fires: In fire rings only
Alcohol: Permitted
Vehicles: 2 vehicles per site; 30-foot length limit
Other: 7-day stay limit; firewood; tribal/state fishing permits required; campground host

MAP

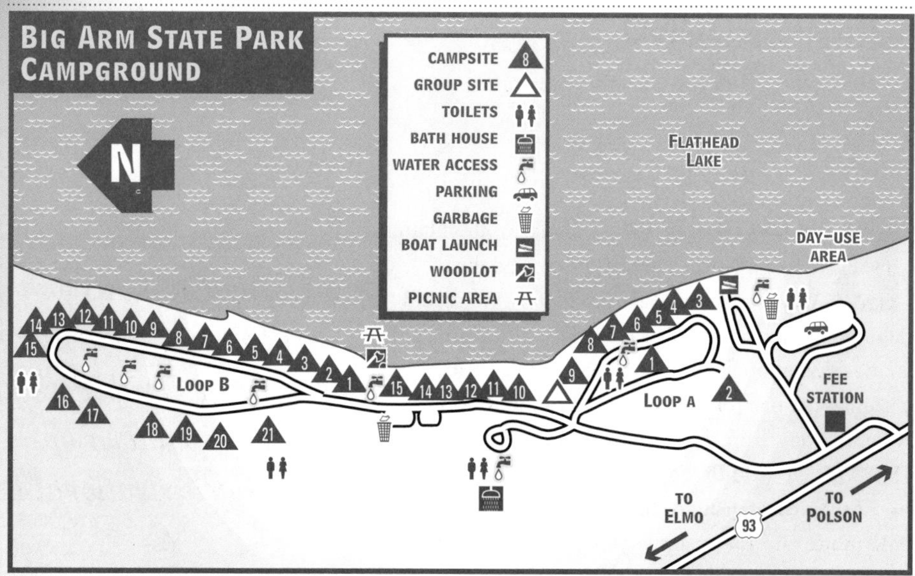

GETTING THERE

From Polson, take US 93 north for 14 miles to the campground entrance on the right.

collection of islands and other points around the lake that can be accessed by sea kayak. Maps and brochures detail the specifics of the lake's over 128 miles of shoreline. You can easily design a day trip between nearby sites or plan a week-long excursion. An extra perk is that a few campsites in designated areas are reserved for marine-trail use until 6 p.m. Less experienced paddlers should stay closer to shore, and those crossing the lake are warned that a calm morning can shift to wicked winds and five-foot waves very quickly.

BIG CREEK CAMPGROUND

Columbia Falls

BIG CREEK SITS ON the banks of the Flathead River's North Fork at the front door of Glacier National Park. Flowing along and defining the park's western boundary, the North Fork is one of Montana's premier rivers and in 1976 was designated a part of the National Wild and Scenic River System from the Canadian border to its confluence with the Middle Fork.

Big Creek sits on the banks of the wild and scenic North Fork at the front door of Glacier National Park.

At the campground, the sites are set among lodgepole pines, and the rushing waters of the North Fork can be heard everywhere. The best sites are 5 through 15, since they back up to the river and have plenty of space between them. If these aren't available, sites 16, 17, and 19 through 22 also have a fair amount of privacy, since they are on the outside loop with no other sites behind them. Site 22 sits even farther apart on a slight rise overlooking a large, open field.

In August 2001, a lightning strike started the 71,000-acre Moose Fire that burned right through this campground. Fortunately, conditions at the time mitigated the damage, and the fire burned little of the crown cover. Ground-cover vegetation, however, was affected and is slowly making a comeback. You'll see the regeneration for yourself as the new plants fill in space between you and your neighbor. Fire visited again in 2003 when the Robert Fire burned much of the area south of the campground.

With only 22 sites, you may find it difficult to get a spot in mid-summer after 6 p.m., so plan accordingly. The Glacier area gets over 1.5 million visitors each year, and camping within the park and at surrounding campgrounds is limited. If you wait until late in the day to set up camp, it may be challenging to find a site anywhere.

Big Creek is busy in the summer. The day-use area is crowded even during the week, and the adjacent

RATINGS

Beauty: ☆ ☆ ☆ ☆
Privacy: ☆ ☆ ☆
Spaciousness: ☆ ☆ ☆ ☆
Quiet: ☆ ☆ ☆ ☆
Security: ☆ ☆ ☆ ☆ ☆
Cleanliness: ☆ ☆ ☆ ☆ ☆

KEY INFORMATION

ADDRESS: Hungry Horse and Glacier View Ranger Districts P.O. Box 190340 Hungry Horse, MT 59919

OPERATED BY: Flathead National Forest

INFORMATION: (406) 387-3800; www.fs.fed.us/r1/flathead

OPEN: Memorial Day–Labor Day

SITES: 22

EACH SITE HAS: Picnic table, fire grate

ASSIGNMENT: First come, first served; no reservations

REGISTRATION: On-site self-registration

FACILITIES: Hand-pump well, vault toilets, boat launch, day-use area

PARKING: At campsites

FEE: $10

ELEVATION: 3,300 feet

RESTRICTIONS: **Pets:** On leash only
Fires: In fire rings only
Alcohol: Permitted
Vehicles: 40-foot length limit
Other: 14-day stay limit; bear country food-storage restrictions; pack in/pack out; campground host

Glacier Institute is a nonprofit organization offering a full range of educational classes, workshops, and field trips for youth and adults. In addition, Big Creek is a popular put-in and takeout for rafters and floaters.

Independent and guided floating on the North Fork is very popular, and the 18-mile section between Polebridge and Big Creek is easiest for novices once the spring runoff has ended, usually by July. This section is also less crowded, since more experienced floaters generally head for the 8-mile whitewater section running south of the campground to the Glacier Rim takeout.

Many fish and wildlife species can be found at the point where Big Creek drains into the North Fork. The river provides cold, clear, fast-moving water, which is a vital link in sustaining the native bull trout *(Salvelinus confluentus)* as it ascends the North and Middle forks of the Flathead River to seek out smaller tributary streams and creeks in which to spawn. These strikingly colorful fish are also known by the name Dolly Varden. If you've brushed up on your Charles Dickens you may remember the book *Barnaby Rudge* and the character Dolly Varden, who, like the bull trout, dressed quite colorfully in flashes of green with pink polka dots. The bull trout is federally listed as a threatened species, and the state of Montana has been aggressively managing those found here to ensure that the population does not further decline and move from threatened to endangered. These efforts have been successful to the point that regulations have been relaxed in some waterways, but, as always, be familiar with current regulations before you wet your hook.

The fairly difficult Glacier View Mountain Trail #381 begins at the campground trailhead and is an 8-mile round-trip that gains nearly 3,000 feet in elevation ascending the mountain peak. From there, Demers Ridge Trail #266 continues another 4 miles to Outside North Fork Road (Forest Service Road 486) near the Camas Creek entrance to Glacier. Both trails offer excellent views of Glacier and the North Fork area. Trailheads for the 17-mile Ralph Thayer Memorial National Recreation Trail and 10-mile Smoky Range National Recreation Trail are within driving

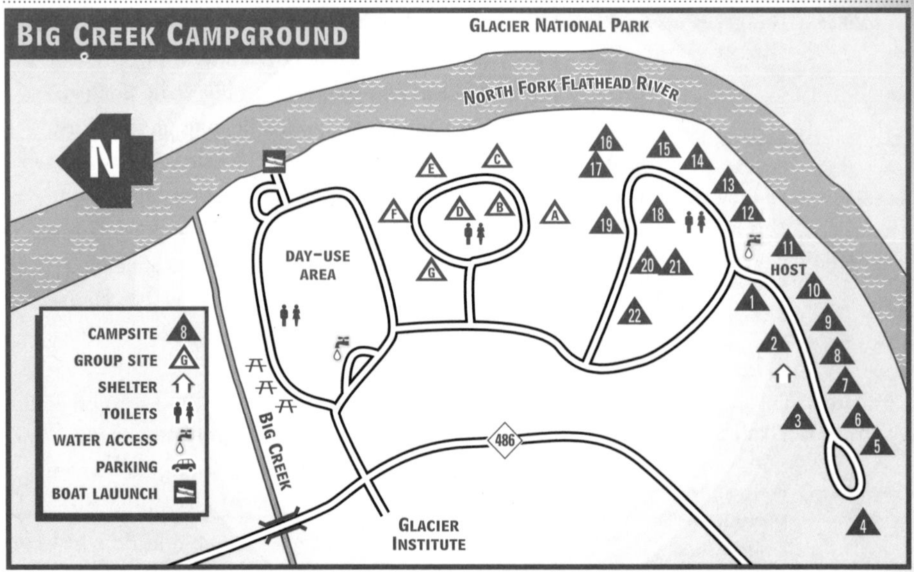

distance. Additional information and maps can be obtained from the Ranger District headquarters.

The closest hike in Glacier begins near the Camas Creek entrance. This 6-mile round-trip to Huckleberry Lookout traverses an area partially burned in the 2001 Moose Fire, but there are pockets that haven't burned since the 1967 fire. These pockets are maturing and provide an educational contrast to the land you'll encounter at Big Creek and elsewhere on your hike. The trail takes you along the creek and up some steep slopes before hitting the ridge, where you'll be above the tree line. Wildflowers dazzle here all summer, especially through the first mile or so. Over 200 bird species have been seen in the North Fork area, so maybe you'll be one of the lucky visitors who glimpses a great gray owl or a Le Conte's sparrow.

GETTING THERE

From Columbia Falls, take County Road 486 north for 20.5 miles to the campground.The road turns into dirt after 12.5 miles.

BIG THERRIAULT CAMPGROUND

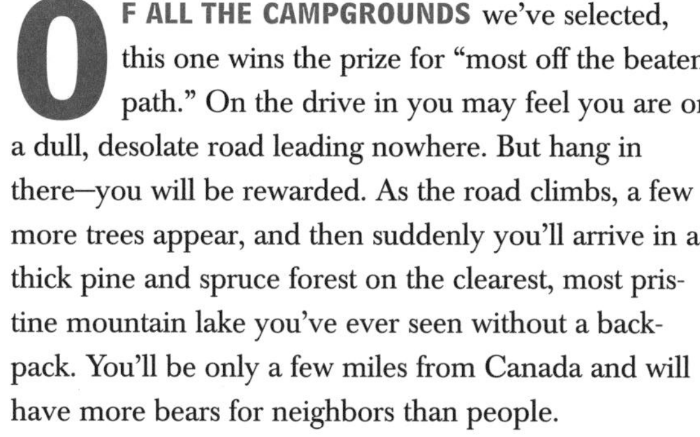

Big Therriault wins the prize for 'most off the beaten path.'

OF ALL THE CAMPGROUNDS we've selected, this one wins the prize for "most off the beaten path." On the drive in you may feel you are on a dull, desolate road leading nowhere. But hang in there—you will be rewarded. As the road climbs, a few more trees appear, and then suddenly you'll arrive in a thick pine and spruce forest on the clearest, most pristine mountain lake you've ever seen without a backpack. You'll be only a few miles from Canada and will have more bears for neighbors than people.

The campground itself is small, only five acres, and the ten sites are set on a hillside around a single loop with plenty of understory for privacy. Most sites are suited for tents, although the two pull-through spots are better left for RVs. None of the sites sit directly on the lake, and there aren't any with clear views due to the thick forest, but most are adjacent to the 1-mile trail around the lake. This trail provides a short course in glacial geology; you will see grooves carved by the glaciers and moraines formed by the debris left behind.

Highlights of the trail include wildflower-strewn meadows and a variety of wildlife—deer, elk, osprey, eagles, the occasional mountain lion, and, if you're extremely lucky, a wolverine. Centered within the loop is a 55-acre lake with its multihued rock bottom and wealth of cutthroat trout. An afternoon spent canoeing in this serene spot is an ideal antidote for the tension of everyday life. In the morning you'll awaken to songbirds, and in the evening you'll hear the call of loons.

Just down the road is Little Therriault Lake Campground, with six roomy and secluded campsites. This lake is smaller (28 acres), but you'll find a lakeside trail here as well. At the north end of the lake is a trailhead into the Ten Lakes Scenic Area, where hikers and horses are allowed but ATVs are not.

RATINGS

Beauty: ✩ ✩ ✩ ✩ ✩
Privacy: ✩ ✩ ✩ ✩ ✩
Spaciousness: ✩ ✩ ✩ ✩
Quiet: ✩ ✩ ✩ ✩ ✩
Security: ✩ ✩ ✩ ✩ ✩
Cleanliness: ✩ ✩ ✩ ✩ ✩

While not an officially designated wilderness area, this 40,000-acre, unspoiled slice of roadless area extends to the Canadian border and is managed by the Kootenai National Forest as if it were one. Prehistoric glaciers carved the deep cirques and rocky basins that ultimately became alpine lakes. The waters are spectacularly clear, wildflowers bloom profusely, and huckleberries are abundant for those who keep their eyes open. Waterfalls appear unexpectedly, and you can literally hike all day without seeing anyone else.

There is a day-hike loop from the south end of Big Therriault Lake, over Therriault Pass, along the Highline Trail and St. Clair Peak that ends at the south end of Little Therriault Lake. This route takes you up about 1,500 feet and provides dramatic vistas across the Whitefish Range into Canada. From the same trailhead, you can take Highline Trail left for a hike to the summit of Stahl Peak. The view from this lookout is to the south, where you'll have a pretty good chance of seeing bighorn sheep along the mountainsides throughout the summer months.

From the trailhead northwest of Little Therriault Lake you can take the 5-mile out-and-back hike to Bluebird Lake. Elevation gain on this hike is less than 1,000 feet, and you won't encounter any super-steep or difficult sections. If you start early enough, you can spend a relaxing day at the lake before heading back. A longer option is to continue past Bluebird Lake to Wolverine Lakes. You can make this hike either a 9-mile out-and-back or an 11.5-mile loop. The loop option brings you back on Tie Thru Trail #82; it is best spread over two or three days and is one of only several combinations that take hikers deep into this lush backcountry.

Stocking up on supplies, topping off the gas tank, and checking the air in your spare while passing through Eureka is a prudent idea. It's 36 long, bumpy miles to the campground. Cell-phone reception is nonexistent, bears don't make the best auto mechanics, and if you get a yearning for a cold glass of milk, a nice juicy orange, or a super gooey s'more, it will take you at least half the day to satisfy your craving. Wouldn't you rather be out hiking or just sitting by the lake enjoying the peace and quiet?

KEY INFORMATION

ADDRESS: Fortine Ranger District, P.O. Box 116, Fortine, MT 59918

OPERATED BY: Kootenai National Forest

INFORMATION: (406) 882-4451; www.fs.fed.us/r1/kootenai

OPEN: July–Labor Day (maybe earlier depending on the weather)

SITES: 10

EACH SITE HAS: Picnic table, fire grate, bear-resistant box

ASSIGNMENT: First come, first served; no reservations

REGISTRATION: On-site self-registration

FACILITIES: Hand-pump well, vault toilets, boat launch

PARKING: At campsites

FEE: $5

ELEVATION: 5,560 feet

RESTRICTIONS: Pets: On leash only
Fires: In fire rings only
Alcohol: Permitted
Vehicles: 32-foot length limit
Other: 14-day stay limit; bear country food-storage restrictions; pack in/pack out; campground host

MAP

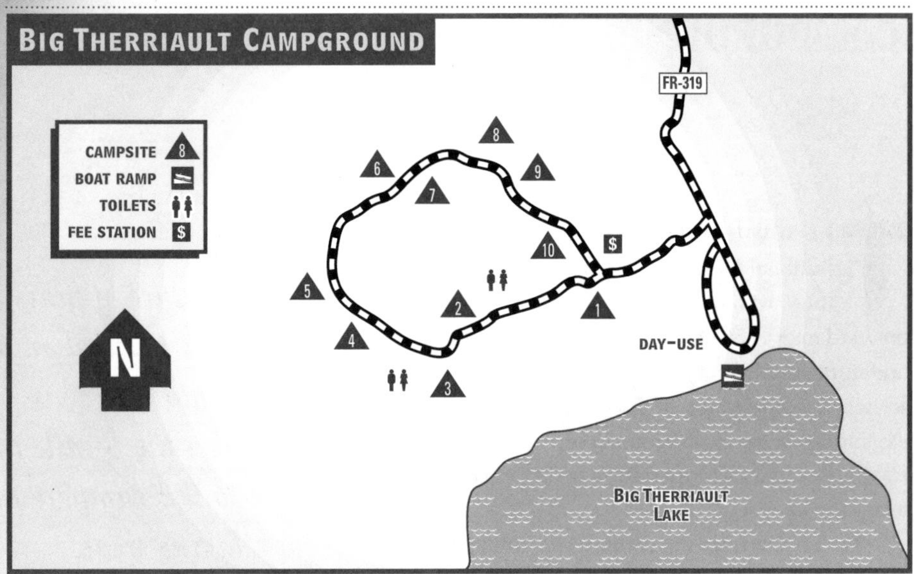

GETTING THERE

From Fortine, take US 93 northwest 3 miles. Turn right on Grave Creek Road (FR 114) and go 12 miles to Therriault Lakes Road (FR 319). Continue straight on Therriault Lakes Road (FR 319) and follow signs for 16 miles to the campground. Therriault Lakes Road is a narrow, winding dirt road that requires patience.

CUTBANK CAMPGROUND

St. Mary

THE SOUTHEASTERN CORNER of Glacier National Park is an area few people see, but those who do are surprised at the contrast to the verdant western half of the park, where the thick undergrowth often obscure the spectacular mountain scenery. In this section of the park you'll encounter expansive views, scrub ground cover mixed with pockets of trees, and lush riparian edges. The scenery seems to stretch forever.

Such is life from the comfort of Cutbank. A mixture of pines and aspens painted on a mountain canvas makes the 5-mile drive into this campground a relaxing treat. Open-range cattle graze both sides of the road, so drive cautiously to avoid a situation where your car will be the loser. In Montana, we don't fence in cattle, we fence them out.

The campground is small, and RVs are discouraged from making the trip, so you will probably only be sharing space with nylon neighbors. Choose from 14 gravel tent pads framed in wood timbers—further evidence that RVers should keep looking. A mixture of fir, aspen, cottonwood, and ponderosa pine provide shade in this otherwise exposed area. Although sites are fairly close together, each offers enough space to make you feel like it's your own private piece of Glacier. In keeping with the wilderness theme, restrooms are rustic wood, not concrete, with one hole each. Bear-proof food-storage boxes remind you to be conscientious and practice bear-aware camping techniques. Additional information is stapled to picnic tables, and park staff patrols the area, just in case you need help remembering.

Sites 8 and 10 on the outside loop are most desirable, with lots of room and the most privacy. Site 11 is roomy as well but isn't as private, since it adjoins the host's site. Overall, it's a quiet area with most people

> *A mixture of pines and aspens painted on a mountain canvas makes the 5-mile drive into this campground a relaxing treat.*

RATINGS

Beauty: ✩ ✩ ✩ ✩ ✩
Privacy: ✩ ✩ ✩ ✩ ✩
Spaciousness: ✩ ✩ ✩
Quiet: ✩ ✩ ✩ ✩ ✩
Security: ✩ ✩ ✩
Cleanliness: ✩ ✩ ✩ ✩ ✩

KEY INFORMATION

ADDRESS:	Glacier National Park P.O. Box 128 West Glacier, MT 59936
OPERATED BY:	National Park Service
INFORMATION:	(406) 888-7800; www.nps.gov/glac
OPEN:	June–September
SITES:	14
EACH SITE HAS:	Picnic table, fire grate
ASSIGNMENT:	First come, first served; no reservations
REGISTRATION:	On-site self-registration
FACILITIES:	Hand-pump well, vault toilets
PARKING:	At campsites
FEE:	$12
ELEVATION:	5,500 feet
RESTRICTIONS:	**Pets:** On leash only **Fires:** In fire rings only **Alcohol:** Permitted **Vehicles:** 22-foot length limit **Other:** 7-day stay limit; bear country food-storage restrictions

out on the trails during the day. Since it stays light until around 10 p.m. in summer, you can enjoy plenty of peaceful down time even if you just hang out around camp. Early morning and dusk are the best times to view wildlife such as black and grizzly bears, deer, and elusive wolves, but eagles and hawks can be seen anytime. Check with the Ranger Station for current high-activity areas.

Fishing for brook and rainbow trout or mountain whitefish in the North Fork of Cutbank Creek wiles away the hours for many, while others rise to the challenge of a hike from the trailhead. There are several options, but for the first 4 miles, all follow the same route through meadows along the creek before beginning to gradually climb. At the junction near Atlantic Creek, the left fork takes you 2.6 miles to Medicine Grizzly Peak (8,315 feet) and its waterfalls and then on to Morningstar Lake. From there it's a steep 3-mile climb (quite possibly through snowfields) to Katoya and Pitamakan Lakes and Pitamakan Pass. Along the way, you'll see Red Mountain (9,389 feet) to the east and Mount Phillips (9,627 feet) to the southwest.

Choose to veer right at the junction, and in one-half mile you'll have another decision—Medicine Grizzly Lake or Triple Divide Pass. Many people do both, since it's only 1.5 miles to the lake and 2.5 miles to the pass, but this requires a pretty early start. The 14.4-mile round-trip to the pass is a gradual climb without steep pitches or switchbacks, and views are continuous. This hike also brings you to the base of Triple Divide Peak (8,020 feet), a unique geographic location where a three-sided glacial horn formed as separate glaciers eroded the mountain's sides. The result is that water or snow collecting on the northeast side drains into the Saskatchewan River, Hudson Bay, and then the Arctic Ocean; water on the west side drains into Flathead River, Clark Fork River, and on into the Columbia River and Pacific Ocean. From the south side, water makes its way to the Missouri River via Atlantic Creek and Marias River and then on into the Mississippi River and Gulf of Mexico.

MAP

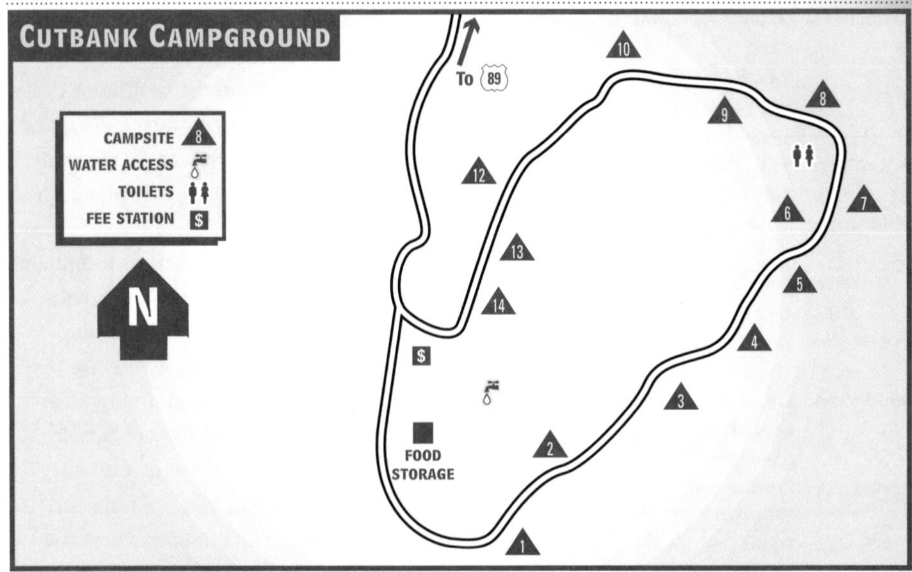

Along any of these trails you'll encounter plenty of wildflowers and wildlife along with an ever-changing assortment of rain, snow, sunshine, and hail. Be prepared, be aware, and have fun.

GETTING THERE

From St. Mary, take US 89 south for 15 miles to the park entrance road. Turn right and go west for 5 miles to the campground.

From East Glacier Park, take MT 49 north for 11.8 miles to US 89. Continue north on US 89 for 5 miles to the park entrance road. Turn left and go west for 5 miles to the campground. MT 49 is a narrow, winding road that requires caution and patience.

FISH CREEK CAMPGROUND

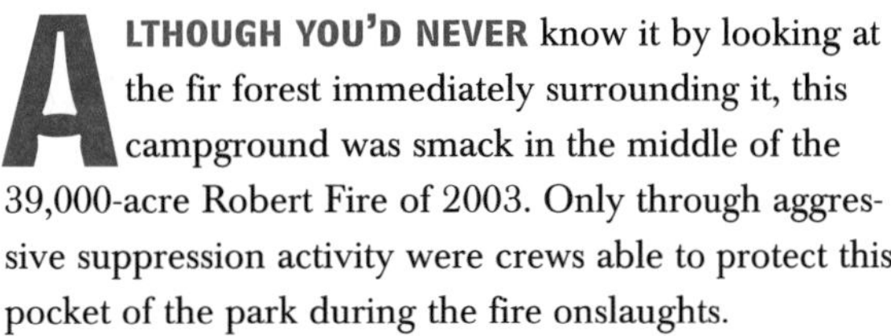

"Smack in the middle of the 2003 Robert Fire, Fish Creek emerged unscathed."

RATINGS

Beauty: ✩ ✩ ✩ ✩ ✩
Privacy: ✩ ✩ ✩ ✩
Spaciousness: ✩ ✩ ✩ ✩
Quiet: ✩ ✩ ✩ ✩
Security: ✩ ✩ ✩ ✩ ✩
Cleanliness: ✩ ✩ ✩ ✩ ✩

ALTHOUGH YOU'D NEVER know it by looking at the fir forest immediately surrounding it, this campground was smack in the middle of the 39,000-acre Robert Fire of 2003. Only through aggressive suppression activity were crews able to protect this pocket of the park during the fire onslaughts.

On the drive to the campground from the park entrance, about one-half mile past the Apgar area, you'll see Bullhead Lodge on the shore of Lake McDonald. The lodge once served as artist Charlie Russell's private home. Private homes were common in the park's early days, but only a few are left, and they aren't for sale. They remain only because they've been in the same families for a long time.

As one of only two campgrounds at Glacier accepting reservations (the other is St. Mary), it's surprising Fish Creek rarely fills up, even during July and early August. Three of the four loops (B, C, and D) sit between Fish Creek and Lake McDonald, but few sites have clear water views due to the dense forest. That's okay, since the trees provide more privacy than you'd expect at such a large campground.

None of the sites on loop A stand out as exceptional, but most are well suited for tents. The most coveted sites on loop B are the odd-numbered sites that lie along the loop's south side. Sites 42 and 43 are nice as well, but they're opposite the restrooms and path to loop C. Sites 47 and 49 offer a unique option–both are raised and require a bit more energy to set up camp, but it's definitely worth the effort for the sense of privacy. Loop C provides spectacular lake views from sites 106, 108, and 110. Site 150, on the connecting road between loops C and D, is the most private.

When we visited here in July, it was the same weekend First Lady Laura Bush was in the area with some friends. Don, the campground supervisor, advised us not to miss the "Presidential Suite." He wasn't divulging state secrets about her location when he sent us to site 174 on loop D; he simply wanted us to see the site used by her father-in-law and his entourage when he visited during his tenure as vice-president. This site, along with site 173, is the most private and these have the best lake views, but they're tough to get and very popular with RVs.

Due to restrictions that protect the habitat of nesting Harlequin ducks, Fish Creek is one of the park's tributaries where fishing is not allowed. But feel free to visit the creek and the ducks. You might even try braving the chilly waters to wade a bit.

A hike along the northern shore of Lake McDonald gives you an up-close view of the fire damage along with the regrowth already transforming the devastation. This trail is 6.6 gentle miles from end to end with several lakeshore overlooks. Fishing along the shoreline is easy, and no license is required to pursue the cutthroat, rainbow, and lake trout. Early morning and early evening, when the wind is calm, are the best times for fishing the clear, cold water of this glacial lake.

An easy hike to Rocky Point begins near the campground, and dozens more hiking trails exist throughout the park. A few miles north, on Camas Road, is the trailhead for the Huckleberry Mountain Trails—a level 0.9-mile interpretive trail and a 6-mile out-and-back trail to a manned lookout. Ultimately, it will come down to a question of time and stamina. Obtain a trail guide and be prepared to have trouble choosing from the wealth of options, which range from quick jaunts to multiday backpacking trips.

Nightly amphitheater programs explain the park's flora and fauna and provide historical anecdotes and insight into the weather patterns. Questions are welcome and the discussion often extends well into the evening. Rangers also lead hikes along Huckleberry Nature Trail to observe the regeneration occurring after various fires.

More options are available at nearby Apgar, where programs are held at the amphitheater four nights a week. At the Discovery Center, visitors can explore hands-on exhibits about the park's natural residents

KEY INFORMATION

ADDRESS: Glacier National Park
P.O. Box 128
West Glacier, MT 59936

OPERATED BY: National Park Service

INFORMATION: (406) 888-7800; www.nps.gov/glac; reservations (800) 365-CAMP or reservations.nps.gov

OPEN: Mid-June–early September

SITES: 180

EACH SITE HAS: Picnic table, fire grate

ASSIGNMENT: First come, first served; reservations available

REGISTRATION: On-site self-registration

FACILITIES: Water spigots, flush toilets, pay phone, dump station, amphitheater, interpretive activities and programs

PARKING: At campsites

FEE: $17

ELEVATION: 3,150 feet

RESTRICTIONS: **Pets:** On leash only, not permitted on trails or along lakeshores
Fires: In fire rings only
Alcohol: Permitted
Vehicles: 35-foot length limit; 2 vehicles per site
Other: 7-day stay limit; bear country food-storage restrictions; no firearms; no firewood gathering; special fishing regulations

MAP

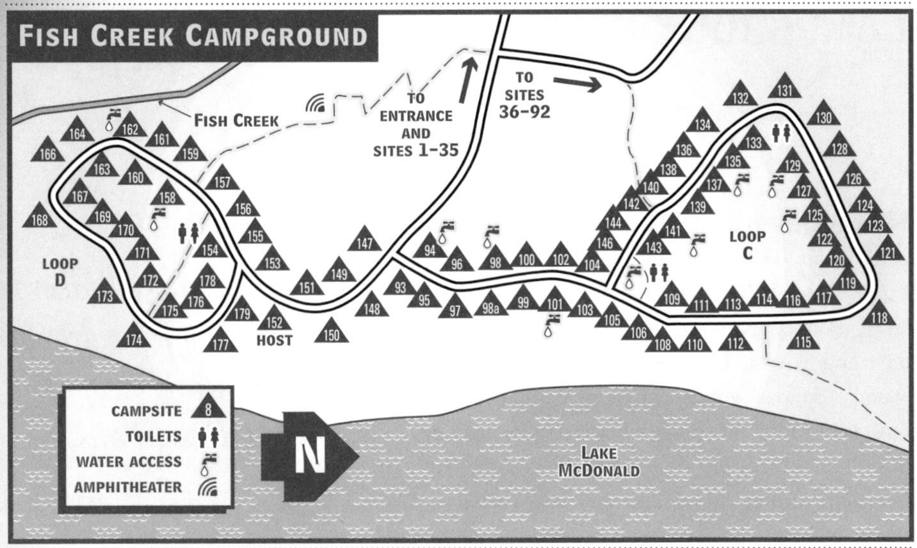

GETTING THERE

From West Glacier entrance, take the park road 2 miles east to Camas Road. Turn left and go northwest for 5 miles to the campground.

and geological creation. Food service, gift shops, and basic supplies are also available at Apgar.

MAP

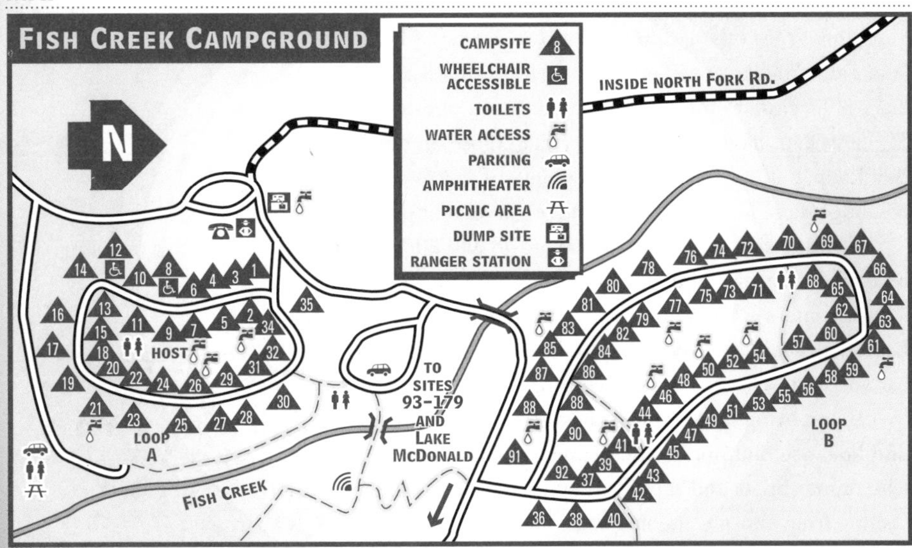

HOLLAND LAKE CAMPGROUND

Condon

TUCKED BETWEEN the Swan Range to the east and the Mission Range to the west, the Seeley-Swan Valley is a popular outdoor paradise with lakes, mountains, rivers, small streams, and trails. Visitors can enjoy the best Mother Nature has to offer year-round. You may wonder why a place that sounds this busy is included in a book where the idea is to get away from it all. It's simple: the setting is awesome, and, especially during the week, it isn't as crowded as you might expect.

Holland Lake was formed when the last glacial ice melted from this area some 10,000 years ago. The receding glaciers deposited sediments, forming moraines, which now hold back a lake fed by runoff from the spectacular mountains surrounding it. This 427-acre lake is one of the deepest in the area at 155 feet. The clarity of the water can make the depth deceiving, so be prepared when boating.

Campsites here are in two loops, and the very best sites (1, 2, and 6) lie in the Larch Loop, which is the first loop off the entrance road. Sitting atop a lakeshore bluff, these sites offer a dramatic postcard view of Holland Falls. You'll also get a nice view from sites 3 and 5 but will be close to the restroom and trash dumpster. The sites here have less understory than those on the Bay Loop, but they're large, with plenty of space for pitching a tent, and uneven sites have gravel tent pads.

The best sites on the Bay Loop are 18 and 30, right on the lake, but we think this loop is less desirable since it attracts more RVs. It also puts you closer to Holland Lake Lodge and its activity, although the lodge's rustic bar and dining room are a draw for many.

If you bring a boat, head for deeper waters to find kokanee, but not during prime weekend hours when motorboats and Jet Skis may be overwhelming. Fishing from shore is quieter and yields perch, cut-

"Sites atop a lakeshore bluff offer a dramatic postcard view of Holland Falls."

RATINGS

Beauty: ✩ ✩ ✩ ✩ ✩
Privacy: ✩ ✩ ✩ ✩
Spaciousness: ✩ ✩ ✩ ✩
Quiet: ✩ ✩ ✩ ✩
Security: ✩ ✩ ✩ ✩
Cleanliness: ✩ ✩ ✩ ✩

KEY INFORMATION

ADDRESS: Swan Lake Ranger District
200 Ranger Station Road
Bigfork, MT 59911

OPERATED BY: Flathead National Forest

INFORMATION: (406) 837-7500; www.fs.fed.us/r1/flathead

OPEN: Mid-May–September

SITES: 40

EACH SITE HAS: Picnic table, fire grate

ASSIGNMENT: First come, first served; no reservations

REGISTRATION: On-site self-registration

FACILITIES: Water spigots, vault toilets, boat ramp, beach, dump station

PARKING: At campsites

FEE: $12

ELEVATION: 4,050 feet

RESTRICTIONS: **Pets:** On leash only
Fires: In fire rings only
Alcohol: Permitted
Vehicles: 50-foot length limit
Other: 14-day stay limit; bear country food-storage requirements; campground host

throat, and rainbow trout. Just be sure you know how to identify a bull trout so you don't mistake it for a cutthroat and end up with a hefty fine. Bull trout are currently protected in Montana, and you'll be preventing the species from reproducing by frying one up for dinner.

Several years ago we took our canoe out on Holland Lake. The sun was shining, the water sparkled, and we were the only ones out—nothing ahead of us but an idyllic day outdoors. Idyllic until we decided to head for shore. The afternoon became a classic example of Montana's unpredictable weather. The sky turned black, the temperature dove, a headwind blew in, and there we were paddling with all our strength just to stay in one place, certain we would never see shore again. Then, just as suddenly, it was over. We took advantage of the reprieve, using our remaining strength to reach shore. Our son Tyler (age seven at the time) had slept through the entire storm—as usual—and as he awoke he said, "I thought you were going to let me paddle back to shore. You only let me paddle when it's really hard. This would have been an easy one." We looked at each other and tried to laugh, but we just didn't have the energy.

By all means, try a swim in the crystalline lake if it's late July. But even then it may be too cold for comfort. Less hearty souls are content to seek out a nice spot along the shoreline to wade and enjoy the mirrored image of the Swan Range peaks or to take the 0.6-mile nature trail along the shore. Elk and deer frequent the lakeshore, and an occasional bear shows up to keep things interesting.

No visit to Holland Lake is complete without a hike to Holland Falls at the base of the Swan Range. This 3.5-mile hike is along National Recreation Trail 416, which begins at the north end of the lake and climbs steadily to the 40-foot falls and a spectacular view of the Swan Valley and the Mission Mountains. You'll find several natural nooks and crannies along the way for picnics and just enjoying the day. It's a popular trail on weekends, so early-morning treks are best for campers seeking solitude. In addition, bugs can be fierce along the trail, especially after it rains.

MAP

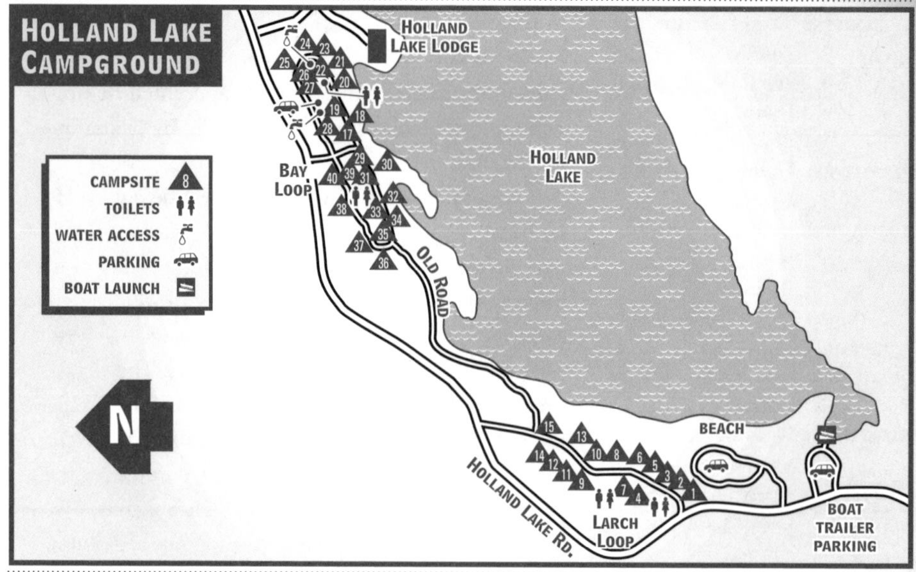

If you still have energy, this trail continues on as the Upper Holland Loop, a fairly strenuous additional 10 miles that climb 3,000 feet to Upper Holland Lake and Sapphire Lake on the edge of the Bob Marshall Wilderness before returning to the falls. From this loop, you can hike spurs to the Holland Lookout, Necklace Lakes chains, Big Salmon Lake, and Gordon Pass. Except on the trail to the falls, you'll be sharing the path with horses, but motorized vehicles and bikes are prohibited.

GETTING THERE

From Condon, take MT 83 southeast for 9 miles, and turn left and go east for 3 miles on Forest Service Road 44 (Holland Lake Road) to the campground.

From Seeley Lake, take MT 83 northeast for 35 miles, and turn right and go east for 3 miles on FR 44 (Holland Lake Road) to the campground.

KINTLA LAKE CAMPGROUND

Camp near an isolated mountain lake at the base of towering, snowcapped mountains.

RATINGS

Beauty: ☆ ☆ ☆ ☆ ☆
Privacy: ☆ ☆ ☆ ☆
Spaciousness: ☆ ☆ ☆ ☆
Quiet: ☆ ☆ ☆ ☆ ☆
Security: ☆ ☆ ☆ ☆ ☆
Cleanliness: ☆ ☆ ☆ ☆ ☆

DRIVING THE INSIDE North Fork Road to Kintla Lake offers an excellent chance to view wildlife, wildflowers, and the rebirth of Glacier after the fires of 1988 and 2003. But getting here isn't easy. You won't need four-wheel drive, but the road is extremely rough, and you should plan on averaging 15 mph. This was the first road in the area, developed by oil barons in the early 1900s as they began drilling near Kintla Lake. Things were going well (no pun intended) until they hit a gas vein, causing the whole operation to explode into flames. Meanwhile, the area was already on track for designation as a national park. When Glacier became the country's tenth national park in 1910, oil exploration ended, but drilling on the Rocky Mountain front and on land adjoining the park remains a divisive issue today.

Kintla is off the main track for Glacier's typical drive-through visitors who often don't realize this region exists. But if you like isolated lakes at the base of towering, snowcapped mountains where deer, elk, and black bears are abundant and eagles are frequent visitors, this is a prime choice. The campsites themselves are not very private since much of the understory was removed as a fire precaution, but the splendid location and potential for being one of the few people here are distinct advantages that more than offset the lack of screening. Sites here are similar to one another, with none actually situated on the lake, although sites 9 through 11 do sit along the creek that runs between the lake and North Fork Flathead River.

The trailer near the lake is actually a Ranger Station that is infrequently staffed, another indication that camping here requires preparation and self-reliance. The weather can be unpredictable—yes, it has snowed in every month of the year—and it's 15 miles to limited services in Polebridge. Cell phones probably won't work, no matter what your provider tells you, and you need to take the food-storage restrictions seriously.

Fishing on the 8-mile-long lake, either from shore or from a canoe, is good for cutthroat trout and whitefish. If you're planning to wade or use a float tube, insulated gear is essential since the water is always cold.

Hiking trails fan out along the shore and lead to backcountry sites on Upper Kintla Lake. Dramatic views of forested peaks along the northern shore contrast with those of the lake's southern shore, which were devastated in the 2003 Wedge Canyon fire. The campground itself was miraculously spared even though the fire burned 53,000 acres over a period of two months. About 2 miles from the campground, on Inside North Fork Road, is the trailhead for HeKishenehn Creek Trail. This easy 4-mile trail includes two creek crossings and an excellent chance to see elk, moose, and maybe even a bear. Whenever hiking in Glacier, be sure you understand and follow safety precautions. They aren't tough or complicated, but they will help you have a safe and enjoyable hike.

When you're seeking a bit of civilization, it's about an hour by car to the hamlet of Polebridge. This tiny enclave is the stalwart heart of the North Fork region. Threatened by the Red Bench fire in 1988 and essentially shut down during the 2003 fire season, it survives. Folks here are tough, resilient, and creative at keeping their community and way of life alive. Whether it's world-class music festivals or holiday celebrations, Polebridge attracts an eclectic mix of visitors and locals. A stop here is not complete without sampling the baked goods at the Polebridge Merchantile and reading the well-preserved news clippings that tell the area's history. Sit on the porch of this building, listed on the National Register of Historic Places, sip a cool drink, and plan the next phase of your visit to Glacier. If you've brought your mountain bike, the ride to Polebridge is a fairly level 29-mile round-trip. It can be a dusty ride at times but is an excellent opportunity for wildlife viewing, which just isn't possible when you're driving.

Another biking option is Hornet Peak Loop, which begins just north of Polebridge on Outside

KEY INFORMATION

ADDRESS: Glacier National Park
P.O. Box 128
West Glacier, MT 59936

OPERATED BY: National Park Service

INFORMATION: (406) 888-7800; www.nps.gov/glac

OPEN: Year-round if accessible; full services mid-May–mid-September

SITES: 13 tent sites

EACH SITE HAS: Picnic table, fire grate

ASSIGNMENT: First come, first served; no reservations

REGISTRATION: On-site self-registration

FACILITIES: Hand-pump well, vault toilets

PARKING: At campsites

FEE: $12

ELEVATION: 4,008 feet

RESTRICTIONS: Pets: On leash only, not allowed on trails or along lakeshore
Fires: In fire rings only
Alcohol: Permitted
Vehicles: RVs not recommended, 2 vehicles per site
Other: 7-day stay limit; bear country food-storage restrictions; no firearms; nonmotorized boats only; special fishing regulations

MAP

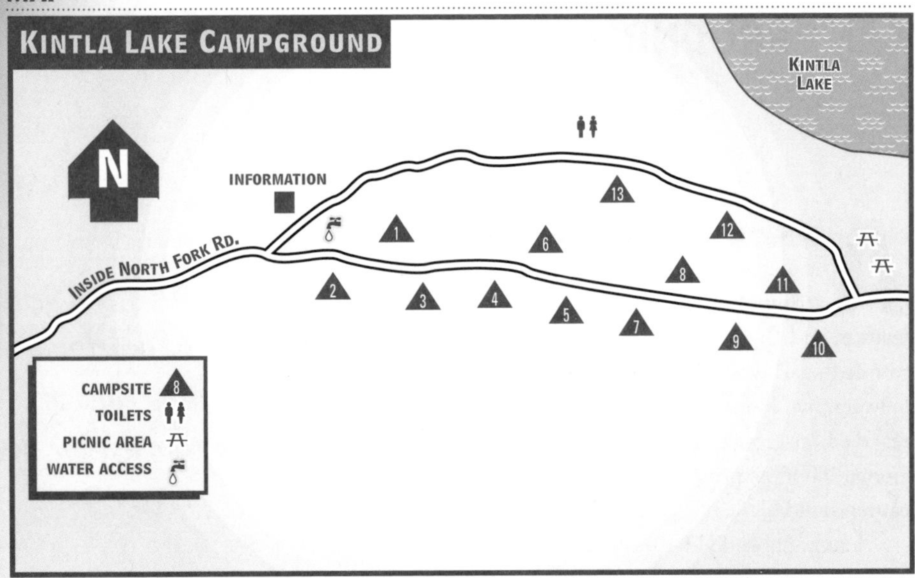

GETTING THERE

From Polebridge, take Inside North Fork Road north for 15 miles to the campground.

From West Glacier, take Inside North Fork Road north for 44 miles to the campground.

North Fork Road. This is a 21.5-mile ride (with a 1-mile spur trail you can hike to the lookout) along the southern edge of the area burned by the Wedge Canyon fire. The ride up is tough, with an elevation gain of more than 2,000 feet, but the descent will literally take your breath away.

LAKE ALVA CAMPGROUND

Seeley Lake

ALONG THIS STRETCH of the Clearwater River is a chain of lakes nestled in the valley like a string of pearls, each having its own unique features and characteristics. Lake Alva is a gentle, wooded pearl where the campsites are divided between two loops, with a third loop on the lake reserved for groups. The sites are well spaced and among the most private to be found at a developed campground.

"Lake Alva is a gentle, wooded pearl where the haunting calls of loons echo through the night."

Larch, fir, and alder trees anchor the screening between most sites. These trees buffer so well that even if a large RV is on the adjacent site, you probably won't know it. Each site is different, but our favorites—27, 37, 38, and 40—are on the northern loop. These are the most private, with plenty of room for tents.

The haunting calls of common loons echo throughout the day and into the night here, adding to the sense of wilderness even though you're not far from the highway. If you're lucky you'll see them dive far beneath the surface and stay underwater for long periods of time using their dagger-like beaks to ferret out food.

The day-use area is busy on weekends and provides a boat ramp and a grass-and-gravel beach with a well-marked swimming area. Fishing on this 310-acre lake yields a well-mixed bag of northern pike; cutthroat, brown, and rainbow trout; and an occasional kokanee. Wildlife viewing takes a backseat to the wealth of birds found here, but deer sightings are fairly common along the shore at dusk, and bears have been seen in the campground.

Sitting around the campfire or awakening to a symphony of birds, it's hard to imagine the bustle of activity around here during the logging boom years of the early 1900s. Back then, this river was a super-highway used to float logs to the Blackfoot River and on to

RATINGS

Beauty: ☆ ☆ ☆ ☆
Privacy: ☆ ☆ ☆ ☆ ☆
Spaciousness: ☆ ☆ ☆ ☆
Quiet: ☆ ☆ ☆ ☆
Security: ☆ ☆ ☆ ☆ ☆
Cleanliness: ☆ ☆ ☆ ☆ ☆

KEY INFORMATION

ADDRESS: Seeley Lake Ranger District
3583 MT 83
Seeley Lake, MT 59868

OPERATED BY: Lolo National Forest

INFORMATION: (406) 677-2233; www.fs.fed.us/r1/lolo

OPEN: Mid-May–September

SITES: 43

EACH SITE HAS: Picnic table, fire grate

ASSIGNMENT: First come, first served; no reservations

REGISTRATION: On-site self-registration

FACILITIES: Water spigots, vault toilets, boat ramp, beach

PARKING: At campsites

FEE: $10; $5 per extra vehicle

ELEVATION: 4,100 feet

RESTRICTIONS: **Pets:** On leash only
Fires: In fire grates only
Alcohol: Permitted
Vehicles: 22-foot length limit
Other: 14-day stay limit; bear country food-storage requirements; campground host

Bonner. These log drives consisted of damming up sections of the Clearwater to collect a large raft of felled logs. This wasn't a simple Huck Finn and Tom Sawyer raft, it was a serious number of trees. As a log reservoir would fill up, dynamite was used to blow the dam, allowing the load to rush into the next dammed section, where the process would be repeated until it reached Salmon Lake.

A logjam on the river could stretch for 2 miles. To prevent jams, agile men called "river hogs" or "river pigs" skillfully stepped from log to floating log, prodding them along to keep things moving. If a jam occurred it was their job to find the log or series of logs holding up progress and set a charge to blow them free.

Today the only objects floating on the river, besides ducks, are canoes. The Clearwater Canoe Trail is nearby and well worth your time. If you don't have a canoe, rentals are available in Seeley Lake. The trail's put-in is 8 miles south of the campground, and is clearly marked on MT 83. Allow about two-and-a-half hours for this leisurely float. If you leave early enough, you may be able to catch a moose looking for a meal. Don't worry about a shuttle vehicle; the takeout is located at the Seeley Lake Ranger Station, which also serves as the trailhead for the level, 1.5-mile trail leading back to the parking lot.

Along the canoe trail, it's bird city. Shorebirds such as American bittern, great blue heron, and belted kingfisher will keep you entertained along the water's edge. Look a little farther inland to see warblers, eagles, and osprey. When you paddle the short distance across Seeley Lake, your chances of seeing waterfowl, particularly loons, are pretty good.

If you'd rather travel by car, the Clearwater Chain-of-Lakes driving tour runs about 18 miles from Salmon Lake to Rainy Lake and provides designated viewing areas at four different lakes. It isn't quite the same as the view from the water, but you should see loons, eagles, and osprey throughout the day.

Located off MT 83, 11 miles south of the campground, is Morrell Creek Road. Follow the signs to the Morrell Falls National Recreation Trail #30. This popular 5.4-mile route takes hikers through dense forests

MAP

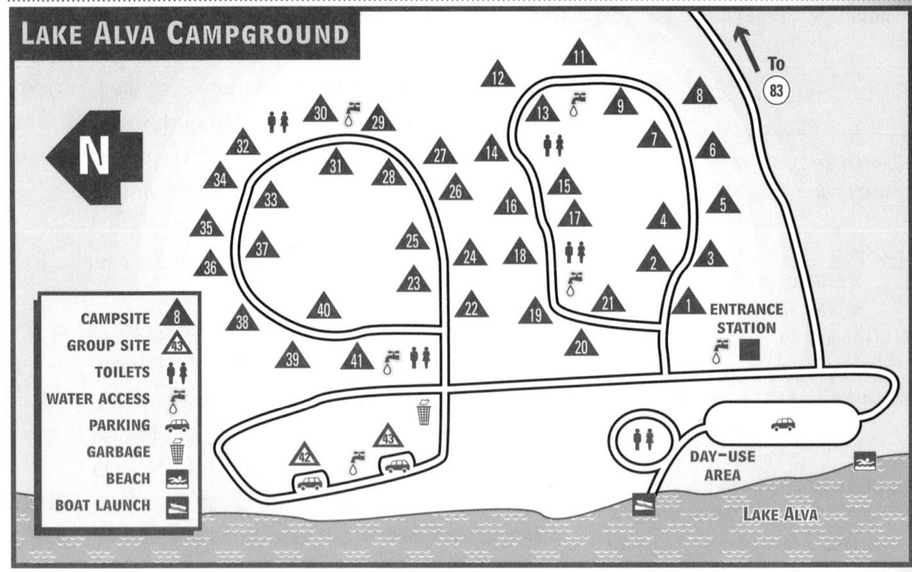

of lodgepole pine, fir, larch, and spruce on the way to Morrell Lake and Morrell Falls. It's 2.3 miles to the lake, and a view of the Swan Mountains is breathtaking. Another half mile takes you to the 90-foot double falls, where agile, fearless hikers often ascend a steep scramble to the top of the falls. Remember that this is grizzly bear country, so traveling in groups is advised.

GETTING THERE

From Seeley Lake, take MT 83 north for 12 miles. The campground is on the left.

PETE CREEK CAMPGROUND

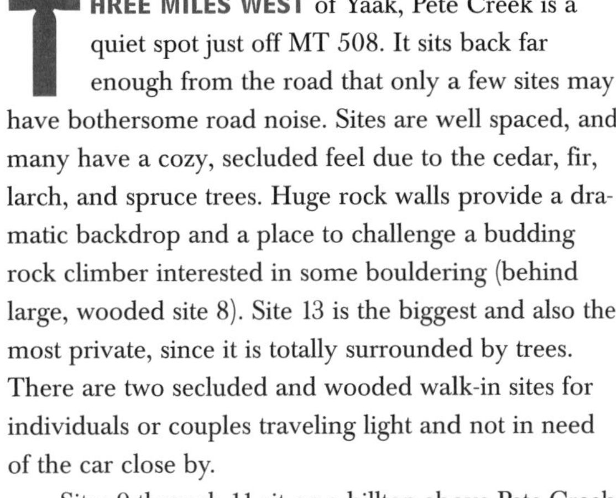

"Along the river you'll find delightful waterfalls and plenty of pools with trout and whitefish."

THREE MILES WEST of Yaak, Pete Creek is a quiet spot just off MT 508. It sits back far enough from the road that only a few sites may have bothersome road noise. Sites are well spaced, and many have a cozy, secluded feel due to the cedar, fir, larch, and spruce trees. Huge rock walls provide a dramatic backdrop and a place to challenge a budding rock climber interested in some bouldering (behind large, wooded site 8). Site 13 is the biggest and also the most private, since it is totally surrounded by trees. There are two secluded and wooded walk-in sites for individuals or couples traveling light and not in need of the car close by.

Sites 9 through 11 sit on a hilltop above Pete Creek, with a trail leading down to a nice swimming hole complete with small beach area. Site 11 is the best of the trio, set farther off the trail and offering a little more privacy from other campers using the trail to access the creek and the Yaak River. Site 1 is small and right off the road, but it is on the creek, and a waterfall dampens the road noise. Also along the river are delightful waterfalls and plenty of pools with trout and whitefish.

Wildlife viewing is abundant, with deer, elk, and moose in the area, along with more-than-occasional sightings of mountain lions, coyotes, and grizzly and black bears. Despite the highway, this is a sparsely populated, rugged region.

Down the road, the Yaak Mercantile hums with activity. Its sparse shelves hold only the most essential items. If your tires need air, ask for the air chuck at the counter. If your whistle needs wetting, beer and pop are in the cooler. If you're planning to fish—don't fret—tackle and sage advice are readily available. You're also likely to hear what the locals think about wilderness and winter. But the Mercantile and adjoining bar are not the only game in town. Across the street,

RATINGS

Beauty: ☆ ☆ ☆ ☆
Privacy: ☆ ☆ ☆ ☆
Spaciousness: ☆ ☆ ☆ ☆
Quiet: ☆ ☆ ☆ ☆
Security: ☆ ☆ ☆ ☆
Cleanliness: ☆ ☆ ☆ ☆ ☆

another bar offers refreshments alongside a tiny Laundromat.

From Yaak, take South Fork Pipe Creek Road (Forest Service Road 68) to Vinal Lake Road (FR 746) and go north 6 miles. Here you'll find the trailhead for The Vinal–Mount Henry–Boulder National Recreation Trail #9, which leads to the Mount Henry Lookout. This 16-mile round-trip requires an early start. You'll pass Turner Creek Falls and follow the ridge to get a 360-degree view from the mountaintop. Along the way, you'll see red cedars over 25 feet in diameter, and probably some deer and elk.

Another option, even though it's a 22-mile drive, is the Northwest Peaks Scenic Area. Take Pete Creek Road (FR 338) north to the trailhead, and you'll find yourself only a few miles from the Canadian and Idaho borders. There are several trails in the area, but Northwest Peak Trail #169 is an excellent day hike. It's a strong possibility you'll have the trail to yourself, since few people know about the area and even fewer venture this far off the track. This is a 4.6-mile out-and-back hike to the top of Northwest Peak (7,705 feet), the highest point in the Purcell Range, where you'll enjoy views of the Cabinet Mountains and Canadian Rockies in the distance. It's an easy hike, except for the final climb to the top, where the grade increases to 35 percent.

If the campground at Pete Creek is full, try Whitetail, another Forest Service site, 4 miles west on MT 508. The sites along the water here are more like an incredibly spacious backyard than a standard campground. It's a perfect place for kids to run off steam and for everyone to wade, skip rocks, and fish along this scenic stretch of the Yaak River, but it isn't as quiet as Pete Creek.

About 500 yards west of the Whitetail entrance is an open meadow where the river bends and pools, and where we stumbled upon one of those rare, breathtaking moments that are easy to miss. A family of moose was calmly dining on lush aquatic vegetation. Water sparkled in the twilight as it cascaded from the bull's massive rack each time he dramatically surfaced after feasting on river-bottom delicacies. The cow and her

KEY INFORMATION

ADDRESS: Three Rivers Ranger District
1437 North US 2
Troy, MT 59935

OPERATED BY: Kootenai National Forest

INFORMATION: (406) 295-4693; www.fs.fed.us/r1/kootenai

OPEN: Year-round; full services mid-May–mid-September

SITES: 12

EACH SITE HAS: Picnic table, fire grate

ASSIGNMENT: First come, first served; no reservations

REGISTRATION: On-site self-registration

FACILITIES: Water spigots, vault toilets

PARKING: At campsites

FEE: $7

ELEVATION: 3,120 feet

RESTRICTIONS: **Pets:** On leash only
Fires: In fire rings only
Alcohol: Permitted
Vehicles: 24-foot length limit
Other: 14-day stay limit; bear country food-storage restrictions; campground host

MAP

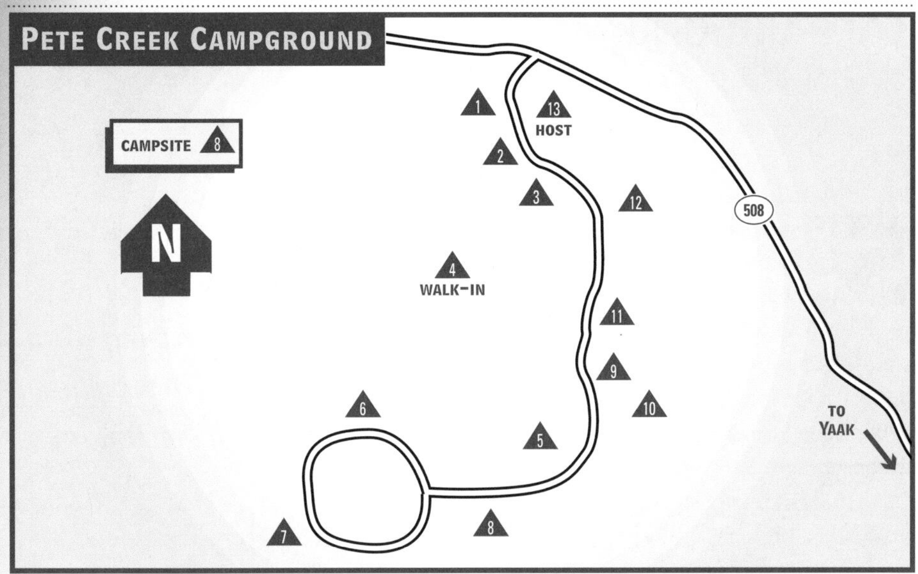

GETTING THERE

From Yaak, take MT 508 southwest for 3 miles to the campground.

From Troy, take US 2 west for 10 miles to MT 508. Turn right and go northeast for 36 miles to the campground.

calf frolicked downstream a hundred yards, while we stood mesmerized by this unexpected gift from Mother Nature after a long, hot day on the road.

PETERS CREEK CAMPGROUND

Hungry Horse

SIGNS AT BOTH ENDS of the town of Hungry Horse read "The Best Dam Town in the West," and you will certainly find some friendly people here. The town is named after–of all things–a couple of hungry horses. It's true. Tex and Jerry were hungry after wandering off during a tough winter in 1900. They both survived, and the town was named in their honor. Weird, eh?

At this small campground, each site offers a peaceful view of the mountains.

Hungry Horse Dam, built across the South Fork of the Flathead River in 1953, is just 15 miles from the west entrance to Glacier National Park, but it doesn't get as much use as you might think. Many visitors just rush right by, not even knowing it's here.

Tucked in a narrow canyon adjacent to both the Great Bear and Bob Marshall Wilderness areas, this 34-mile-long, 3-mile-wide reservoir is up to 500 feet deep in sections and holds more than 3.5 million acre-feet of water managed both for flood control and power production. Before the reservoir was formed, native bull trout and Westslope cutthroat migrated from Flathead Lake up the Flathead River to spawn in the river's South, Middle, and North Fork tributaries. The dam's construction blocked the fish from making the annual trip to Flathead Lake, and they adapted by spawning between the South Fork of the Flathead and Hungry Horse Reservoir. As a result, there is an unusual fishery here made up primarily of native species instead of introduced species like brook, brown, and rainbow trout. Visitors are requested to assist in protecting this resource by taking the time to familiarize themselves with how to identify bull trout and reviewing the most recent regulations. Fishing pressure is typically light on the reservoir, and you should find a variety of quiet spots to try your luck.

The road around Hungry Horse Reservoir is 115 miles long, and only the first 15 miles on the west side

RATINGS

Beauty: ✰ ✰ ✰ ✰
Privacy: ✰ ✰ ✰ ✰ ✰
Spaciousness: ✰ ✰ ✰ ✰ ✰
Quiet: ✰ ✰ ✰ ✰ ✰
Security: ✰ ✰ ✰
Cleanliness: ✰ ✰ ✰

KEY INFORMATION

ADDRESS: Spotted Bear Ranger District
P.O. Box 190340
Hungry Horse, MT 59919

OPERATED BY: Flathead National Forest

INFORMATION: (406) 387-3800; www.fs.fed.us/r1/flathead

OPEN: May 15–November

SITES: 5

EACH SITE HAS: Picnic table, fire grate

ASSIGNMENT: First come, first served; no reservations

REGISTRATION: Not required

FACILITIES: No water, vault toilets

PARKING: At campsites

FEE: Free

ELEVATION: 3,600 feet

RESTRICTIONS: **Pets:** On leash only
Fires: In fire rings only
Alcohol: Permitted
Vehicles: 30-foot length limit
Other: 14-day stay limit; bear country food-storage requirements; pack-in/pack-out

(Forest Service Road 895) are paved. Although the gravel surface isn't as bad as the road to Kintla Lake, it does have a reputation for eating tires. We can honestly report that the reputation is well earned and, having failed to heed our own excellent advice about being prepared, found our spare somewhat deflated. It was a Sunday afternoon, we were more than 50 miles from a gas station, and the bars on the cell phone were nonexistent. Fortunately, the Spotted Bear Ranger Station at the south end of the reservoir—only 13 bumpy miles away—is open seven days a week (very unusual, but greatly appreciated), and the staff helped us get back on the road.

After that adventure, pulling into Peters Creek was a welcome surprise. Located on the east shore (FR 38 out of Martin City), it offers the reservoir's best option for tent camping, with sites nestled among a heavy forest of aspens, larch, ponderosa pine, and Douglas fir. Sites are well spaced, and each has a peaceful view of the mountains surrounding the reservoir. This is a small campground, and every site could easily be considered the best. Short trails lie behind the campsites and leading down to the reservoir and a nice area where you can enjoy a morning cup of coffee or a relaxing dinner. There is no water available at the campground itself, and the closest option is 14 miles south at Spotted Bear Campground, so be sure to bring your own.

The west-shore campgrounds (FR 895 out of Hungry Horse) pale in comparison to those on the east shore. The Forest Service has completed an assessment of the recreational facilities around the reservoir in the hope that additional funding will be made available for much-needed improvements. Many of the campgrounds are old and worn and need an infusion of TLC.

If you can't find a spot at Peters Creek, try Murray Bay (15 miles north), where some of the 18 sites have nice views of the reservoir. Another 17 miles north is Emery Bay, where seclusion is minimal but maintenance is good.

Hiking opportunities are plentiful here. The trailhead for Logan Creek Trail #62 is a few miles north on FR 38. This 12-mile round-trip enters Great Bear

MAP

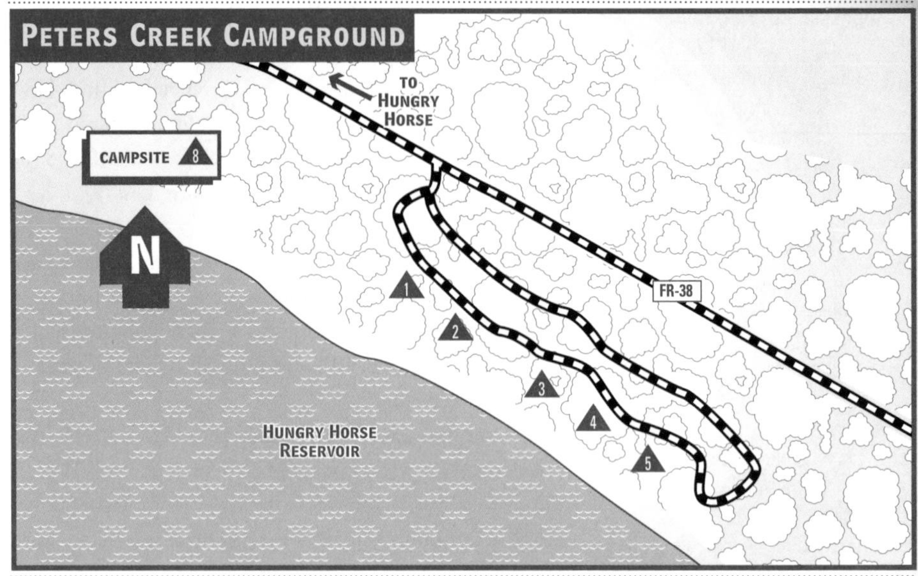

Wilderness area and rises more than 2,000 feet through dense forests, rugged cliffs, and wildflower meadows. Panoramic views of a lofty waterfall and Unawah and Red Top Mountains reward those who try this trail.

As you drive south on FR 38, you'll find several trailheads. At the Ranger Station you can continue south to Meadow Creek Gorge, where a suspension bridge crosses the designated Wild and Scenic South Fork of the Flathead River, or you can head east on FR 568 to another assortment of trailheads. Many trails in this region follow small tributaries to their headwaters in nearby alpine lakes. Be sure to get trail maps and current information from the Ranger Station. You'll be hiking in the wilderness, whether it's inside the official boundaries or not, and precautions and common sense are required. Problems you could encounter are far worse and more dangerous than a flat tire.

GETTING THERE

From Hungry Horse, take US 2 east for 0.6 miles to the East Side Hungry Horse sign. Turn right and go south on FR 38 for 28 miles to the campground.

SPRAGUE CREEK CAMPGROUND

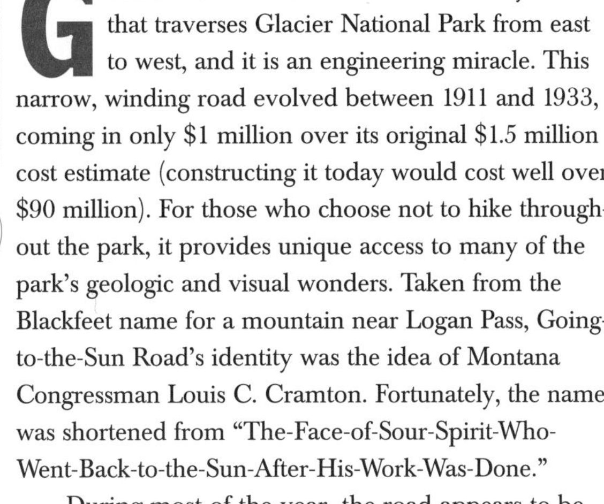

Towering cedars define this small loop on Lake McDonald.

RATINGS

Beauty: ✰ ✰ ✰ ✰ ✰
Privacy: ✰ ✰ ✰ ✰
Spaciousness: ✰ ✰ ✰ ✰
Quiet: ✰ ✰ ✰ ✰
Security: ✰ ✰ ✰ ✰ ✰
Cleanliness: ✰ ✰ ✰ ✰ ✰

GOING-TO-THE-SUN ROAD is the only road that traverses Glacier National Park from east to west, and it is an engineering miracle. This narrow, winding road evolved between 1911 and 1933, coming in only $1 million over its original $1.5 million cost estimate (constructing it today would cost well over $90 million). For those who choose not to hike throughout the park, it provides unique access to many of the park's geologic and visual wonders. Taken from the Blackfeet name for a mountain near Logan Pass, Going-to-the-Sun Road's identity was the idea of Montana Congressman Louis C. Cramton. Fortunately, the name was shortened from "The-Face-of-Sour-Spirit-Who-Went-Back-to-the-Sun-After-His-Work-Was-Done."

During most of the year, the road appears to be going more toward the North Pole, as heavy snows create drifts up to 80 feet deep, so the opening date fluctuates from mid-May to mid-June, depending on when work crews finally get everything plowed. On a Father's Day weekend trip, we walked through drifts in our shorts and had a snowball fight with our kids at Logan Pass.

Until the roadway was completed, visitors traveled through the park by foot or on horseback, spending days and weeks exploring. Today, a majority of those who enter the park spend a few hours driving Going-to-the-Sun Road and proudly proclaim they've "seen Glacier." Sadly, what they miss is an opportunity to experience this jewel by camping, hiking, or just relaxing along a creek or in a meadow to enjoy the sights, the smells, and the sounds.

Of the five campgrounds along the road, this is the best one for tenters due to its size and the restrictions against towed units. Towering cedars define this small loop on Lake McDonald, and sites range from spectacular to those that are too close for comfort.

Understory is quite sparse, but most sites provide at least some privacy. Two of the 25 sites are reserved for hikers and bicyclists and provide secure bear-proof food storage, while site 8 is the most coveted for its size and incredible lake and mountain views from the picnic table. Decent lake views are also available from sites 10, 12, and 13, but there are more trees through which to peer.

Avoid sites on the inside of the loop. These sites sit on top of one another and adjoin the restrooms. They may, however, be preferable for a group of families with small children. If these or sites 20 through 24 are all that's left, you might want to try Fish Creek. It's not that sites 20 through 24 are bad, but they lack privacy and get a lot of noise from traffic on Going-to-the-Sun Road. Keep in mind that this campground fills early, and during July and August there may be days when no sites open up at all. Fish Creek is a good alternative, since it fills later in the day.

Along the lakefront is a pleasant pebbled beach with a designated swimming area. The crystalline water is fairly cold throughout the year, so wading is generally the preferred method of experiencing the lake. For those who want to fish, no license is required, and dawn and dusk, when the wind is calm, are the best times to catch cutthroat, rainbow, and lake trout.

Within walking distance is Lake McDonald Lodge, where you can board an historic boat for tours of the lake or attend nightly programs that divulge the park's history and secrets. Across the road from the lodge is a trailhead leading to Fish Lake, Lincoln Lake, Mount Brown Lookout, and Sperry Chalet. The hike to Fish Lake is a 4.8-mile round-trip along Snyder Creek that gently climbs through fir and pine forests and along benches to the lake. The setting is peaceful and highlighted by the call of loons, but the heavy forest surroundings do prevent views of the mountains. Hiking to Mount Brown Lookout is a challenge. Most of this 10.8-mile trek consists of switchbacks, but there are huckleberries along the way, and views of Lake McDonald and the surrounding mountains, including the Little Matterhorn, are awesome.

KEY INFORMATION

ADDRESS: Glacier National Park
P.O. Box 128
West Glacier, MT 59936

OPERATED BY: National Park Service

INFORMATION: (406) 888-7800; www.nps.gov/glac

OPEN: Mid-May–mid-September

SITES: 25

EACH SITE HAS: Picnic table, fire grate

ASSIGNMENT: First come, first served; no reservations

REGISTRATION: On-site self-registration

FACILITIES: Water spigots, flush toilets, pay phone

PARKING: At campsites

FEE: $15

ELEVATION: 3,200 feet

RESTRICTIONS: **Pets:** On leash only, not permitted on trails or along lakeshore
Fires: In fire rings only
Alcohol: Permitted
Vehicles: No towed units, only Class C RVs allowed
Other: 7-day stay limit; bear country food-storage restrictions; no firearms; no firewood gathering; special fishing restrictions

MAP

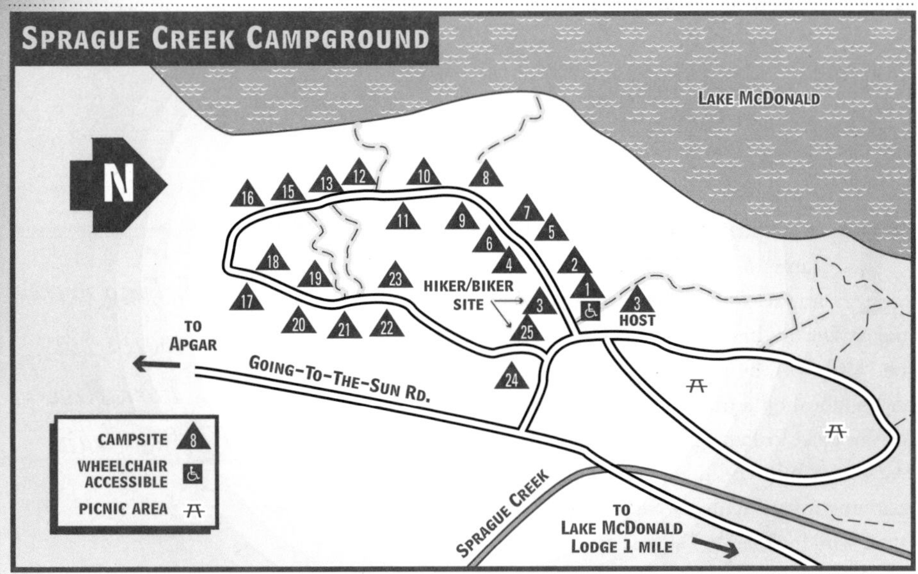

GETTING THERE

From West Glacier entrance, take Going-to-the-Sun Road northeast for 8 miles to the campground.

Wildlife viewing at Sprague Creek is not as good as at some of the other campgrounds due to the road traffic, but deer and elk are usually sighted in the early evening, and as dusk settles, you may hear brakes squealing as animal–vehicle collisions are avoided.

THOMPSON FALLS STATE PARK CAMPGROUND

Thompson Falls

THIS PARK IS ONE of many places bearing the name of David Thompson, a tribute to the impact of the Canadian explorer and mapmaker. During his 28-year, 55,000-mile exploration of the Northwest, he settled nearby, from 1809 to 1811, and established a trading post, Saleesh House, named for the local Indians. The tribes demonstrated their respect for him and their awe of his telescope and mapping instruments by calling him Koo-koo-sint (man who looks at the stars).

> *Easy fishing access to the world-class Clark Fork River is a prime draw.*

Like many campgrounds set amid a canopy of towering pines, the lack of understory affects privacy, but these sites are roomy, well spaced, and peaceful. Site 10 is unique and well designed for tenters: the tent area is perched on a terraced area set below the picnic table and fire ring, which mitigates the open view to site 11 across the road. The most popular site is 7 because it overlooks the Clark Fork River, but it is next to the boat ramp and its daytime bustle. River access is also easy from sites 15, 16, and 17. They aren't exactly riverfront but do adjoin a short trail to the Clark Fork.

Even though a group site occupies its own corner close to the access road and large RVs do camp here, the campground host keeps everyone under control and maintains quiet. As a result, deer are usually spotted several times a day by kids riding their bikes around the campground loops. Osprey sightings are frequent as well.

Fishing in the Clark Fork is a prime draw, particularly for fly-fishing devotees. But this world-class river is tricky, and novices may want to focus on the experience rather than the quantity of their catch. Rainbow, brown, and cutthroat trout, along with largemouth and smallmouth bass, are prevalent, and rods and reels are available in town for those who aren't equipped but can't resist the temptation to wet a line.

RATINGS

Beauty: ☆ ☆ ☆
Privacy: ☆ ☆ ☆ ☆
Spaciousness: ☆ ☆ ☆ ☆ ☆
Quiet: ☆ ☆ ☆ ☆ ☆
Security: ☆ ☆ ☆ ☆ ☆
Cleanliness: ☆ ☆ ☆ ☆

KEY INFORMATION

ADDRESS: Region 1
490 North Meridian
Kalispell, MT 59901

OPERATED BY: Montana Fish, Wildlife & Parks

INFORMATION: (406) 293-1790; www.fwp.state.mt.us

OPEN: May–September

SITES: 17

EACH SITE HAS: Picnic table; fire grate

ASSIGNMENT: First come, first served; no reservations

REGISTRATION: On-site self-registration

FACILITIES: Water spigots, vault toilets, boat ramp, picnic shelters

PARKING: At campsites

FEE: $12

ELEVATION: 2,473 feet

RESTRICTIONS: **Pets:** On leash only
Fires: In fire rings only
Alcohol: Permitted
Vehicles: 30-foot length limit
Other: 14-day stay limit; bear country food-storage requirements; campground host

Floating the Clark Fork is an excellent way to spend a sunny day whether you're in a raft or canoe. Inner tubes are often the craft of choice for the young (and the young at heart), and since the river runs along the highway, shuttles are fairly easy. If you are planning a long float, outfitters and supplies are available in Thompson Falls.

When you're ready to explore the area, don't spend your time looking for the falls in the park's name; they disappeared years ago when the Clark Fork was dammed, but there are a variety of other sights nearby. In town, a pedestrian bridge leads to a river island with several nature trails—prime territory for wildlife enthusiasts. Three miles southeast on MT 200 is the Mount Silcox Wildlife Management Area, where white-tailed and mule deer, elk, black bears, and turkey are visible throughout the summer, and mountain goats can be seen on the surrounding cliffs. KooKooSint Sheep Viewing Area is another 5 miles south on MT 200. Although peak viewing opportunities are during the fall mating season, sightings are still possible during the summer, when sheep perch on the rocky outcroppings.

The state's best huckleberry-hunting country is found throughout this area. You can try asking locals for suggestions, but most patches are closely guarded secrets. Don't be afraid to strike out on your own beginning about mid-June at lower elevations and into July for the higher mountainsides. Patches sprout at elevations between 3,500 and 7,000 feet, where tree cover is less than 50 percent so they can receive necessary sunlight. Burn areas that are a few decades old are also good possibilities for patches, as are south-facing slopes. Generally, no permit is required to pick up to ten gallons per person, but check with the Forest Service on current regulations and be sure your newfound berry patch isn't on private land before you pick.

A drive along the Vermillion River on Blue Slide Road (off MT 200 at Trout Creek Bridge) brings you to a short hike down to the waterfall and a great picnic spot. Trailheads for several longer trails dot both sides of this forest road, and most follow a creek or stream.

West of Thompson Falls on Prospect Creek Road is Blossom Lake Trail #404. You may share the way

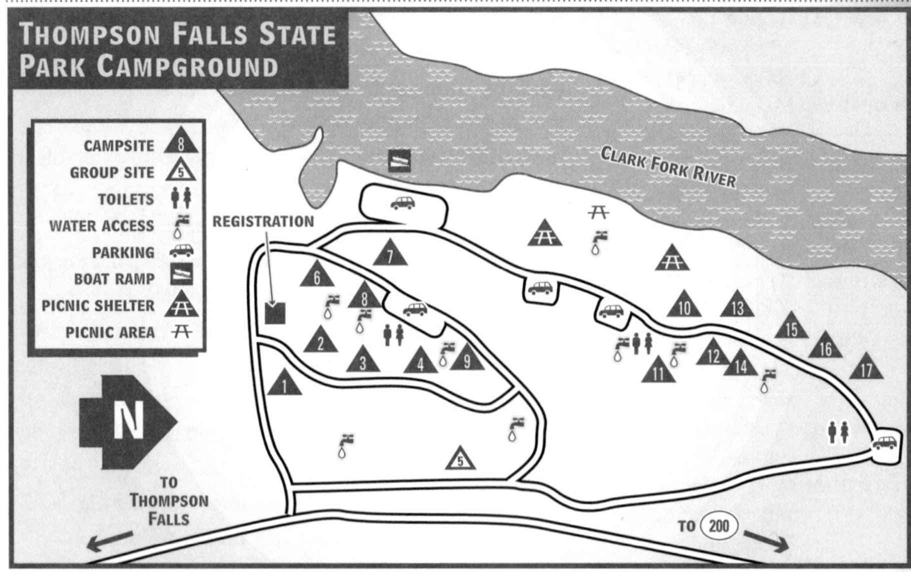

with an occasional horseback party, but it isn't a problem on this isolated, 10-mile round-trip to a series of high mountain lakes. The trail itself runs along the Idaho-Montana border, and your trek can continue all the way to the Coeur d'Alene River near Lookout Pass.

GETTING THERE

From Thompson Falls, take MT 200 northwest for 1 mile (milepost 50). Turn right into the campground.

NORTH CENTRAL **MONTANA**

CAVE MOUNTAIN CAMPGROUND

Choteau

VIEWS OF THE ROCKY MOUNTAIN front are spectacular as you drive along the Teton River to Cave Mountain. Ahead of you are Wind Mountain and flat-topped Ear Mountain. This is actually part of the original Old North Trail, used for centuries as a travel corridor between Canada and points south. Limestone cliffs rise 500 feet on either side of you, and viewpoints provide panoramic 360-degree vistas.

The road enters a gap in the cliffs, and not far beyond, a sign points the way to Cave Mountain. Two bridge crossings, one over the North Fork Teton River and one over the Middle Fork, lead to the campground entrance. Set under a beautiful mix of birch, aspen, and pines, the campground's 14 sites are perfect for tenters looking for quiet and solitude. Sites here are spacious, and sites 1, 3, 4, 6, 8, 10, and 12 back up to and are only a short walk from the North Fork of the Teton. You won't go wrong picking any one of these pine-needle–covered sites. Site 14, on the back end of the loop at the end of the road, is nicely secluded. Sites 5 and 7 are also well separated with plenty of space to spread out for a few days.

This campground makes a great base camp for fishing, hiking, or mountain biking. The trailhead for Middle Fork Teton River Trail #108 is at Cave Mountain. It's actually more of a stroll than a hike, as it follows the river bottoms: no mountain vistas, no dramatic canyons, just a walk in the woods along a stream where you can relax, watch industrious beavers, or fish for mountain whitefish or trout. From this trail you can also access the Bob Marshall Wilderness.

A mile east of the campground is the trailhead for Clary Coulee Trail #177. This 12-mile out-and-back trail follows an open bench with views of vast plains to the east and Rocky Mountain peaks to the west. Small stream crossings necessitate some short, steep up-and-

Enjoy spectacular vistas of the Rocky Mountains as you drive along the Teton River.

RATINGS

Beauty: ☆ ☆ ☆ ☆ ☆
Privacy: ☆ ☆ ☆ ☆ ☆
Spaciousness: ☆ ☆ ☆ ☆ ☆
Quiet: ☆ ☆ ☆ ☆ ☆
Security: ☆ ☆ ☆
Cleanliness: ☆ ☆ ☆ ☆ ☆

KEY INFORMATION

ADDRESS:	Rocky Mountain Ranger District P.O. Box 340 1102 Main Avenue NW Choteau, MT 59422
OPERATED BY:	Lewis and Clark National Forest
INFORMATION:	(406) 466-5341; www.fs.fed.us/r1/lewisclark
OPEN:	Memorial Day–October
SITES:	14
EACH SITE HAS:	Picnic table, fire grate
ASSIGNMENT:	First come, first served; no reservations
REGISTRATION:	On-site self-registration
FACILITIES:	Hand-pump well, vault toilets
PARKING:	At campsites
FEE:	$6
ELEVATION:	5,200 feet
RESTRICTIONS:	**Pets:** On leash only **Fires:** In fire rings only **Alcohol:** Permitted **Vehicles:** 22-foot length limit **Other:** 14-day stay limit; pack-in/pack-out; bear country food-storage restrictions

down climbs, but overall this is a moderate trail that isn't heavily used.

Another hiking option is North Fork Teton Trail #107, which winds along the river through narrow Box Canyon. During summer, the many river crossings on this trail are pretty simple, but during spring runoff, it's quite possible that the depth and speed of the water will make them impassable. The trailhead for this 8-mile out-and-back trip is 4 miles west of the campground.

You can climb to the peak of Mount Wright on a day hike from the trailhead 10 miles west of the campground. The trail follows West Fork Trail #144 for the first quarter mile, and from there it's a steep 4-mile climb through prime habitat for mountain goats and bighorn sheep. The descent can be challenging as well, but if you're in good shape, the view from the 8,875-foot summit is spectacular and worth the effort. On a clear day you'll see peaks at Glacier National Park and part of the Chinese Wall running through the Bob Marshall Wilderness.

About 5 miles east of the campground is a turnoff for Our Lake Trail and the Pine Butte Swamp Preserve, an 18,000-acre wetland owned by The Nature Conservancy that provides significant grizzly bear habitat. At the preserve, the A.B Guthrie Trail across from the information board is the only hiking access provided, although you can obtain permission to hike the butte from the preserve manager. You may not see any bears while you're here, but dozens of other mammals like elk, deer, and coyote will draw your attention. Over 100 bird species have been sighted here, from songbirds to sand-hill cranes.

If you're heading for the trails instead of the preserve, take a left as you cross the river and follow South Fork Road (Forest Service Road 109) for 9 miles to the trailhead. Our Lake Trail #184 is a 5-mile out-and-back that climbs steeply in places and can be slippery before the snow melts in late June. Bears are seen often in this area, and many people see mountain goats clinging to the slopes on the other side of the lake. A waterfall about halfway to the lake is usually less crowded than the lake itself. If you are thinking about

MAP

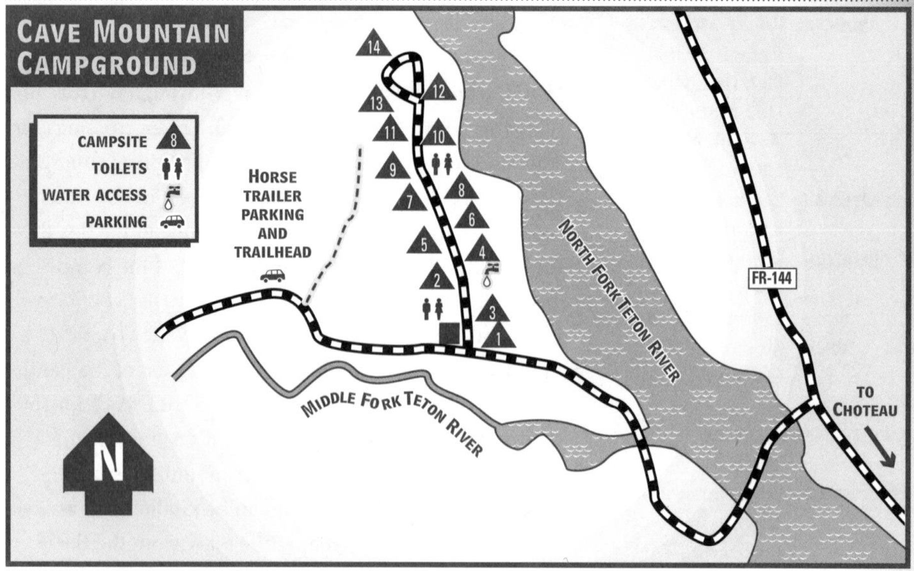

making this an overnight hike, camping is allowed near the waterfall, but not near the lake.

The Choteau area is famous for more than ranching and spectacular scenery. Nearby Egg Mountain is where paleontologist Jack Horner discovered fossilized dinosaur eggs and embryos, establishing the Willow Creek Anticline as an active site where finds are still being made. If you want to take part in a dig, stop at the Old Trail Museum in Choteau for information.

GETTING THERE

From Choteau, take US 89 north for 4 miles to Teton Pass Winter Sports Area/ Eureka Reservoir signs. Turn left at the signs (FR 144) and go 23 miles to the campground. (Last 5 miles are gravel and dirt road.)

HOME GULCH CAMPGROUND

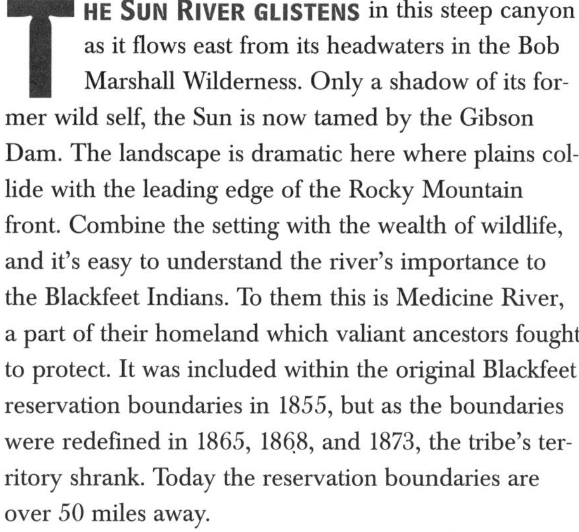

This spectacular canyon invites tenters to make camp in the shadow of overthrust formations along the shoreline.

THE SUN RIVER GLISTENS in this steep canyon as it flows east from its headwaters in the Bob Marshall Wilderness. Only a shadow of its former wild self, the Sun is now tamed by the Gibson Dam. The landscape is dramatic here where plains collide with the leading edge of the Rocky Mountain front. Combine the setting with the wealth of wildlife, and it's easy to understand the river's importance to the Blackfeet Indians. To them this is Medicine River, a part of their homeland which valiant ancestors fought to protect. It was included within the original Blackfeet reservation boundaries in 1855, but as the boundaries were redefined in 1865, 1868, and 1873, the tribe's territory shrank. Today the reservation boundaries are over 50 miles away.

As you drive to the campground along Sun Canyon Road you'll see a bighorn-sheep viewing area. One of the largest herds in North America lives here, lured by the same spectacular topography that invites tenters to make camp in the shadow of overthrust formations along the shoreline. Set among thick stands of aspens, sites are well spaced, and most have a nice amount of ground cover providing privacy between them. Of the eight sites with river access, our favorites are sites 1, 3, 5, and 7, with thick ground cover as a privacy barrier and short trails leading to the river for fishing, wading, or stone skipping in the cold, clear water. Water levels in the river can fluctuate significantly depending on discharge from the reservoir, but fishing is still good for rainbow, brown, and cutthroat trout in the deep pools throughout the canyon.

Rafting the Sun River's 3 miles of Class V whitewater between Gibson Reservoir and Sun River Dam (just west of Home Gulch) can be a challenge even for experienced rafters. Fishing from boats is not allowed here for obvious reasons. The section through the

RATINGS

Beauty: ★ ★ ★ ★ ★
Privacy: ★ ★ ★ ★
Spaciousness: ★ ★ ★
Quiet: ★ ★ ★ ★
Security: ★ ★ ★ ★
Cleanliness: ★ ★ ★ ★

canyon and Home Gulch is a little calmer, with Class II and III rapids, but rocks and underwater ledges are frequent in this section. Beyond the canyon to Willow Creek Reservoir, the river winds and twists relentlessly with some occasional Class II spots.

To the east is Sun River Game Range, home to one of the state's largest elk populations. The range's 20,000 acres are open to the public in summer, and visitors can hike, bike, or drive throughout the area to see wetlands, wildlife, and maybe a black or grizzly bear set against a magnificent backdrop.

Mortimer Gulch Campground lies 2.5 miles west. This camping alternative sits directly on the reservoir and is a major trailhead, but it's usually full of RVs and motorboats. If you do decide to camp here, you'll choose between two loops. Sites 18 through 20, on the first loop you'll encounter, are large and more secluded than the others. You won't be right on the water at any of the sites here, but you'll be close enough to still hear an occasional boat motor during the day.

Home Gulch–Lime Trail #267 is a 15-mile point-to-point hike with gentle grade changes. The scenery is spectacular, but don't forget to turn back before you're exhausted. Not heavily used, this trail is ideal for families or those looking for easy terrain. The trailhead is 0.5 miles from Home Gulch, north of the Sun Canyon Lodge gate.

A variety of trails lead from the area into the Bob Marshall Wilderness to the northwest. Just past Home Gulch is Hannan Gulch Trail #240, which begins near the guard station and climbs nearly 2,400 feet along its 6.5-mile length to the head of the gulch. This is a good mountain-bike trail due to its width and relatively low usage by hikers.

Mortimer Gulch Trail #252 begins at Mortimer Gulch Campground and runs the 7-mile length of the gulch to Blacktail Creek Trail #223. It's surprising that this isn't a more heavily used trail, since the elevation gain is minimal and it provides excellent views of Sawtooth Ridge, Norwegian and French Gulches, and Gibson Reservoir. This is an especially good wildlife-viewing area in the spring and early summer

KEY INFORMATION

ADDRESS: Rocky Mountain Ranger District
1102 Main Avenue NW, P.O. Box 340
Choteau, MT 59422

OPERATED BY: Lewis and Clark National Forest

INFORMATION: (406) 466-5341; www.fs.fed.us/r1/lewisclark

OPEN: Memorial Day–October

SITES: 15

EACH SITE HAS: Picnic table, fire ring

ASSIGNMENT: First come, first served; no reservations

REGISTRATION: On-site self-registration

FACILITIES: Hand-pump well, vault toilets, boat ramp at Gibson Reservoir

PARKING: At campsites

FEE: $6

ELEVATION: 4,580 feet

RESTRICTIONS: **Pets:** On leash only
Fires: In fire rings only
Alcohol: Permitted
Vehicles: 22-foot length limit
Other: 14-day stay limit; bear country food-storage requirements; pack-in/pack-out; only non-motorized boats on river

MAP

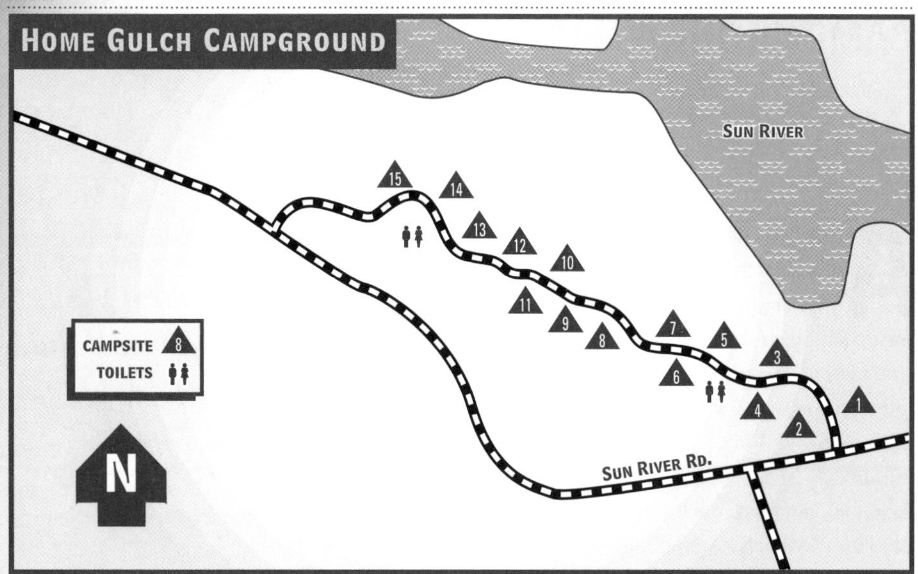

GETTING THERE

From Augusta, take Manix Street west toward Gibson Reservoir for 3.7 miles (this turns into FR 108). At the reservoir-sign intersection, turn right and go 16.8 miles on Sun River Road (FR 180). Turn right at the sign to the campground.

before the deer, elk, mountain goats, and bighorn sheep head for higher elevations.

North Fork Sun River Trail #201 also begins at the Mortimer trailhead. This trail follows the north side of Gibson Reservoir for 2 miles before it intersects with Big George Gulch Trail #251, a more difficult trail that continues another 6 miles on a high bench. The trail drops and climbs steeply in sections over the pass, but switchbacks ease the effort. Views to the south are of Sawtooth Ridge and Gibson Reservoir, and you'll see plenty of wildlife here as well.

INDIAN HILL CAMPGROUND

Hobson

AS A CHILD IN MISSOURI, Charles M. Russell played hooky to sketch landscapes along the Mississippi River. He dreamt of being a Wild West cowboy, and at 15 he journeyed to Montana to visit a family friend, began working as a sheepherder, and never returned home. He was captivated by the dramatic colors and views across north central Montana and quickly became less than enthusiastic about herding sheep. He devoted more and more time to his art and, ultimately, Russell became internationally renown for his renderings of Western history, Indians and their homelands, and the wild and domestic animals that graced the landscape. The vibrantly colored skies he loved, and captured so well, are frequently seen at dawn and sunrise. When they appear above our house, we call one another to the window to see the "Charlie Russell sky."

> *Enjoy great views of the rock walls lining South Fork Judith River canyon.*

The Judith River Basin is the heart of Charlie Russell country. The river, named by explorer William Clark for his fiancée, sparkles as it flows through this wonderful canyon. The road to the campground follows the river and is part of the C. M. Russell Auto Tour, designed by the Forest Service and local tourism agencies. This particular section is called "Memorial Way," and an interpretive brochure illustrated with several of Russell's paintings is available from visitor centers and the Judith Ranger District headquarters.

The road passes through Utica, once considered the liveliest town in the West, where hundreds of cowboys would converge in the fall and raise a major ruckus. Now the annual celebration revolves around haystacks. These aren't ordinary haystacks; these grand and elaborate sculptures dot the landscape and are the source of an intense but friendly competition among surrounding ranchers.

Farther down the road you'll come to Sapphire Village and Yogo Gulch, identified in 1952 as one of

RATINGS

Beauty: ✩ ✩ ✩ ✩
Privacy: ✩ ✩ ✩
Spaciousness: ✩ ✩ ✩ ✩
Quiet: ✩ ✩ ✩ ✩ ✩
Security: ✩ ✩ ✩ ✩
Cleanliness: ✩ ✩ ✩ ✩

KEY INFORMATION

ADDRESS: Judith Ranger District
109 Central Avenue
Stanford, MT 59479

OPERATED BY: Lewis and Clark National Forest

INFORMATION: (406) 566-2292; www.fs.fed.us/r1/lewisclark

OPEN: Memorial Day–September, depending on conditions

SITES: 7

EACH SITE HAS: Picnic table, fire ring

ASSIGNMENT: First come, first served; no reservations

REGISTRATION: None required

FACILITIES: No water, vault toilets

PARKING: At campsites

FEE: Free

ELEVATION: 5,265 feet

RESTRICTIONS: **Pets:** On leash only
Fires: In fire rings only
Alcohol: Permitted
Vehicles: 20-foot length limit
Other: 16-day stay limit; pack-in/pack-out

the most important gem localities in the world. The name hints at the rich deposit of gemstones beneath the surface but doesn't come close to revealing that millions of dollars' worth of the world's most beautiful sapphires have been mined here. The Yogo Gulch Sapphire Mine is privately owned and not open to the public like some sapphire mines around the state, but you will find these cornflower blue gemstones in jewelry shops across Montana.

Just to the west of Sapphire Village is the Judith River Wildlife Management Area, a 7,745-acre range for elk, deer, antelope, and black bears. You'll be able to view white-tailed deer, antelope, raptors, and a variety of songbirds from the road. Elk are more plentiful during the fall and winter but may occasionally be seen by summer visitors.

As you near Hay Canyon the road narrows, becoming single-lane gravel with turnouts. Along this stretch there are actually two campgrounds from which to choose—Indian Hill and Hay Canyon campgrounds—both of which have quiet sites along the South Fork Judith River. Please note that no water is available at either of these spots, so bring plenty of your own.

Indian Hill is the better choice, with its seven scenic sites. The first two sites are right on the river, and even though there isn't much space between them, the sound of the water flowing past makes them very inviting. A short bridge over the river leads to a loop with the five remaining campsites. Our top picks are the three nearest the water on the north side of this loop. The spruce-and-pine forest offers great shady spots, and fantastic views of the rock walls lining the canyon are revealed between the trees. The river here is narrow and shallow, which makes wading a joy and turns fishing into a challenge. If you're patient and cagey enough, you might land some sly brook trout.

If Indian Hill is full, you can choose between the dispersed sites across the road or one of the sites at Hay Canyon Campground. Hay Canyon lies 2 miles southwest and offers nine sites split between two areas. The sites don't sit on the river, and the surroundings aren't quite as scenic. Beyond the campground is the

MAP

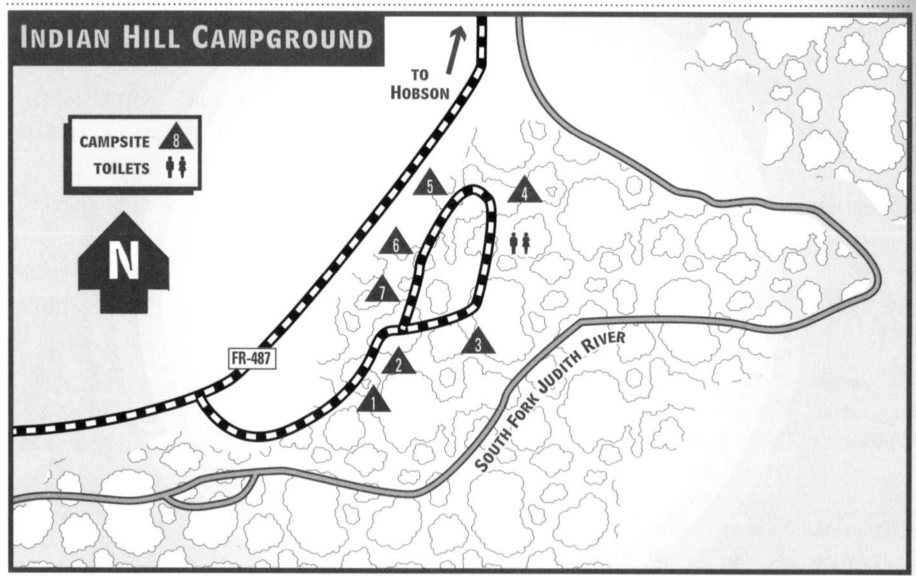

Hay Canyon Trailhead, starting point for a 4.5-mile hike that begins at the canyon floor and climbs above the canyon rim.

GETTING THERE

From Hobson (US 87), take MT 239 southwest for 12 miles through Utica and Sapphire Village. Continue on FR 487 for the last 3 miles to the campground.

Elliston

KADING CAMPGROUND

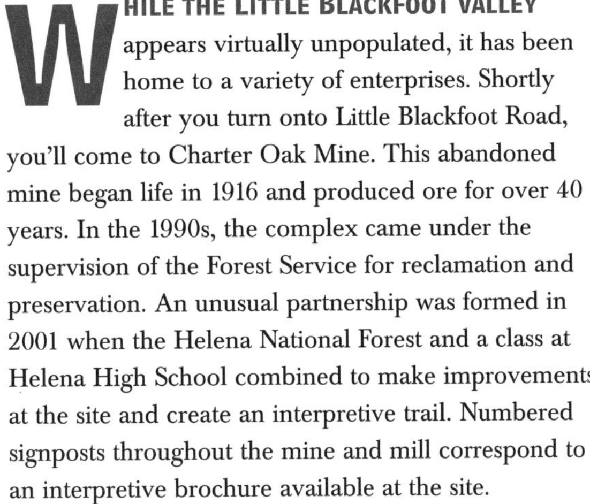

> *Brook trout are easy to catch in the pools of cool water held back by downed logs and large rocks.*

WHILE THE LITTLE BLACKFOOT VALLEY appears virtually unpopulated, it has been home to a variety of enterprises. Shortly after you turn onto Little Blackfoot Road, you'll come to Charter Oak Mine. This abandoned mine began life in 1916 and produced ore for over 40 years. In the 1990s, the complex came under the supervision of the Forest Service for reclamation and preservation. An unusual partnership was formed in 2001 when the Helena National Forest and a class at Helena High School combined to make improvements at the site and create an interpretive trail. Numbered signposts throughout the mine and mill correspond to an interpretive brochure available at the site.

About the same time Charter Oak began full-scale operation, two enterprising settlers sought their fortune from a different natural resource. You'll see the remains of their handiwork if you take the hike to Blackfoot Meadows. The marshy pond in the meadows was dammed by two men who started a beaver farm here in the 1920s. After about five years, the economic windfall they anticipated failed to materialize, and they left seeking greener pastures.

On your drive to the campground, you'll follow the Little Blackfoot River almost to its headwaters. Along the way, watch for white-tailed deer and small mammals in the roadside meadows, and those who are especially observant should see raptors or grouse. Nestled on the west side of the Continental Divide along a trout-filled river, Kading is a popular weekend escape for those in Helena and the surrounding communities. On weekdays, however, you will likely have your choice of sites to set up camp.

Sites here are spacious and set among songbird-filled trees with a minimal amount of understory. Our favorite sites for location are 1, 2, 4, and 5 on the river

RATINGS

Beauty: ★★★★
Privacy: ★★★★★
Spaciousness: ★★★★★
Quiet: ★★★★
Security: ★★★★
Cleanliness: ★★★★★

side of the road. They lie closest to the riverbank, which makes dropping a line or casting a fly extremely easy. The downside is their proximity to the day-use parking areas. Sites 8 and 10, on the river side at the end of the road, are quieter and well covered by trees, but it's farther to the water.

The Little Blackfoot is narrow here, and brook trout are plentiful. They're easy to catch in the pools of cool water held back by downed logs and large rocks, making this a great stop for those with young anglers in tow. Not as plentiful, but very much in evidence, are rainbow and brown trout along with longnose suckers. Bull trout are also found here, so be sure you're current on fishing regulations.

Choose from a variety of hiking opportunities. You can easily spend a few days here exploring the area. For starters, try the easy 11-mile out-and-back hike to Blackfoot Meadow Trail #329, which begins from the trailhead half a mile past the campground. The trail runs for about a mile along an old road until you take the fork that gently heads down to the riverbank and across a small bridge. The next section is fairly marshy, so keep that in mind when you're selecting footgear. The surrounding hillsides are painted in beargrass, Indian paintbrush, bluebells, and grouse whortleberry (where, you guessed it, grouse like to hang out). There is nothing as heart-stopping on a leisurely hike as a grouse bursting into flight only a few feet away from you! There will be another river crossing where you can try the downed logs or just wade across. Another mile or so brings you mountain views and the broad, wildflower-strewn Blackfoot Meadow. Relax and have lunch here before retracing your route to the campground.

Both mountain bikers and hikers may want to take a 13-mile loop that follows Trail #329 to Blackfoot Meadow and then continues northeast on Trail #362 to the ridge, picking up Trail #359. This trail takes you into Larabee Gulch and ends at Forest Service Road 227. From there it's 2 miles west to the campground to complete the loop.

Adjacent to the campground is Kading Cabin, named for the area rancher who originally owned the

KEY INFORMATION

ADDRESS: Helena Ranger District
2001 Poplar Street
Helena, MT 59602

OPERATED BY: Helena National Forest

INFORMATION: (406) 449-5490; www.fs.fed.us/r1/helena

OPEN: June–September

SITES: 11

EACH SITE HAS: Picnic table, fire grate

ASSIGNMENT: First come, first served; no reservations

REGISTRATION: On-site self-registration

FACILITIES: Hand-pump water, vault toilets

PARKING: At campsites

FEE: $5

ELEVATION: 6,200 feet

RESTRICTIONS: **Pets:** On leash only
Fires: In fire rings only
Alcohol: Permitted
Vehicles: 22-foot length limit
Other: 14-day stay limit; bear country food-storage restrictions; pack-in/pack-out

MAP

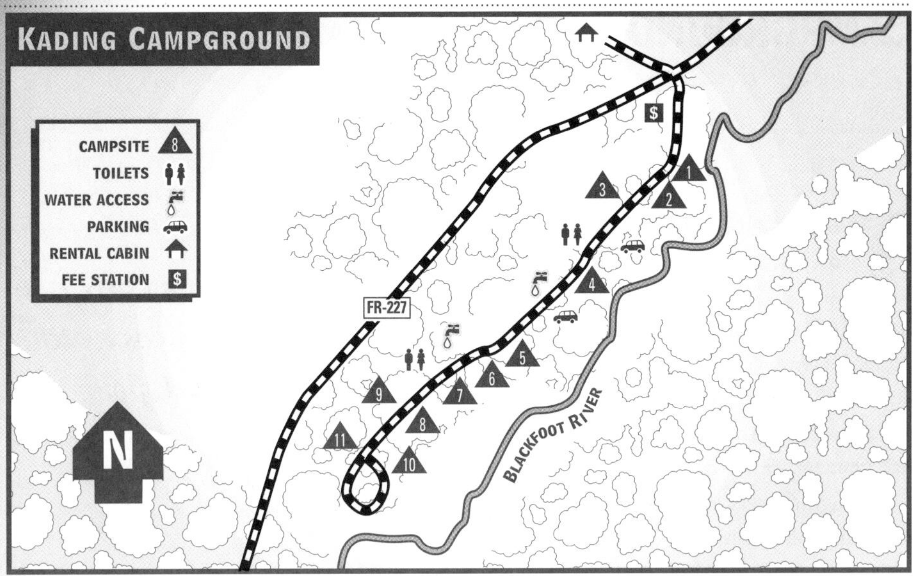

GETTING THERE

From Elliston, take US 12 east for 1 mile to Little Blackfoot Road (FR 227). Turn right and go 13 miles southwest to the campground.

From Helena, take US 12 west for 18.5 miles to Little Blackfoot Road (FR 227). Turn left and go 13 miles southwest to the campground.

land and built by the Civilian Conservation Corps in the 1930s. Today it is a year-round rental cabin and the site of various Forest Service summer programs.

LOGGING CREEK CAMPGROUND

Monarch

THE TWO ROUTES into Logging Creek are as diverse as the countryside. On the tamer ride along MT 227, your teeth won't chatter nearly as much as they will on the narrow, single-lane track called Logging Creek Road. If you're in a rental car or borrowed a good friend's Lexus, you should seriously consider the highway route, unless you're willing to risk your insurance or your friendship.

> *Camping here is as relaxing as watching the creek flow.*

Logging Creek is tucked on the northern edge of the Little Belt Mountains. Your drive in will be a visual education about the Madison Limestone Formation that makes the views around this campground worth the drive. This formation lies beneath much of Montana's surface and is unique because of the many caves, fissures, and seams that allow water to run through it. It's like a giant slab of Swiss cheese. Water enters above the surface but in some places moves beneath the surface and splits off in many directions, all the while continuing to flow downhill. Surrounding this limestone formation are other geologic formations that developed before and after the limestone; these formations seal the water into the porous rock channel.

No matter which route you take, you will cross Belt Creek, which is a great example of how the Madison Limestone Formation works. At certain points, during periods of low water, the creek bed runs dry while the upstream and downstream ends continue to flow. After your stay at Logging Creek, visit Giant Springs State Park in Great Falls. The pristine water flowing from these springs originated in the Little Belt Mountains that surround Logging Creek. But don't expect the water flowing underground today to come out at Giant Springs next week. It takes thousands of years for each drop of water to make the circuitous underground trip.

Belt Creek also runs through nearby Sluice Boxes State Park, a narrow box canyon sliced into the lime-

RATINGS

Beauty: ✩ ✩ ✩ ✩
Privacy: ✩ ✩ ✩ ✩ ✩
Spaciousness: ✩ ✩ ✩ ✩
Quiet: ✩ ✩ ✩ ✩ ✩
Security: ✩ ✩ ✩
Cleanliness: ✩ ✩ ✩ ✩

KEY INFORMATION

ADDRESS: Belt Creek Ranger District
4234 US 89 North
Neihart, MT 59465

OPERATED BY: Lewis and Clark National Forest

INFORMATION: (406) 236-5511; www.fs.fed.us/r1/lewisclark

OPEN: Memorial Day–September

SITES: 27

EACH SITE HAS: Picnic table, fire grate, some have an upright grill

ASSIGNMENT: First come, first served; no reservations

REGISTRATION: On-site self-registration

FACILITIES: Hand-pump well, vault toilets

PARKING: At campsites

FEE: $10

ELEVATION: 4,500 feet

RESTRICTIONS: Pets: On leash only
Fires: In fire rings only
Alcohol: Permitted
Vehicles: 30-foot length limit
Other: 16-day stay limit; pack-in/pack-out; bear country food-storage requirements

stone. The park's name comes from the water cascading down a limestone formation that resembles a miner's sluice box. Hiking here requires several creek crossings, which often aren't possible until well into the summer. While you're hiking, imagine the complexity of moving train cars filled with limestone across these cliffs. You'll even find remnants of an old mining town awaiting exploration.

Camping at Logging Creek is as relaxing as the flowing creek itself. Well-spaced sites sit among aspen and fir trees. Undergrowth is thin, so you will see your neighbors. Any of the sites along the creek are good, but 14 and 16 are our favorites for their size and access. Sites 24 through 26 have an extra benefit in their proximity to the best wading spot on the creek. Over the years, amateur engineers have built an impressive ring of rocks pooling the water, and children of all ages can be found cooling off here. Wildlife visits the campground on a regular basis, and at least a few bears stop by every summer. Views of the limestone cliffs are dramatic, and exploring them from the creek is a good choice. When you find a perch, relax and watch the anglers below trying to outsmart the trout.

A trailhead 3 miles south on Forest Service Road 839 at Mill Creek is the starting point for a variety of hikes. North Fork Deep Creek Trail #303 isn't an easy trail, but it does provide fishing access to the Smith River and its namesake creek. The 8.8-mile trail sees heavy use by hikers, motorized vehicles, and horses, and it ends at Deep Creek. After a mile on Trail #303, there is a junction with Ming-Coulee Trail #307. Several good vista points dot this trail, and you might even see a few deer.

Other trails spur off from these trails for a variety of hiking options. You'll encounter fewer motorized travelers if you visit during the week. Some of these trails cross private land or require starting from a trailhead on private land. The landowners have agreed to provide access, but you must request permission first. Information about these trails can be found on the signboards at the fee station. Mountain bikers will find any of the trail options rewarding. Taking longer day trips only involves looping onto another trail.

MAP

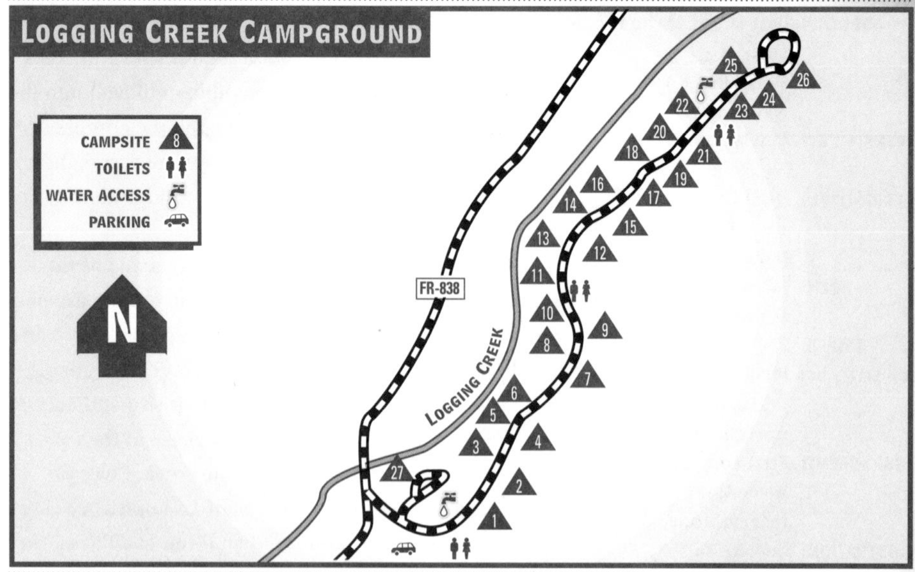

GETTING THERE

From Great Falls, take US 87/89 southeast 40 miles to Armington Junction. Turn right and continue 10 miles on US 89 to Evans–Riceville Road. Turn right and go 7 miles to the Y intersection. Bear left onto a single-lane dirt-and-gravel road and go 4.4. miles to the campground sign at FR 839. Turn right and drive 2.2 miles to the campground.

From Monarch, take US 89 north for 3 miles to CR 427 (Logging Creek Road). Make a sharp left turn and go 11.2 miles to a Y intersection. Bear left and drive 2.2 miles to the campground. (This route not recommended for low-clearance vehicles or RVs).

MANY PINES CAMPGROUND

> *Wildlife and wildflowers abound during summer in this somewhat hidden part of Montana.*

THIS SECTION of US 89 is designated at Kings Hill Scenic Byway and stretches for 71 lovely miles through a somewhat hidden part of Montana. Wildlife and wildflowers abound during summer, and with 450 miles of trails and roads to explore, crowds are not a problem except on the most popular trails.

Many Pines, like all the other campgrounds along the Scenic Byway, has a bit of road noise, but the setting is worth it. Here, 22 campsites are divided between a loop to the right of the entrance road and a straight segment along Belt Creek. On the loop, sites 6 and 7 both have steps up to the campsite from the parking pad. This feature gives a sense of separation, which we liked. Site 8 is well isolated, with no neighboring campsites on this end of the loop.

True to its name, the campground is set in a thick stand of spruce, firs, and lodgepole pines, which limits the amount of understory to provide buffer zones between sites. Of those sites on the creek-road segment, sites 15, 16, and 19 have greater privacy than their neighbors. Half of the sites overlook the creek, but they are also closer to the occasional buzz from the highway. Wading in the creek is fun on hot days, and trout fishing can be rewarding, but it's strictly catch and release.

Neihart (population 50) is the only town you will find between Monarch to the north and White Sulphur Springs to the south. It's a small, friendly place where folks are ready to fill your coffee cup or pour a cold drink and discuss everything from politics to the weather. Just north of town, an area of exposed Precambrian rock enticed miners to stop and explore this mineral-rich area. The discovery of lead, silver, zinc, gold, and sapphires brought an onslaught of treasure-seekers to the heart of the Little Belt Mountains.

RATINGS

Beauty: ✰ ✰ ✰ ✰
Privacy: ✰ ✰ ✰
Spaciousness: ✰ ✰ ✰ ✰
Quiet: ✰ ✰ ✰
Security: ✰ ✰ ✰ ✰
Cleanliness: ✰ ✰ ✰ ✰ ✰

Established in 1881, Neihart has survived the continuing boom-and-bust lifecycles of a mining town. Look carefully and you'll see evidence of mining history. Can you find the old false-front building bearing the sign, "Wu Tang, Laundry, Drugs 1882"?

Another treasure lies above ground, exposed to the impact of the elements, mankind, and fire. The surrounding forest, a treasure of incalculable value, is guarded by day from the Kings Hill fire lookout. Open to visitors, this operational fire watch is one of a shrinking core of fire towers in Montana, as new technology gradually takes over. Fortunately, many towers are old enough to be listed as historic structures, and this may help save them from ultimately being dismantled.

Shelley, the ranger in the Kings Hill tower, watches for fire using the same methods that have been used for decades—with a few twists. Looking around the tower, we jokingly asked if she had a high-speed Internet connection. Sure enough, she does. She uses it to check weather and fire data, records of area lightning strikes, and she punches in GPS coordinates from people in the field to help pinpoint a fire start.

Not everyone is comfortable spending hour upon hour alone, perched above the treetops, watching and waiting. However, the rewards can be priceless: a bird's-eye view of the Northern lights, bear-watching from a safe vantage point, and making a call that prevents disaster.

Just north of the campground, a turnoff leads to the Memorial Falls Trailhead #321 for an easy 15-minute walk to two spectacular waterfalls. On our trek we encountered a budding 11-year-old geologist who was enthralled with a crystal-laden rock exposed along the trail. Other hiking options with trailheads off US 89 are nearby.

Paine Gulch Trail #737 is a 7.6-mile out-and-back to Paine Gulch Creek and the base of Servoss Mountain. This easy trail begins 1 mile south of Monarch and is one of a few in the area designated as off limits to motorized vehicles. Two more difficult trails begin at the Belt Creek Ranger Station, where the staff can assist you with maps and contact information.

KEY INFORMATION

ADDRESS: Belt Creek Ranger District
4234 US 89 North
Neihart, MT 59465

OPERATED BY: Lewis and Clark National Forest

INFORMATION: (406) 236-5511; www.fs.fed.us/r1/lewisclark

OPEN: Memorial Day–September

SITES: 22

EACH SITE HAS: Picnic table, fire grate

ASSIGNMENT: First come, first served; no reservations

REGISTRATION: On-site self-registration

FACILITIES: Hand-pump well, vault toilets

PARKING: At campsites

FEE: $10

ELEVATION: 5,900 feet

RESTRICTIONS: Pets: On leash only
Fires: In fire ring only
Alcohol: Permitted
Vehicles: 30-foot length limit
Other: 16-day stay limit; pack-in/pack-out; bear country food-storage restrictions; campground host

MAP

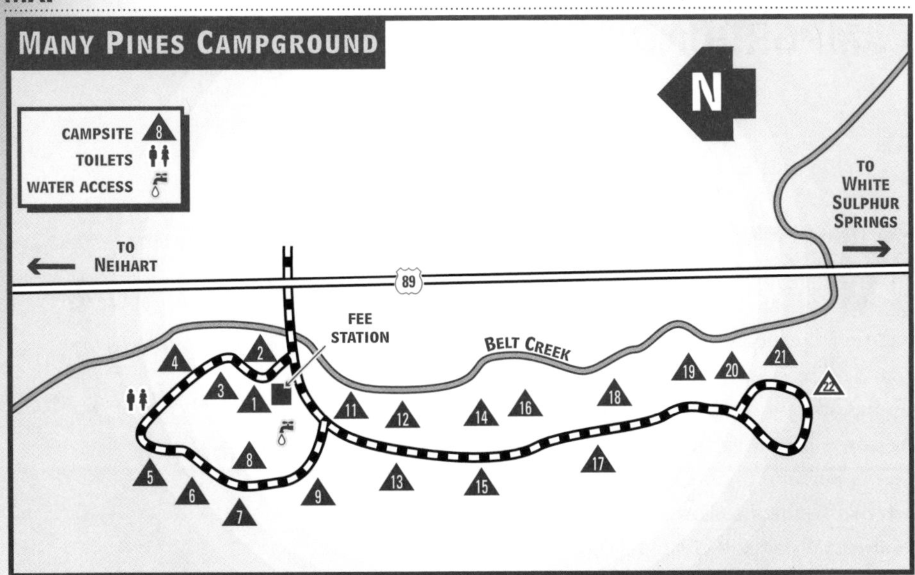

GETTING THERE

From Neihart, take US 89 south for 2.7 miles to the campground.

Access to the Tenderfoot Creek Trail System is west of Kings Hill Campground on Forest Service Road 839. The main Tenderfoot Trail #342 winds down to the creek, and many day visitors frequent this area to fish for trout. Additional trail spurs can be combined for loop hikes throughout the canyon. As with many other trails, several creek crossings may not be passable during spring runoff. Armed with a trail map, plenty of water, and sunscreen, the potential for finding a place of solitude exists if you're persistent.

PARK LAKE CAMPGROUND

Clancy

NESTLED AMONG lodgepole pine and Engelman spruce, this five-acre mountain lake appears as a thoughtful gift from Mother Nature. In reality, it is man-made, part of a late-1800s mountain reservoir system built to provide water for mining operations farther down the mountain. Unlike the mines in nearby Butte, the treasure here was silver, not copper, and the ore mined from this area was so rich that taking it to Fort Benton and shipping it to Swansea, Wales, still created a significant profit for the mining companies. Millions of dollars worth of silver was extracted in the 1890s alone, and reminders of mining history are prevalent for those who take the time to explore.

Park Lake, with its clear blue water shimmering against the lushly forested mountains, proves that not every remnant of placer mining is a blight on the landscape. Keep this setting in mind to soften the hammering you'll encounter on the access road's washboard sections on the climb into the Boulder Mountains. Always a popular escape for Helena Valley residents, this area may be a bit too noisy for those seeking a quiet weekend getaway. But, come Monday, the area returns to its placid mountain splendor.

The 22 campsites set along the looped road provide the perfect place to set up base camp for a multiday stay. Large boulders provide natural play structures for a game of "king of the rock" or a place to perch while reading a book. Trees and shrubs round out the natural barriers providing privacy. Site 17, at the back of the loop, is secluded from the other sites. A few steps down from the parking spur take you to the picnic table and fire ring, and farther below is a great space to pitch a tent. You'll think you're all alone in the mountains. Site 15, also on the back of the loop, is large and secluded as well. These sites are farther from

The lake's clear water shimmers against lushly forested mountains.

RATINGS

Beauty: ★★★★
Privacy: ★★★★
Spaciousness: ★★★★
Quiet: ★★★
Security: ★★★★★
Cleanliness: ★★★★

KEY INFORMATION

ADDRESS: Helena Ranger District
2001 Poplar Street
Helena, MT 59601

OPERATED BY: Helena National Forest

INFORMATION: (406) 449-5490; www.fs.fed.us/r1/helena

OPEN: May–November

SITES: 22

EACH SITE HAS: Picnic table, fire grate

ASSIGNMENT: First come, first served; no reservations

REGISTRATION: On-site self-registration

FACILITIES: Water spigots, vault toilets, boat launch, pay phone

PARKING: At campsites

FEE: $8

ELEVATION: 6,360 feet

RESTRICTIONS: **Pets:** On leash only
Fires: In fire rings only
Alcohol: Permitted
Vehicles: 50-foot length limit
Other: 14-day stay limit; nonmotorized boats; campground host

the lake, but since none of the sites is lakefront and it isn't that far, the privacy is a nice perk. Site 10 is very large and has access to both the trail to the lake and the trail to the wetland area.

For those who venture here before mid-June, be prepared for sudden snow squalls one day and blue skies and balmy temperatures the next; temperature swings of 40 degrees or more are not uncommon. Summer weather settles in during July and August, and sites fill quickly on Fridays when the weather is good, but during the week you will find yourself with very few, if any, neighbors.

Most people spend at least part of their time here on the water—boating, swimming, or fishing. The lake supports a healthy population of Arctic grayling, rainbow trout, and Yellowstone cutthroat trout, and the restriction against motors makes a canoe- or float-tube–fishing excursion with fly rod in hand an enticing option. This five-acre lake is crystal clear, and its tiny islands make good resting places for one or two people. There isn't a designated beach area, but many visitors wade and swim from several access points. Well-spaced lakefront picnic sites offer a sense of privacy and some sound buffering.

Nearby hiking trails offer a variety of day hikes, ranging from a 2-mile hike around the lake to short spurs leading away from the campground. As you hike around the lake you'll see remnants of mining cabins and many wildflowers. Full-day hiking routes head toward the Continental Divide and other tiny lakes, or you can take a loop around Frohner or Cataract basins. Mountain bikers have plenty of options, although you will be sharing those nice wide trails with four-wheelers on occasion. The trailhead for Lava Mountain Trail #244 is about a mile north of Park Lake and is probably the best choice for bikers. This 8-mile trail is wide but steep and will challenge hikers and bikers alike.

At this altitude, the wealth of surrounding wetlands doesn't attract a lot of mosquitoes, but it does provide excellent habitat for a variety of species. On an early evening hike from the campground, our three-year-old son was rewarded with his first up-close view

MAP

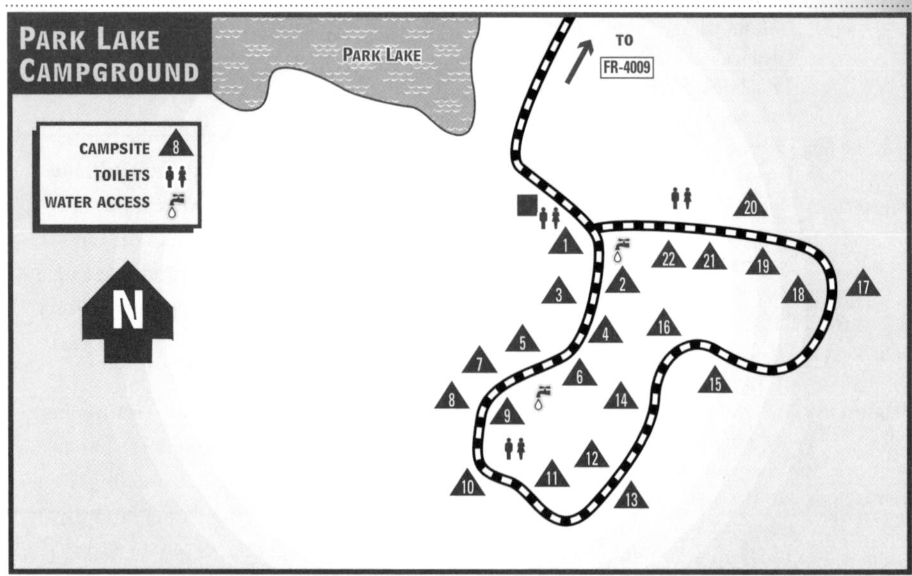

of a moose. Other sightings have included elk, black bear, mule deer, and even hard-to-spot wolverines. The potential for wildlife viewing and bird watching combined with excellent fishing and nearby trails make this site a gold mine for campers.

GETTING THERE

From Clancy, take exit 182 off I-15 south of Helena. Following Park Lake signs, go 7.3 miles northwest on Lump Gulch Road to the Y intersection. Take Forest Service Road 4009 southwest for 6.2 miles to the campground.

THAIN CREEK CAMPGROUND

Streams in the Highwood Mountains carve a colorful quilt of meadows and forests filled with wildflowers and wildlife.

RATINGS

Beauty: ✩ ✩ ✩ ✩
Privacy: ✩ ✩ ✩ ✩ ✩
Spaciousness: ✩ ✩ ✩ ✩
Quiet: ✩ ✩ ✩ ✩
Security: ✩ ✩ ✩ ✩
Cleanliness: ✩ ✩ ✩ ✩ ✩

THE ROUTE TO THAIN CREEK travels through ranch country in the lowlands of the Highwood Mountains. Named "espi-toh-tok" by the Blackfeet Indians due to the timber that runs high along its slopes, this is one of Montana's island mountain ranges, created by volcanic eruptions over 50 million years ago. Streams carve a colorful quilt of meadows and forests filled with wildflowers and wildlife, and ranches seem to stretch forever.

While gold miners were seeking their fortune to the west, cattlemen began staking their claims as well. Expansive ranches spread across open prairies and mountain valleys, and cattle became as commonplace as antelope. This is open rangeland, with cattle grazing throughout the national forest. Every fall cowboys create a bit of historic déjà vu when they gather for the community round-up.

In the early twentieth century, legends began to circulate about an enormous white wolf named Old Snowdrift whose mythical prowess and intelligence helped him evade trappers and wardens for years. Those who believed in his existence were rewarded when, in 1923, he and his mate were both caught. He was killed and his pelt put on display, but two of his pups were spared and shipped to Hollywood, where they starred on the silver screen for several years.

Set on a hillside above the creek, this campground is a place where RVs and tents peacefully coexist among a lodgepole-pine-and-aspen forest. Site 5 is the best as far as size and location, with plenty of room to spread out, a fair amount of privacy, and frontage on the creek. Site 6, across the road, is on the creek as well but isn't as big. In general sites are open, without a lot of overstory, but they are separated by thick undergrowth, and most have plenty of room for tents.

A nice group area is made by combining sites 7 and 8, which can be reserved in advance with the ranger district. If you're traveling with another family or a lot of kids, this would be an ideal place for a base camp. Hiking and exploration options will keep everyone busy for more than a week.

Hiking is the primary draw here. A well-connected network of trails winds through the creeks and ridges of the surrounding mountains. Most trails are open to horses, mountain bikes, and motorbikes (although visiting during the week should reduce your trail neighbors significantly). From the campground, Thain Creek Trail #411 is a short 0.75-mile loop combining the first section of Trail 411 with the final leg of Trail 431. This route is popular with kids, and there's plenty of room for them to explore. Another short trail is on Forest Service Road 8841, about a mile from the campground. This is a 1.5-mile environmental education trail with an accompanying interpretive brochure.

North Fork Highwood Creek Trail #423 lies west of the campground. Take FR 8840 south along the creek to the trailhead for this 14-mile out-and-back hike through meadows and along the river to its headwaters. The trail climbs 1,300 feet to the saddle before dropping to the Cottonwood Creek drainage, and the climb to the saddle is the only strenuous section. Combining Windy Mountain Trail #454 and Briggs Creek Trail #431 creates a 7-mile loop that climbs to a saddle south of Windy Mountain and then gently drops to a wildflower meadow. You'll encounter another saddle following Briggs Creek and then descend toward the trailhead.

A mile west on County Road 8830 is Highwoods Environmental Education Trail #452. This 1.5-mile interpretive trail is easy, informative, and for hikers only. Another nonmotorized option is Deer Creek Trail #453 off CR 121 southwest of the guard station. Although it doesn't actually make it to Highwood Baldy, this 3-mile out-and-back trail follows the creek and ends in a meadow from which a route along the ridge is possible.

Nearby as the crow flies are two significant geological features. To the northeast is Shonkin Sag, a 500-

KEY INFORMATION

ADDRESS: Judith Ranger District
109 Central Avenue
Stanford, MT 59479

OPERATED BY: Lewis and Clark National Forest

INFORMATION: (406) 566-2292; www.fs.fed.us/r1/lewisclark

OPEN: Memorial Day–November; full services through Labor Day

SITES: 8

EACH SITE HAS: Picnic table, fire ring

ASSIGNMENT: First come, first served; no reservations

REGISTRATION: On-site self-registration

FACILITIES: Water spigots, vault toilets

PARKING: At campsites

FEE: $5

ELEVATION: 4,520 feet

RESTRICTIONS: **Pets:** On leash only
Fires: In fire rings only
Alcohol: Permitted
Vehicles: 22-foot length limit
Other: 16-day stay limit; pack-in/pack-out; campground host

MAP

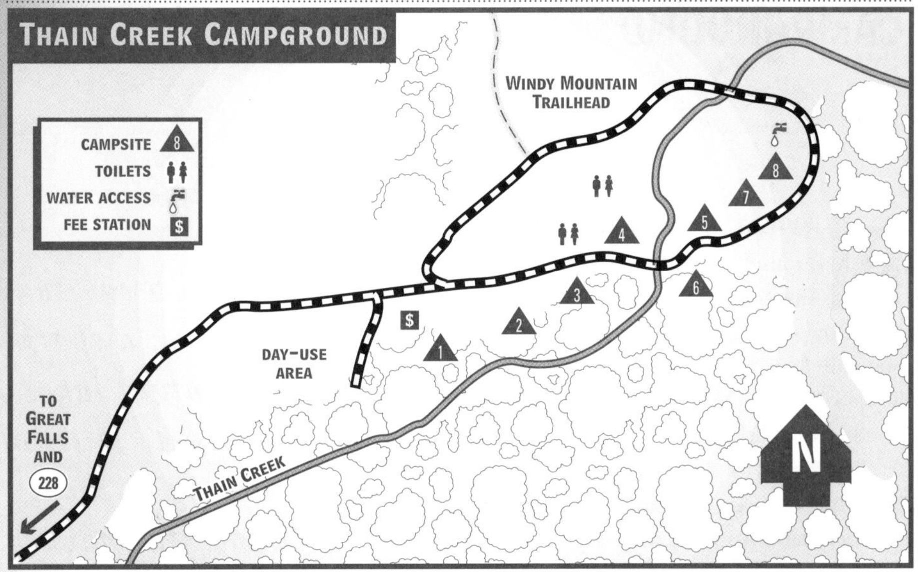

GETTING THERE

From Great Falls, take US 87/89 east for 6 miles to MT 228. Turn left and continue 13.9 miles on MT 228 to a stop sign. Go straight for 20 miles on the gravel road to the campground.

foot-deep, 1-mile-wide U-shaped valley that was cut by an ancient river draining glacial melt-off. Farther east, rising 2,500 feet above the plain, is Square Butte Natural Area. Visible for 100 miles across the eastern Montana plains, it was named "Fort Mountain" by Meriwether Lewis in 1805 and is featured in many of Charlie Russell's paintings.

WOOD LAKE CAMPGROUND

Augusta

NESTLED IN WOOD CANYON, this campground offers dramatic mountain views to the north and rugged rock walls to the southwest. Except for breathtaking scenery, the sparkling mountain lake, and access to miles of hiking trails in the Bob Marshall Wilderness Area, you may find Wood Lake a little dull.

> *Enjoy breathtaking scenery, a sparkling mountain lake, and access to miles of hiking in the Bob Marshall Wilderness Area.*

The campground lies along the eastern edge of the wilderness area, and since the parking areas and roadway are narrow, it's perfectly suited for tent camping. RVers head for nearby South Fork and Benchmark campgrounds, which offer wider spaces. The campground is on the opposite side of the road from the lake, but it's only a short walk to the lakeshore. This is a place where you can expect to see wildlife and have long debates about which trail to hike.

This isn't a large or heavily wooded campground, but with fewer trees, the views extend in every direction. If privacy is important to you, Site 4, on the outside edge of the loop, sits farthest from the road and is the quietest and most secluded spot. If you're traveling with another group, opt for sites 7 and 8, set off to the left before you get to the main loop.

You'll find brook, cutthroat, and rainbow trout in the lake, and if you decide not to fish, a lazy afternoon of canoeing will keep you near the water when the temperature rises. Deer, elk, and bears frequent the area, and many campers are lucky enough to see at least one of the peregrine falcons that nest here.

Drive to the parking area at Benchmark Campground (6 miles farther west on Forest Service Road 235) to sit beside the creek on a mellow summer afternoon and watch the high mountain snowmelt cascade over boulders. This is Bob Marshall country: 1 million acres of trees, rivers, mountains, and wildlife in a wilderness preserved against the impact of progress

RATINGS

Beauty: ✩ ✩ ✩ ✩ ✩
Privacy: ✩ ✩ ✩ ✩ ✩
Spaciousness: ✩ ✩ ✩ ✩
Quiet: ✩ ✩ ✩ ✩
Security: ✩ ✩ ✩
Cleanliness: ✩ ✩ ✩ ✩ ✩

KEY INFORMATION

ADDRESS: Rocky Mountain Ranger District
P.O. Box 340
1102 Main Avenue NW
Choteau, MT 59422

OPERATED BY: Lewis and Clark National Forest

INFORMATION: (406) 466-5341; www.fs.fed.us/r1/lewisclark

OPEN: Memorial Day–October

SITES: 9

EACH SITE HAS: Picnic table, fire ring

ASSIGNMENT: First come, first served; no reservations

REGISTRATION: On-site self-registration

FACILITIES: Hand-pump well, vault toilets

PARKING: At campsites

FEE: $6

ELEVATION: 5,500 feet

RESTRICTIONS: Pets: On leash only
Fires: In fire ring only
Alcohol: Permitted
Vehicles: 22-foot length limit
Other: 14-day stay limit; pack-in/pack-out; nonmotorized boats; bear country food-storage requirements

and technology. You'll understand what Marshall meant when he wrote that wilderness is "the lapping of waves against the shoreline and the melody of wind in the trees."

Bob Marshall is the man responsible for developing the framework to protect this expansive pocket of Montana and others like it. He knew the area well, taking legendary day hikes of 30 to 70 miles that were more than simply a physical challenge; they intensified his passion for the wilderness—a passion that focused on preserving a place where everyone can experience days when the cycles of nature (not the hours on a clock) dictate the schedule.

Born and raised in New York City, Marshall was instrumental in the growth of the country's fledgling wilderness system. In the late 1930s, as a division chief with the Forest Service, he single-handedly brought more than 5 million acres under its protection. Two years after his untimely death at the age of 38, the Bob Marshall Wilderness area was formally designated and protected. "The Bob," as it is affectionately called by many Montanans, is a lasting legacy to the impact of one man's vision. Woody, a friend of ours, is an example of those who keep Marshall's spirit alive—hearty souls who hike across The Bob in a single day.

For those seeking something a bit shorter in distance, several options exist, but the closest are Wood Lake Trail #263, a short, easy stroll, and Patrol Mountain Trail #213, which begins just up the road. Trail #213 follows Straight Creek Trail for the first 3 miles, with refreshing creek crossings along the way. One particularly wide crossing is on Straight Creek, but when it's shallow it shouldn't be a problem. The trail then branches off for the final steady, steep 3-mile climb to a Forest Service lookout. This trail climbs just above 8,000 feet at the lookout, and you should expect to encounter some snow here and in Honeymoon Basin well into the early weeks of summer.

Petty Ford Creek Trail #244 begins 4 miles east of Wood Lake near Double Falls. It climbs briefly above Ford Creek and then gradually drops 400 feet over 3 miles to Petty Creek. You'll glimpse plenty of mountain views along the way, and you should have the trail

MAP

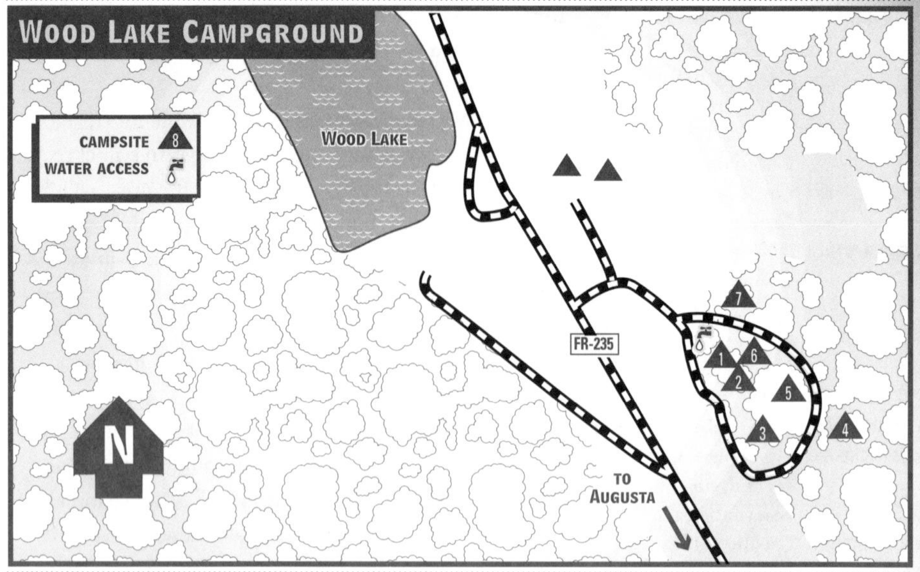

pretty much to yourself. At Petty Creek you can continue on Smith Creek Trail #215 through the forests with a few shallow creek crossings. This is a lightly traveled area, and you might have the waterfalls along the way all to yourself.

GETTING THERE

From Augusta, take Benchmark Road (FR 235) west for 24 miles to the campground.

EASTERN **MONTANA**

BEAVER CREEK COUNTY PARK CAMPGROUNDS

Havre

MOST PEOPLE PROBABLY haven't heard of Fort Assinniboine, but when it was built in 1879 near the Milk River, it was the largest fort west of the Mississippi, encompassing all of the Bears Paw Mountains. The fort was built in response to concerns about Indian attacks after General Custer's defeat at Little Big Horn in 1876 and Chief Joseph's surrender in 1877 at Bear Paw Battlefield, 37 miles southeast. Before the fort was abandoned in 1911, General John Pershing served here as a lieutenant, and two companies of the 10th Cavalry "Buffalo Soldiers" trained here prior to their service in the Spanish-American War. Some of the fort's buildings still stand 6 miles southwest of Havre on US 87, and walking tours are available.

After the fort was abandoned, much of the land was designated as the Rocky Boy's Reservation, and the section that ultimately became Beaver Creek County Park bounced between the federal government, the state, and the city of Havre until it was finally established as a Hill County park in 1948.

Nestled on the northern edge of the Bears Paw Mountains, this park is an anomaly: it is possibly the country's largest county park but receives no county funds, and is set along a sparsely populated stretch of a state that, unlike many Midwestern and Eastern states, has very few county parks. Located in an island mountain range, where the highest peaks are generally buttes topping out around 5,000 feet, this is a 17-mile-long, 10,000-acre oasis that straddles Beaver Creek amid both vast areas of grasslands and groves of pines, cottonwoods, box elders, and willows that line the creek. It includes two large lakes and numerous feeder streams, and while there are no officially designated trails, bushwhacked trails are common. Geologists delight in the variety they find here, with glacial

> *"This 17-mile-long, 10,000-acre oasis straddles Beaver Creek."*

RATINGS

Beauty: ✩ ✩ ✩ ✩
Privacy: ✩ ✩ ✩
Spaciousness: ✩ ✩ ✩ ✩ ✩
Quiet: ✩ ✩ ✩ ✩
Security: ✩ ✩ ✩ ✩
Cleanliness: ✩ ✩ ✩ ✩

KEY INFORMATION

ADDRESS: Beaver Creek County Park
17863 Beaver Creek Road
Havre, MT 59501

OPERATED BY: Hill County Parks

INFORMATION: (406) 395-4565

OPEN: Year-round

SITES: 120–150

EACH SITE HAS: Picnic table, fire grate

ASSIGNMENT: First come, first served; reservations accepted at largest sites

REGISTRATION: Purchase daily and annual passes at the park office

FACILITIES: Water available at park office, vault toilets, boat launch

PARKING: At campsites

FEE: $6

ELEVATION: 3,171–4,113 feet

RESTRICTIONS: **Pets:** On leash only
Fires: In fire rings only
Alcohol: Permitted
Vehicles: No length restrictions
Other: 14-day stay limit; bear-country food-storage restrictions; pack-in/pack-out

deposits in the northern section, volcanic evidence in the middle, and fossil-filled sedimentary cliffs in the south.

This is considered excellent terrain for ATVs and motorcycles, but they are banned from mid-May to mid-September, leaving plenty of room for hikers and mountain bikers. If you're driving the park road, you probably won't notice it, but if you're on a bicycle, you'll definitely feel the 1,000-foot elevation gain from the north end to the south end of the park.

You won't find just one campground here, but about two dozen different ones, in addition to group sites, picnic areas, and a youth camp. Even the superintendent's office isn't sure how many campsites exist, since sites within designated campgrounds are not always well defined. Each of the campgrounds has vault toilets, and several have shelters that can be reserved. There are no iron rangers or fee-collection booths; you must stop at the park office (adjacent to the youth camp) to purchase a daily or annual pass.

Beaver Creek is welcomed and heavily used by local residents and those traveling the Hi-Line, but there always seems to be room for one more. (The Hi-Line extends across northern Montana following US 2 and the east/west railroad tracks originally laid by the Great Northern Railroad in the 1800s.) Fishing is excellent, with rainbow and brook trout stocked at both lakes and in Beaver Creek, while Lower Beaver Creek Lake also offers anglers the opportunity to land perch, northern pike, and walleyes. The park is also a wildlife-watcher's paradise, ripe with white-tailed and mule deer, eagles, hawks, bobcats, and several areas where beavers create intricate dams.

At the south end of the park is access to the Rocky Boy's Reservation, thousands of rolling acres owned by members of the Chippewa Cree tribe. The tribe holds its annual powwow each August, and the public is invited to view and participate in a variety of cultural demonstrations and try a full menu of traditional foods.

Life in Montana, particularly along the Hi-Line, can be hard, and adaptability is crucial. Business owners in Havre proved their flexibility when a January 1904 fire destroyed most of the town and they simply

MAP

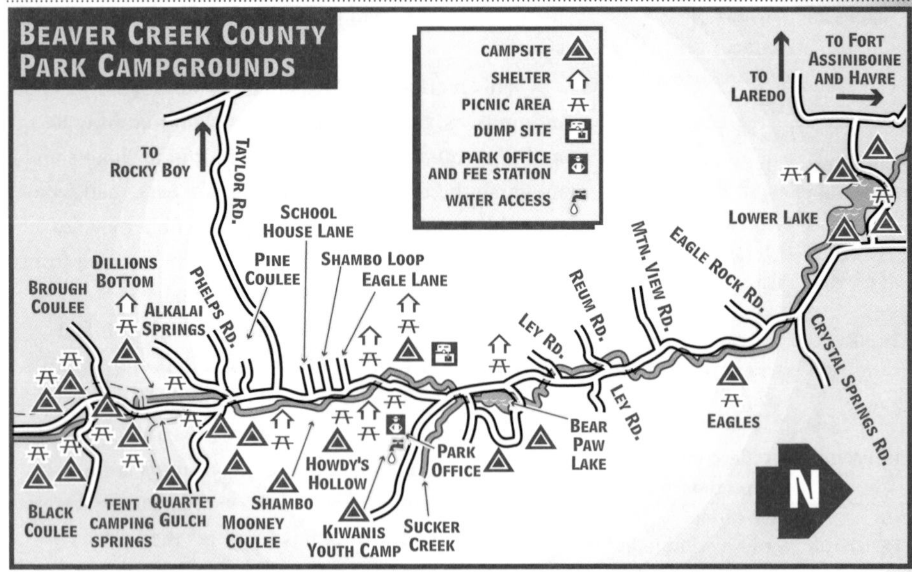

moved their establishments underground until reconstruction could begin. Today, places like Sporting Eagle Saloon, a Chinese laundry, and an opium den have been restored to their early 1900s appearance, and guided tours are given.

Havre is one of the Great Northern Railroad's original stops and still serves as a station for daily Amtrak trains to Chicago, Seattle, and Portland. Train lovers will want to stop at the city's railroad museum and spend some time chatting with the volunteers, whose knowledge and stories are a delight.

GETTING THERE

From Havre, take Beaver Creek Road south for 7 miles to the first campground.

CAMP CREEK CAMPGROUND

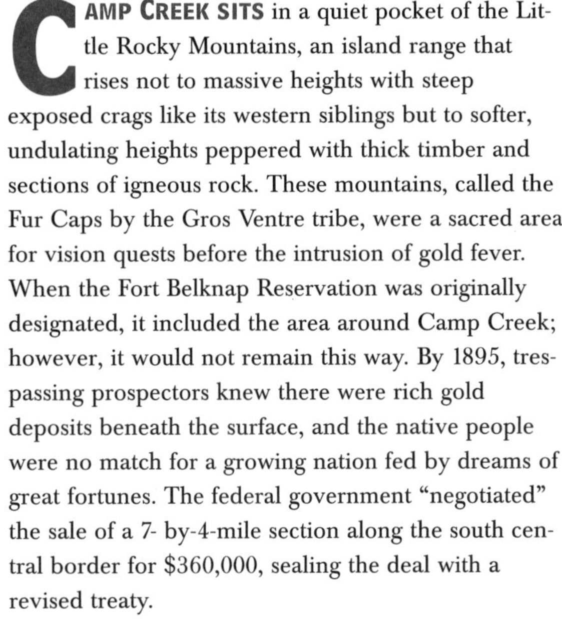

The forest surrounding Camp Creek is an unexpected surprise in this region of vast plains and few trees.

CAMP CREEK SITS in a quiet pocket of the Little Rocky Mountains, an island range that rises not to massive heights with steep exposed crags like its western siblings but to softer, undulating heights peppered with thick timber and sections of igneous rock. These mountains, called the Fur Caps by the Gros Ventre tribe, were a sacred area for vision quests before the intrusion of gold fever. When the Fort Belknap Reservation was originally designated, it included the area around Camp Creek; however, it would not remain this way. By 1895, trespassing prospectors knew there were rich gold deposits beneath the surface, and the native people were no match for a growing nation fed by dreams of great fortunes. The federal government "negotiated" the sale of a 7- by-4-mile section along the south central border for $360,000, sealing the deal with a revised treaty.

Within this tiny section was a mother lode that miners had been illegally accessing for years, and after the 1895 treaty, the mining furor increased. Pike Landusky struck it rich but was killed in his own saloon by outlaw and local resident Kid Curry. Pete Zortman established his mill and the town that bears his name, and soon miners were extracting more than $10,000 of gold a day. World War I and several fires impeded things a bit, but the mines were not totally closed until the mid-1930s.

The historic mining town of Zortman still remains, just down the road from Camp Creek, and is often referred to as a ghost town. In reality, this is a thriving, close-knit community with a general store that serves as information central. Despite the impact of mining, this area still has beautiful mountains filled with big game, songbirds, eagles, coyotes, and beavers. Camp Creek is unexpectedly nestled in the trees and is often

RATINGS

Beauty: ✩ ✩ ✩ ✩
Privacy: ✩ ✩ ✩ ✩
Spaciousness: ✩ ✩ ✩ ✩
Quiet: ✩ ✩ ✩ ✩ ✩
Security: ✩ ✩ ✩ ✩
Cleanliness: ✩ ✩ ✩ ✩ ✩

used by those seeking an overnight stop as they explore the Hi-Line area of the state. The Hi-Line extends across northern Montana followin US 2 and the east–west railroad tracks originally laid by the Great Northern Railroad in the 1800s.

Sites here vary from perfect for tenters to a few that offer no place to pitch a tent except for the gravel RV pull-through pad. The first six sites on the loop road have covered picnic tables, and sites 1 and 2 are across the road from a nice pair of horseshoe pits. Site 5 is the most private, with dense understory and plenty of room for a pair of tents. Sites 8 and 9 accommodate tents but offer little privacy, and sites 7, 10, and 11 have no tent area at all.

A designated auto-tour route through the Charles M. Russell National Wildlife Refuge begins 37 miles south on US 191. This 19-mile driving tour stops at 13 interpretive points, and it takes a minimum of two hours to travel. The gravel roads provide excellent access to unspoiled Missouri Breaks scenery and wildlife viewing. This land remains close to what it was when Lewis and Clark saw it in 1805, and it offers the vistas that artist Charles M. Russell loved best. Plan to stop along the way and explore by hiking off the main roads. You won't see the wealth of bison or bighorn sheep that the Corps of Discovery saw or the grizzly bears and wolves that plagued early homesteaders, but there are dozens of other mammals and over 200 bird species, which makes a bird guide a welcome companion.

The Missouri River to the west of the refuge is designated as a part of the National Wild and Scenic River System, and much of the land along both sides, from the refuge to Coal Banks Landing, was designated as the Upper Missouri Breaks National Monument in 2001. If you have a canoe, we encourage you to enjoy this spectacular stretch of river. But be sure to contact the Bureau of Land Management in Lewistown for the most current regulations.

To the northwest is Bear Paw Battlefield, part of the Nez Perce National Historical Park. This is where the last battle of the Nez Perce War of 1877 was fought and where Nez Perce Chief Joseph finally surrendered. The museum in Chinook serves as a visitor center, and there

KEY INFORMATION

ADDRESS:	Malta Field Office HC 65, Box 5000 Malta, MT 59538
OPERATED BY:	Bureau of Land Management
INFORMATION:	(406) 654-1240; www.blm.gov
OPEN:	Year-round depending on weather conditions; full services May–September
SITES:	18
EACH SITE HAS:	Picnic table, fire grate
ASSIGNMENT:	First come, first served; no reservations
REGISTRATION:	On-site self-registration
FACILITIES:	Water spigots, drinking fountains, vault toilets, group areas
PARKING:	At campsites
FEE:	$5
ELEVATION:	3,500 feet
RESTRICTIONS:	**Pets:** On leash only **Fires:** In fire rings only **Alcohol:** Permitted **Vehicles:** No restrictions **Other:** 14-day stay limit

MAP

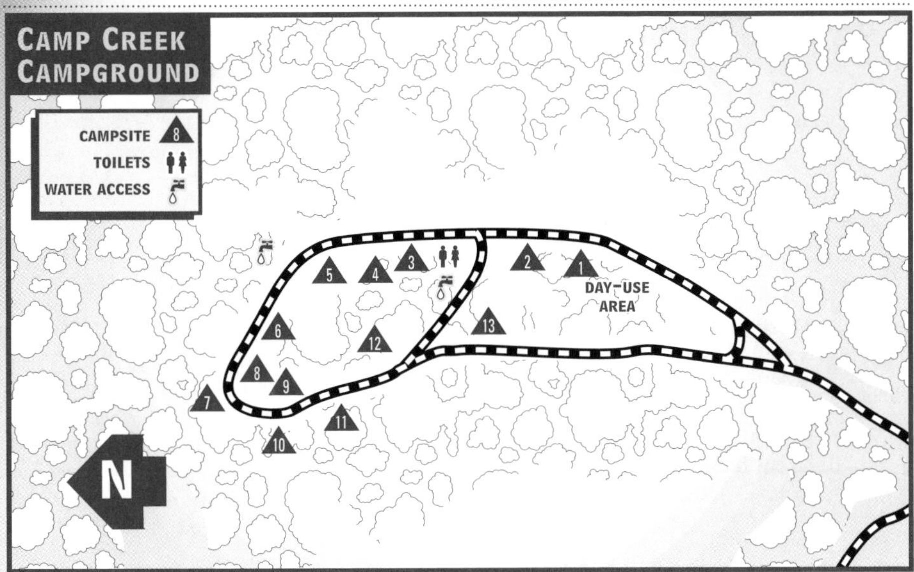

GETTING THERE

From Malta, take US 191 south for 40 miles to Bear Gulch Road. Turn right and go 8 miles east to the campground sign. Turn right and go 1 mile north to the campground.

is a self-guided interpretive trail at the battlefield.

During your visit to Camp Creek, you may still see evidence of the impact of mining. It is estimated that billions of dollars worth of gold was extracted here in the twentieth century, more than $300 million of that from the 1970s to the 1990s. All of this came from a piece of land that cost the United States $360,000 to purchase in 1895 but may cost well over $40 million to partially clean up the mess that was left behind.

CRYSTAL LAKE CAMPGROUND

Lewistown

CRYSTAL LAKE IS DIFFERENT from most high mountain lakes. It's very shallow, about 13 feet deep in the spring after the mountain snowmelt, and by the end of the summer it may dwindle to only 5 feet. The lake's water gradually seeps out through its porous limestone bottom until it is almost nonexistent, and then the snowmelt begins again. As a result, the trout found here are restocked annually, since they can't survive the thick ice cover and lack of oxygen in the winter. The lake is perfect for canoes and float tubes and attracts family groups.

Hiking trails abound in this pristine setting.

The limestone cliffs you'll see were formed about 350,000 years ago, and there are fossils visible in many of them. Also along the cliffs you may see one of the resident mountain goats or the nests of golden eagles or prairie falcons. The mountain goats are not natives, since this island range is too far from their home in the western parts of the state, but they were transported here in 1954 and have adapted well to the Big Snowy Mountains. The range lives up to its name, with peaks that top out above 8,000 feet and are usually snow-capped well into July. The Big Snowies are often called a laboratory range, due to continued geological study of the formation's 400-million-year history and wealth of visible fossils. Hikers and campers may come across fossils or notice the sedimentary aspects, but their appreciation is generally for the recreational aspects of this distinctive island in the midst of the prairies.

Finding a site on summer weekends is a challenge, since there aren't many established campgrounds in this section of the state. When the weather is nice, it often appears that everyone is heading out to camp and hike. Some fairly large RVs manage to navigate the access road, but you'll find several tenters in the mix, and there is enough understory that you may not even be aware of your neighbors. Campsites here are

RATINGS

Beauty: ✩ ✩ ✩ ✩ ✩
Privacy: ✩ ✩ ✩ ✩ ✩
Spaciousness: ✩ ✩ ✩ ✩ ✩
Quiet: ✩ ✩ ✩ ✩
Security: ✩ ✩ ✩ ✩ ✩
Cleanliness: ✩ ✩ ✩ ✩

KEY INFORMATION

ADDRESS: Judith Ranger District
P.O. Box 484
Stanford, MT 59479

OPERATED BY: Lewis and Clark National Forest

INFORMATION: (406) 566-2292; www.fs.fed.us/r1/lewisclark

OPEN: Mid-June–September, depending on the weather

SITES: 28

EACH SITE HAS: Picnic table, fire grate

ASSIGNMENT: First come, first served; no reservations

REGISTRATION: On-site self-registration

FACILITIES: Water spigots, vault toilets, boat launch

PARKING: At campsites

FEE: $10

ELEVATION: 5,700 feet

RESTRICTIONS: Pets: On leash only
Fires: In fire rings only
Alcohol: Permitted
Vehicles: 40-foot length limit
Other: 16-day stay limit; bear country food-storage restrictions; pack-in/pack-out; campground host; electric motors only

well spaced and roomy, with plenty of privacy. None is actually lakeside, and the foliage that creates cozy, private sites also provides a good buffer against hikers on the shoreline trail. Sites 7, 21, and 24 are the largest and most secluded, while sites 16, 17, and 18 are quiet and well hidden by spruce trees. Access to the shoreline loop trail is next to site 4, making it the least private, but it still isn't too bad. The group site is very popular for family reunions, and reservations are required for groups.

Hiking options from this campground may offer the most variety found in a single area in the state. The easiest hike is the Shoreline Loop Trail #404, a 1.75-mile loop marked with interpretive posts that correspond to the informational brochure available from the campground host. From the Loop Trail you can access the 0.5-mile Wildflower Trail, which has signs identifying the flowers, shrubs, and trees along the way. Most wildflowers bloom in July and August, and there is a very detailed brochure available from the ranger district.

Another moderate hike is Crystal Cascades Trail #445, which leads to a delightful waterfall, where the water drops from a cave down stair-step ledges for nearly 100 feet. This trail can be combined with others for an 8-mile-loop day hike.

If your goal is to hit some mountain peaks, take Trail 403 to Grandview Point and West Peak. It's 3.5 miles to Grandview Point, with forest and vista views along the way. From there you'll enjoy a panoramic view of Crystal Lake and the entire Judith Basin. Another 1.5 miles takes you along a ridge to West Peak, one of the highest ridges in the Snowy Range.

For something different, try the 5-mile hike to the Ice Caves. The trailhead for this hike is at the parking lot and leads to permanent ice caves high atop the ridge. To get there, you'll climb 2,200 feet over 3 miles to the top of Snowy Crest and then follow an open ridge marked by cairns for another 2 miles. The view on a clear day extends to the Teton Mountains in Wyoming (220 miles south). You'll be at about 8,000 feet on both this hike and the Grandview/West hike, so don't be surprised if you still see snow in June and even early July.

MAP

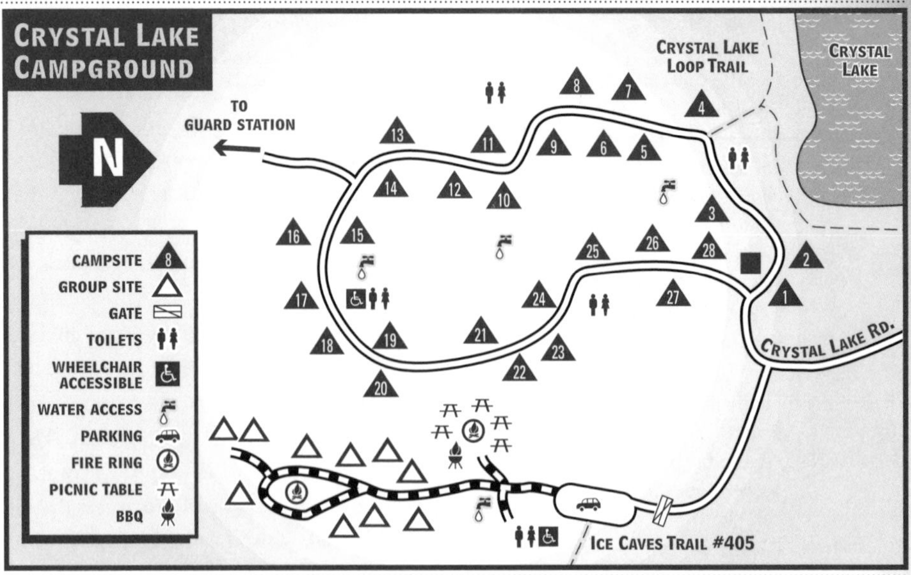

A wealth of additional hiking trails crisscrosses the range, and many are well suited for mountain bikers. Niel Creek Trail #654 branches off near the ice caves, and bikers frequently see black bears along the creek near the trailhead. Horses share most trails with mountain bikers and hikers, but practicing good trail ethics and using common sense will provide a memorable experience for everyone.

GETTING THERE

From Lewistown, take US 87 north for 8.7 miles to Crystal Lake Road. Turn left and go 5.3 miles to a Y intersection. Bear left and go 3.9 miles to the recreation-area sign. Turn left at sign (continuing on Crystal Lake Road) and go 12.7 miles to the campground. The road to the campground varies from narrow two-lane to single-lane and from dirt to paved.

MAKOSHIKA STATE PARK CAMPGROUND

> *Explore this geological and paleontological time clock.*

THE LAKOTA SIOUX called this the "Land of Bad Spirits." Mushroom-shaped cap rocks, flat-topped buttes, spires pointing skyward, razor-sharp hogbacks, and fluted hillsides combine to create a land of curious formations shaped by wind and water.

But wait a minute, you think, as you drive through the Glendive neighborhood that borders the park entrance, this looks like typical, middle-of-nowhere, safe and friendly small-town America. Where is the dramatic landscape of "bad spirits," and what's with those dinosaur tracks on the street? When does the gigantic monster come plodding along to destroy the innocent townies?

Even after you enter the park and arrive at the visitor center, our description will seem more fiction than fact, but just keep driving. A stop at the center will give you an overall view of the park and its history, taking you on a multimillion-year journey.

Tenters will want to bypass the 16-unit lower campground and continue another 1.5 miles up the paved road to Pine on Rocks. Take your time while driving and don't be fooled: this road is steep (a 15-percent grade in some sections), and the switchbacks force a slow speed.

As its name implies, these six tent sites are tucked into a precious oasis of hard-to-find shade, and it is rarely full, since most visitors don't realize it exists. It isn't entirely primitive: there are fire rings, picnic tables, and a vault toilet, and if you need water, it's available at the lower campground, the group picnic area, or the visitor center.

So, did you notice anything yet? Something like a slight change in the landscape? Surreal, isn't it? Mother Nature has carved herself a beauty here, with wind-chiseled sandstone to your left and thick stands of pine

RATINGS

Beauty: ✩ ✩ ✩ ✩ ✩
Privacy: ✩ ✩ ✩
Spaciousness: ✩ ✩ ✩
Quiet: ✩ ✩ ✩ ✩ ✩
Security: ✩ ✩ ✩ ✩ ✩
Cleanliness: ✩ ✩ ✩ ✩ ✩

and junipers to your right. It has taken a few years, actually about 70 million, for this 11,500-acre park to look like this. In the early 1900s, it was promoted as a potential national park. Thankfully, this prehistoric seabed didn't make the cut, and it remains uncrowded and minimally developed. In addition, it has evolved as a paleontologist's dream, where bones from former residents named Triceratops, Edmontosaurus, Tyrannosaurus Rex, and Thescelosaurus protrude, and ancient plant- and sea-life fossils dot the ground, revealing themselves to the patient observer.

If you are lucky enough to find something, state and federal regulations prohibit removing or destroying it. Feel free to take photographs, and be sure to inform the visitor center staff of your find and its location. Who knows? You may have stumbled onto an entirely unknown species that could someday be named after its discoverer—you!

It's hard to believe as you look across the stark landscape that this was once a lush, semitropical environment similar to that found in Louisiana. Everything seems so dry, brown, and dull. But closer inspection reveals a wealth of color, with bands of red, pink, and yellow providing a backdrop for the evergreens and silvery sagebrush. Early morning and dusk provide endless possibilities to experience vibrant sunrises and sunsets, and photographers could spend days taking photos of the sandstone formations from different angles and in different weather.

The weather here provides contrasts as dramatic as the landscape itself. Ever-present winds flapping your tent walls are the same winds that continue to erode the rocks. Rain, which comes infrequently and often lasts only minutes, awakens dry riverbeds and occasionally causes torrents of water to rush through. Like adding water to dry cake mix, the soil becomes thick and heavy quickly, attaching to tires and shoes in large, gooey globs Montanans affectionately call "gumbo." On top of all this, there's the heat. Temperature extremes can be tremendous, shifting the thermometer 50 degrees in a few hours.

Within this dynamic area wildflowers, including lupines, locoweed, prickly pear cactus, Indian paint-

KEY INFORMATION

ADDRESS: Makoshika State Park
1301 Snyder Avenue
Glendive, MT 59330

OPERATED BY: Montana Fish, Wildlife & Parks

INFORMATION: (406) 377-6256 or (406) 232-0900; fwp.state.mt.us/parks

OPEN: May–September full services; no water rest of the year

SITES: 22

EACH SITE HAS: Picnic table, fire grate

ASSIGNMENT: First come, first served; no reservations

REGISTRATION: On-site self-registration

FACILITIES: Water spigots, vault toilets, interpretive center, nature trails, scenic drive, amphitheater, golf course

PARKING: At campsites

FEE: $12

ELEVATION: 2,374 feet

RESTRICTIONS: **Pets:** On leash only
Fires: In fire rings only
Alcohol: Permitted
Vehicles: No length limit at lower campground; tents only at Pine on Rocks
Other: 14-day stay limit; resident park manager; campground host

MAP

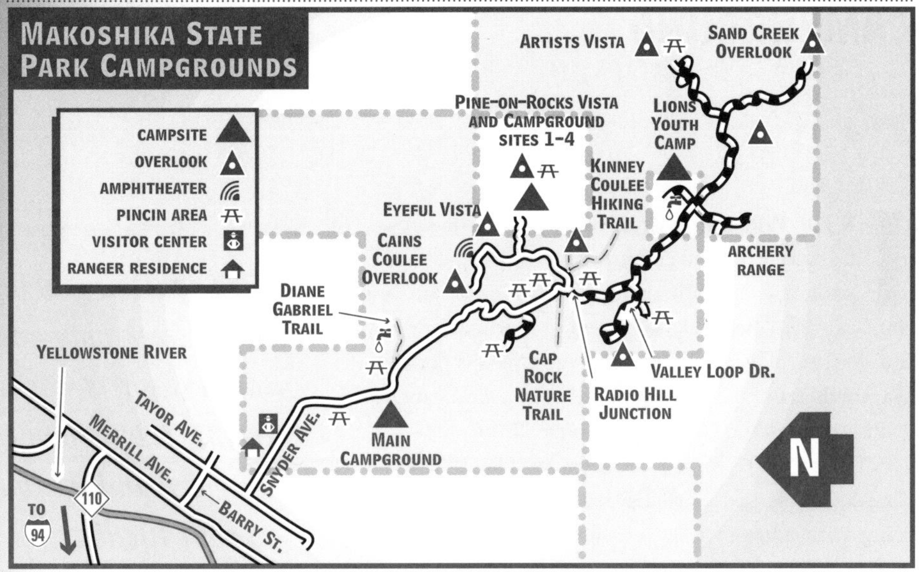

GETTING THERE

From Glendive, take Snyder Avenue southeast for 0.25 miles or follow the hadrosaur tracks to the park.

brush, yucca, and echinacea provide bold pockets of color. Coulees conceal deer, mountain lions, foxes, and coyotes. Sagebrush and grass provide cover for rabbits, bobcats, porcupines, and skunks and the sparse trees and gnarled snags are home to prairie falcons, red-tailed hawks, and golden eagles. Turkey vultures even make an annual pilgrimage, putting on a show by soaring high above the badlands and roosting in trees.

Throughout the park are vista points and picnic areas, an amphitheater, and three short nature trails that lead to very different experiences. The unimproved road climbs and twists into the park's outer reaches, and along the way you'll see prairie rattlesnakes, which necessitate caution while hiking.

Camping here is unlike anything else Montana has to offer. Although it's out of the way except for those traveling through the eastern part of the state, it's a unique opportunity to experience a geological and paleontological time clock that has been virtually untouched for millions of years.

SAGE CREEK CAMPGROUND

Bridger

IN THE WORDS OF Chief Arapooish, "The Crow Country is a good country. The Great Spirit has put it in exactly the right place; while you are in it you fare well; whenever you go out of it, whichever way you may travel, you fare worse." Sage Creek is perched near the heart of the Pryor Mountains in a landscape that is sacred to the Crow (Apsáalooke) Tribe.

The home of another Crow leader, Chief Plenty Coups, is preserved as a state park, in Pryor. As a young man, Plenty Coups retreated to the Pryor Mountains for a vision quest, during which he foresaw the coming of the white people who would take his tribe's land. He told his people, "Education is your most powerful weapon. With education you are the white man's equal; without education you are his victim." Throughout his life, Plenty Coups traveled extensively. He met with leaders and politicians and was instrumental in accomplishing something rare, the designation of his tribe's homelands as their reservation. He was also selected to represent all Indians at the 1921 dedication of the Tomb of the Unknown Soldier in Arlington National Cemetery. He laid his war bonnet and coup stick at the memorial and prayed "that there will be peace to all men hereafter."

Thanks to a facelift by the Forest Service, Sage Creek is no longer a barren, forlorn place. Although there was nothing they could do to change the intense summer heat, the new design does address the lack of shade. New plantings of green ash, ponderosa pine, and cottonwoods help mitigate the fact that trees are hard to come by out here. Shade screens over each picnic table help as well. All campsites have been moved up on a rise, away from the creek. This reduced the mosquito problem dramatically and will allow the regeneration of riparian plants to preserve the stream channel and improve fish habitat. The

> *Bird-watching along Sage Creek may add sage thrashers, rock wrens, ruby-crowned kinglets, and warblers to your life list.*

RATINGS

Beauty: ✩ ✩ ✩ ✩
Privacy: ✩ ✩ ✩ ✩ ✩
Spaciousness: ✩ ✩ ✩ ✩
Quiet: ✩ ✩ ✩ ✩ ✩
Security: ✩ ✩ ✩
Cleanliness: ✩ ✩ ✩ ✩ ✩

KEY INFORMATION

ADDRESS: Beartooth Ranger District
Route 2, Box 3420
Red Lodge, MT 5906

OPERATED BY: Custer National Forest

INFORMATION: (406) 446-2103; www.fs.fed.us/r1/custer

OPEN: Memorial Day–Labor Day

SITES: 10

EACH SITE HAS: Picnic table, fire ring

ASSIGNMENT: First come, first served; no reservations

REGISTRATION: On-site self-registration

FACILITIES: Water spigots, vault toilets

PARKING: At campsites

FEE: $5

ELEVATION: 5,520 feet

RESTRICTIONS: Pets: On leash only
Fires: In fire rings only
Alcohol: Permitted
Vehicles: 32-foot length limit
Other: 10-day stay limit; bear country food-storage restrictions; pack-in/pack-out

vibrant sunsets and cool morning sunrises that you'll enjoy from your campsite are among the best in the state. With the new design, the possibility of having an RV for a neighbor may increase, but the rough road and small number of visitors to the Pryor Mountains still work in your favor.

The Pryor Mountains are one of the most ecologically diverse areas in Montana, offering ten different biological systems, from Great Basin desert to subalpine meadows. Rare plant species can be observed here, including bladderpod and *Shoshonea pulvinata*. The full range of large mammals—black bears, bighorn sheep, mule deer, and an occasional elk—make it a wildlife-watcher's paradise. Bird-watching along Sage Creek may add sage thrashers, rock wrens, ruby-crowned kinglets, and warblers to your life list, and don't be surprised by a hummingbird or green-tailed towhee visiting camp.

If you drive south on Pryor Creek Road, turn left at Warren and head east for about 20 miles on the designated gravel road. You will arrive at the Pryor Mountain National Wild Horse Range. This is a dusty, sweltering drive in the dead of summer, but the dramatic canyons and chance that you might see one of the family groups that make up the herd is worth it.

Twelve miles east of Sage Creek on Forest Service Road 3085 and FR 849 is an amazing geological feature in the heart of the Pryor Mountains. Throughout the year, whether it's December or July, huge icicles form in this cave and the floor is coated with ice. Here at the creatively named Big Ice Cave, all characteristics for a natural deep freeze converge. In winter, cold air flows into the steep cave, forming ice on the floor and walls. In warmer months, the denser cold air sinks and is trapped in the cave chamber by the lighter warm air, and the cycle continues, perpetuating the deep-freeze environment.

Don't expect a guided tour or extensive interpretive signs; the only development here is the walkway to the entrance and an interior viewing platform. Take a jacket—it is cold enough inside to keep ice frozen—and experience one of Mother Nature's refrigerators. While exploring the area, keep your eyes open for

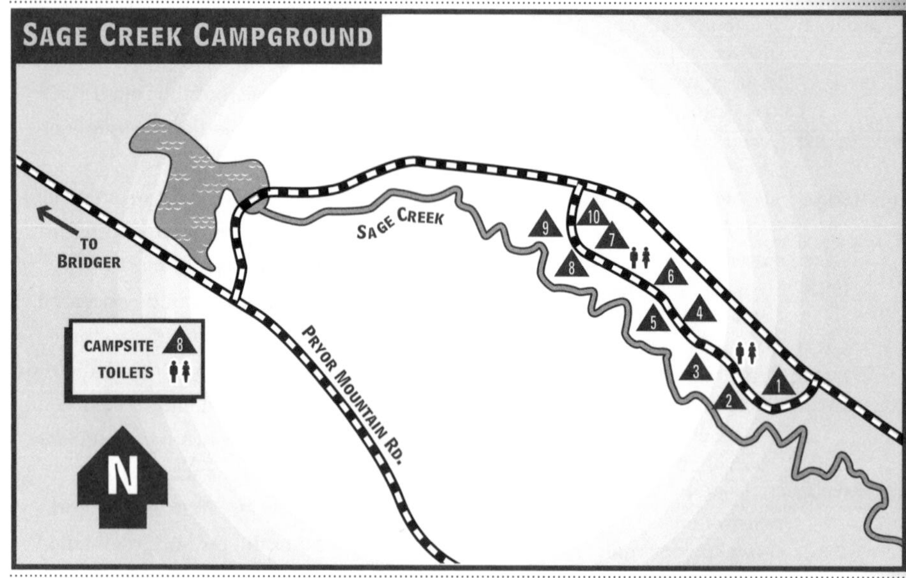

bats. Nearly a dozen species call the Pryors home; see if you can spot the differences between them.

If you continue up the road past the cave, you'll come to Dry Head Vista, where the view extends to Wyoming and the Big Horn Mountains. From here you can hike into Lost Water Canyon, where you may spot some 200-million-year-old fossils, along with a variety of birds and plants, and maybe even a few members of the wild-horse herd.

GETTING THERE

From Bridger, go south 3 miles on US 310 to Pryor Mountain Road. Turn left and go 22 miles east to campground sign. Turn left and cross the creek, and go 1 mile to the campground. Some of these roads are gravel and dirt and can become impassable in wet weather.

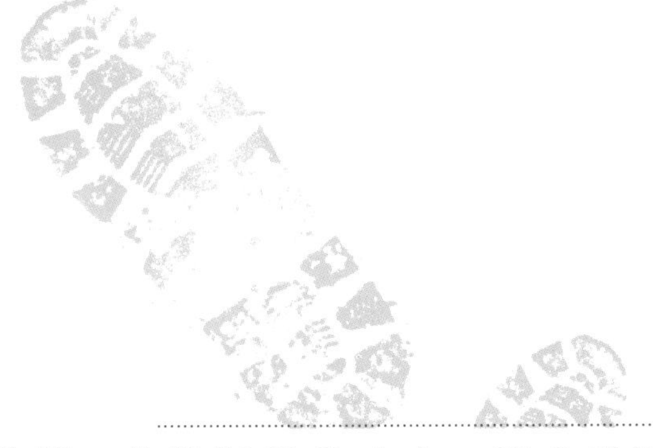

SOUTH CENTRAL **MONTANA**

BEAVER CREEK CAMPGROUND

West Yellowstone

MONTANA IS A LAND of contrasts formed by the continuous shifting of the earth, and on August 17, 1959, the Madison River Valley was the site where it chose to tremble and shake. During that brief moment, which by geologic time is nearly immeasurable, 80 million cubic feet of mountainside slid from its perch, causing a brief but massive windstorm. Before the dust settled, a river was rerouted and a new lake was formed. It was a cataclysmic geologic event, and it was over in an instant.

For the people in the Madison River Valley, however, this nanosecond of geologic time seemed to last forever. Violently awakened on what had been a calm, star-filled night, hundreds of campers, tourists, and residents found themselves in a confusing and disorienting chaos. Twenty-eight people were killed by the quake's power. Nineteen were buried alive under the massive landslide.

It has been nearly 50 years, and a visit to this valley is still humbling. The barren mountainside remains, and absorbing the enormity and suddenness of the event leaves one feeling insignificant and helpless against the forces Mother Nature can unleash.

The same forces of nature that created chaos in 1959 are also responsible for the immense, stark beauty and sense of peace found here today. Placid mountain views and the sparkling water of Quake Lake draw many to this spot between historic Virginia City and Yellowstone National Park.

A long entry road into the campground provides a buffer from the noise on the highway and creates a sense of isolation. The campground is divided into three loops and offers numerous tenting options. The entry road splits, and to the left is Loop A, with beautiful mountain views to the south. A mix of lodgepole pine and aspen divide the spacious sites here. The

"Placid mountain views and the sparkling water of Quake Lake draw many to this spot."

RATINGS

Beauty: ✩ ✩ ✩ ✩ ✩
Privacy: ✩ ✩ ✩
Spaciousness: ✩ ✩ ✩ ✩ ✩
Quiet: ✩ ✩ ✩ ✩
Security: ✩ ✩ ✩ ✩ ✩
Cleanliness: ✩ ✩ ✩ ✩ ✩

KEY INFORMATION

ADDRESS: Hebgen Lake Ranger District
P.O. Box 520
331 US 191 North
West Yellowstone, MT 59758

OPERATED BY: Gallatin National Forest

INFORMATION: (406)823-6961; www.fs.fed.us/r1/gallatin

OPEN: Mid-June–Labor Day

SITES: 64

EACH SITE HAS: Picnic table, fire grate

ASSIGNMENT: First come, first served; no reservations

REGISTRATION: On-site self-registration

FACILITIES: Water spigots, vault toilets

PARKING: At campsites

FEE: $11

ELEVATION: 6,500 feet

RESTRICTIONS: **Pets:** On leash only
Fires: In fire rings only
Alcohol: Permitted
Vehicles: 32-foot length limit
Other: 16-day stay limit; bear country food-storage restrictions; campground host; interpretive center

road drops downhill as you round the backside of the loop, offering additional privacy for sites A4 through A9.

Sites A7 and A8 are near a beaver pond. A8 is the better choice, thanks to a good view of the mountains and more room for a tent. Early in the season these sites might have standing water, making mosquitoes a problem. A10 is the prime site on this loop. You'll need to be a little creative in locating your tent, but you'll have great morning sun and you'll be at the back of the loop, secluded from most of the other sites.

To the right, off the entrance road, is Loop B, and Loop C continues straight ahead. Loop B is heavily forested, and site B5, on the inside of the loop, is perfect for a larger group. Site B6, on the outside of the loop, is raised up slightly from the road and is the pick of the loop. Score this site and you can set your tent back into a secluded grove of trees, with terrific mountain views to the east and west. B8 has a great spot for a tent, perfect morning sun, and a mix of quaking aspen and conifers. This is a beautiful site; however, it isn't as private as some of the others.

Loop C actually sits below Loop B and affords views of Quake Lake and the mountains to the south. As you drop down into Loop C, you'll encounter a delightful aspen grove, and Quake Lake sits just below, full of rainbows, browns, and cutthroats using the dead trees, still standing from 1959, for cover. An interesting hogback ridge runs up the mountainside that dominates the landscape in front of you, and mountain bluebells and lupine provide splashes of color.

A few prime sites exist on Loop C. Site C13 sits back from the road just a bit and offers a picturesque open spot for tents. Site C20 puts you on the outside of the loop, providing a nice backdrop of the mountains and plenty of flat space to set up a tent. Site C18 is on the outside of the loop; back your car in and you will block your neighbor's view of your picnic table while you enjoy your morning tea or coffee and soak in the terrific mountain views.

A walk down to the lake may provide a chance sighting of a moose. On our visit, a cow and two calves

MAP

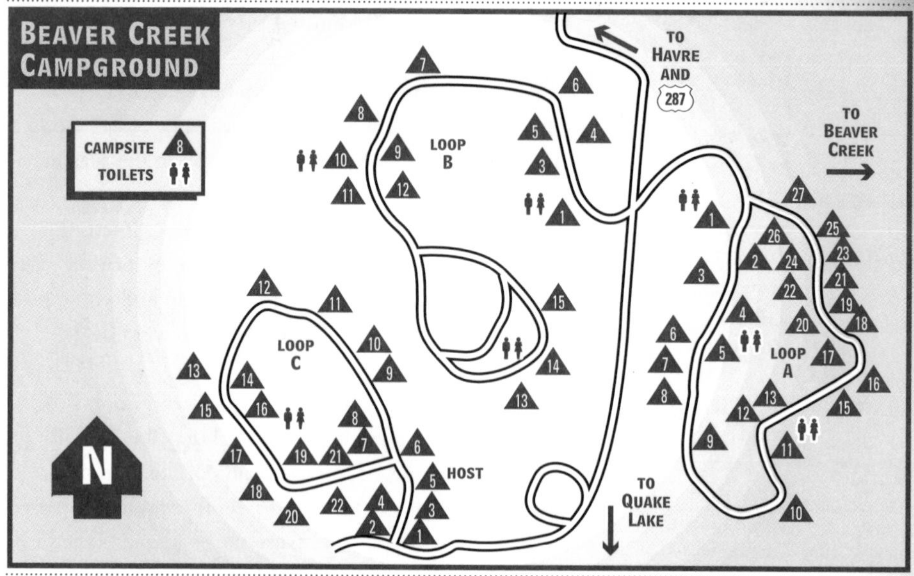

were feeding in the aspen grove. During busy months animals are more likely to seek cover away from the campground.

GETTING THERE

From West Yellowstone, take US 191 north for 8 miles to US 287. Turn left and go west for 16 miles to the campground.

Big Timber

FALLS CREEK CAMPGROUND

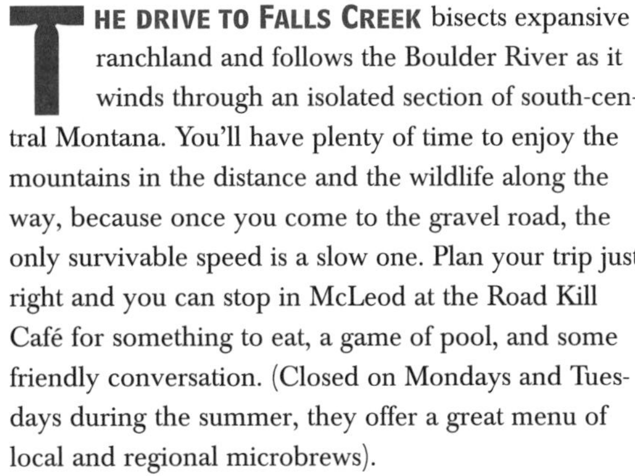

> *Falls Creek is a rare, tents-only campground along the scenic Main Boulder River.*

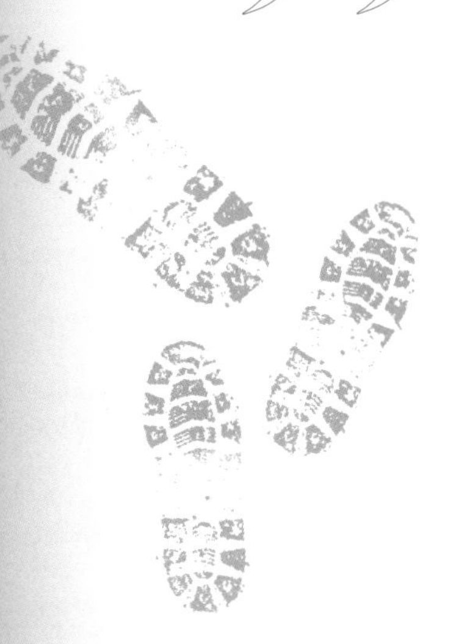

RATINGS

Beauty: ★★★★
Privacy: ★★★★★
Spaciousness: ★★★★★
Quiet: ★★★★★
Security: ★★★★
Cleanliness: ★★★★★

THE DRIVE TO FALLS CREEK bisects expansive ranchland and follows the Boulder River as it winds through an isolated section of south-central Montana. You'll have plenty of time to enjoy the mountains in the distance and the wildlife along the way, because once you come to the gravel road, the only survivable speed is a slow one. Plan your trip just right and you can stop in McLeod at the Road Kill Café for something to eat, a game of pool, and some friendly conversation. (Closed on Mondays and Tuesdays during the summer, they offer a great menu of local and regional microbrews).

A bit farther down the road is Natural Bridge, where a spectacular waterfall show peaks every spring, as the natural rock formations and river come together here in a magical way. Some days, the river cascades over the top of the rocks in a tumbling, frothing, swirling mass. On others, when the water level has dropped, the water disappears beneath the rocks for a distance before pouring from gaps situated at various levels along the canyon. Interpretive signs help visitors understand the geology of the area, and paved trails and overlooks make access easy. Extreme care should be taken, since there are no guardrails along the edge of some trail sections. The easiest hike in the area (but still a challenge) is an 11-mile out-and-back from here to Green Mountain and the East Boulder Campground.

Not much farther down the road is your goal: Falls Creek—a rare find with virtually everything a car camper could ask for, from its setting along the scenic Boulder River to its tents-only design. The river provides world-class trout habitat and lives up to its name with behemoth boulders forcing the flow into a whitewater frenzy. Sites here are all walk-in; they line the river's edge with views of the cliffs on the opposite shore, and the walk is less than 100 yards.

Site 2 is closest to the water, located on a bend in the river and set off from the others, but sites 1 and 3 overlook it since it lies between them and the river. Site 1 is private, and the setting is good, but it is closer to the parking area and a little farther (maybe 30 yards) from the water. Sites 3 and 4 are fairly close to one another, and although there are plenty of firs and cottonwoods between them, the shade prevents much understory privacy. All sites are roomy, and you can easily set up camp without being on top of your neighbor. If you want privacy, Site 8 is totally hidden. The downside is that it isn't on the water, and the surrounding trees and brush block most of the river view. At this end of the campground, site 7 offers the best combination of privacy, proximity to water, and scenic view. Much of the land in this area is privately owned, including property along the river. The water itself is public, as are some portions of the riverbank, but take time to familiarize yourself with the state's stream-access regulations to avoid tresspassing.

This picture-perfect campground still had four sites available when we arrived at 7 p.m. on a balmy Friday in August. But if the campground is full, you'll find several other developed campgrounds as you continue south, and there are two tent-only sites along the river at Chippy Park (4.5 miles south of Falls Creek).

Hiking in this area is not for the weak of heart (or legs). The scenery and wildlife are spectacular but so are the elevation gains. Below 2-Mile Bridge on the west side of the road is the trailhead for Great Falls Creek Trail #18, a hike up several switchbacks to 10,604-foot West Boulder Plateau in the Absaroka-Beartooth Wilderness. It's an extremely strenuous 9 miles to the plateau, making this more than a day hike for all but the heartiest hikers. However, you could hike partway out and back: you'll still be in the Wilderness, and it's all downhill coming home.

Another mile down the road on the east side is Graham Creek Trail #117, which runs between Chrome and Contact Mountains on the way to the East Boulder Plateau. This is another steep (4,300-foot elevation gain) hike that isn't technically in the Wilderness, but you won't be able to tell by the scenery. Off

KEY INFORMATION

ADDRESS:	Big Timber Ranger District 225 Big Timber Loop Road Big Timber, MT 59011
OPERATED BY:	Gallatin National Forest
INFORMATION:	(406) 932-5155; www.fed.fs.us/r1/gallatin
OPEN:	Year-round depending on weather conditions; full services late May–September
SITES:	8 (tent only)
EACH SITE HAS:	Picnic table, fire ring
ASSIGNMENT:	First come, first served; no reservations
REGISTRATION:	None
FACILITIES:	Hand-pump well, vault toilets
PARKING:	At campsites
FEE:	Free
ELEVATION:	5,200 feet
RESTRICTIONS:	Pets: On leash only Fires: In fire rings only Alcohol: Permitted Vehicles: No RVs or trailers Other: 16-day stay limit; bear country food-storage restrictions; pack-in/pack-out

MAP

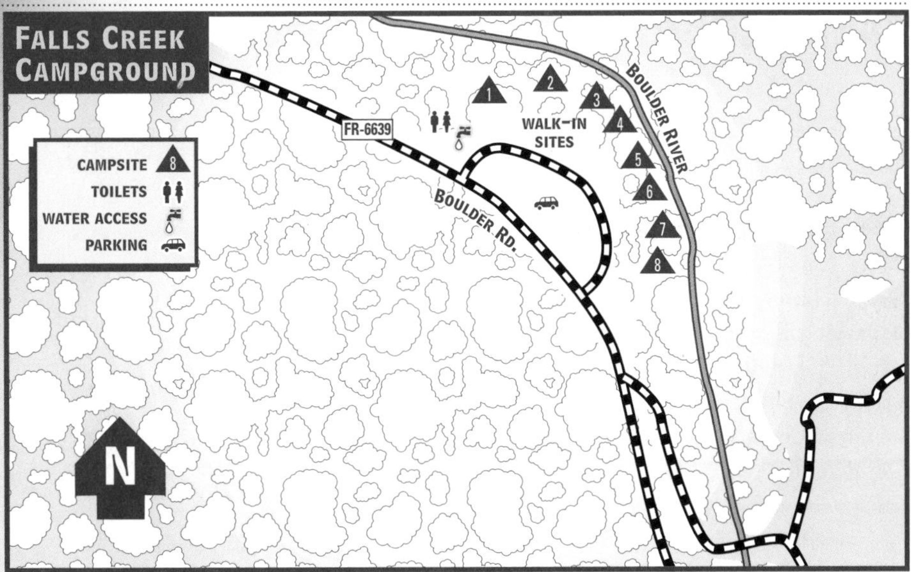

GETTING THERE

From Big Timber, take MT 298 south for 30 miles to the campground. (Don't take the turnoff to East Boulder Road.)

the west side of the road before the entrance to Falls Creek is Grouse Creek Trail #14, which winds 7 miles to West Boulder Campground.

GREENOUGH LAKE CAMPGROUND

Red Lodge

SET AMIDST SPECTACULAR forests and mountain scenery, the narrow Red Lodge Valley has a history of coal mining, colorful and eccentric Old West characters, outdoor recreation, and rodeo royalty. Yes, rodeo royalty. This is the valley where Ben Greenough led pack trains through the steep mountains and across the lofty plateaus of the Beartooths for years, and his eight children grew up riding horses. Five of them participated in rodeos: Turk was named King of the Bronc Riders in 1935, and Alice and Marge rode both bulls and bucking broncos to win a wealth of championships around the world.

The Greenoughs helped bring organized rodeo to Red Lodge and helped build an arena in 1929 for the locals who had been competing at the railroad stockyards since before the turn of the century. Another local hero, Bill Linderman, added more titles to the town's history, even winning the title of "World All-Around Champion" three times. His brother Bud won a world championship as well, and in their honor the Red Lodge rodeo was renamed "Home of Champions Rodeo." Today the tradition continues with Alice's great-nephew, Deb Greenough, continuing as a world-champion bareback rider.

It was at the rodeo grounds, when musician Willie Nelson was giving a concert in August of 2000, that a motorcycle crash ignited a wildfire that spread over 2,000 acres in a few hours. Naming forest fires is a function of the local ranger district, and the name must be distinctive enough to allow differentiation between it and past or future fires. This one was named "Willie," and may make Nelson the only professional entertainer to have a forest fire named after him—a dubious honor, don't you think?

A few miles south of the fire area is Rock Creek Road and the turnoff for Greenough Lake, a canyon

This canyon campground sits in a thick pine-and-fir forest along Rock Creek at the foot of Beartooth Pass.

RATINGS

Beauty: ✩ ✩ ✩ ✩ ✩
Privacy: ✩ ✩ ✩ ✩
Spaciousness: ✩ ✩ ✩ ✩
Quiet: ✩ ✩ ✩ ✩
Security: ✩ ✩ ✩ ✩
Cleanliness: ✩ ✩ ✩ ✩ ✩

KEY INFORMATION

ADDRESS: Beartooth Ranger District
HC 49, Box 3420
Red Lodge, MT 59068

OPERATED BY: Custer National Forest

INFORMATION: (406) 446-2103, www.fs.fed.us/r1/custer; reservations (877) 444-6777, www.reserveusa.com

OPEN: May–September

SITES: 18

EACH SITE HAS: Picnic table, fire ring

ASSIGNMENT: First come, first served; reservations accepted

REGISTRATION: On-site self-registration

FACILITIES: Hand-pump well, vault toilets

PARKING: At campsites

FEE: $10 per night, $6 for 2nd vehicle

ELEVATION: 7,300 feet

RESTRICTIONS: **Pets:** On leash only
Fires: In fire rings only
Alcohol: Permitted
Vehicles: 32-foot length limit
Other: 10-day stay limit; pack-in/pack-out; bear country food-storage restrictions

campground set in a thick pine-and-fir forest along Rock Creek at the foot of Beartooth Pass. The sites along the creek are the best, with 1, 2, and 3 all providing privacy and plenty of room. Of the trio, site 3 is the best, with the most understory buffering the view of the loop road. Sites 5 and 7 are creekside, large, and private; they are also among the few sites you can't reserve. Site 13 is the most unusual, with a huge boulder that just begs you to climb it.

Although deer and elk are the most plentiful, moose frequently visit the area, and at least a few bears will appear throughout the summer. A short trail leads from the campground to Greenough Lake. This small lake, named for the local rodeo dynasty, is stocked with rainbows, and at less than ten feet deep, it's popular for family fishing outings during which kids frequently land good-sized keepers.

Across a bridge and directly on the opposite bank of Rock Creek is Limber Pine Campground, where you can reserve the best sites—Site 9 on a bluff above the creek and Site 8 down below for views of the creek and more privacy.

The trailhead for Glacier Lake Trail #3 is 8 miles down the gravel road past Limber Pine, and if you're driving a regular car, you may want to park and walk the final 800 yards due to the roughness of the road. This trail to the Rock Creek headwaters begins at about 8,600 feet and climbs steeply along Moon Creek for 1.7 miles and ending on a ridge above the tree line before it drops down to the bowl where the lake nestles at 9,700 feet on the Montana-Wyoming border. Trails lead to several other lakes in this basin, but the fishing here and in adjacent Little Glacier Lake generally yields larger cutthroat and brook trout. The wind picks up in the afternoon, and short but severe storms can roll in suddenly, bringing rain, hail, and even snow.

Rock Creek also provides sections of Class III and IV whitewater, with a put-in at Lake Fork Creek, 11 miles south of Red Lodge. Lower Lake Fork Trail #1 into the Absaroka–Beartooth Wilderness is an easy-to-moderate 2.9-mile out-and-back hike through the forest alongside the creek's whitewater and waterfalls. The

MAP

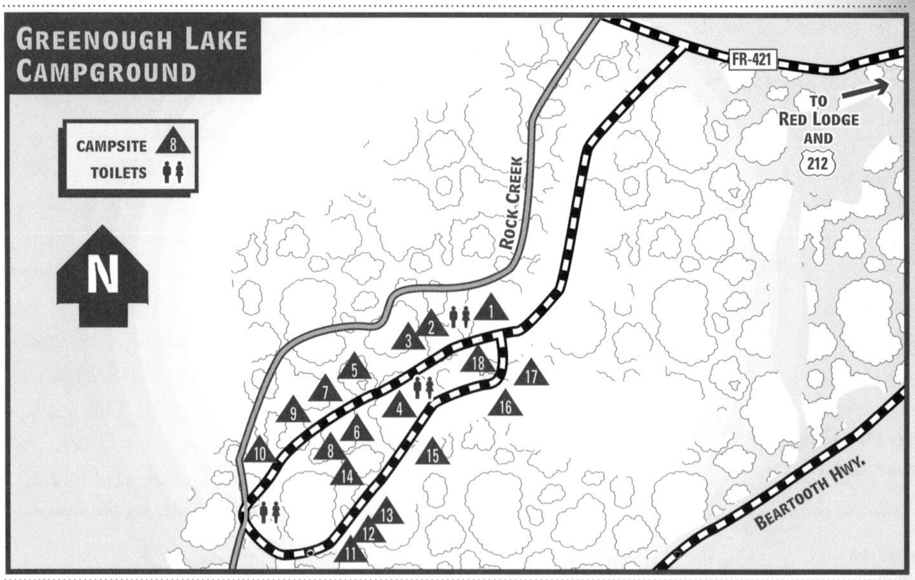

trail skirts Black Pyramid Mountain and is an excellent place to see moose.

On your hikes you may see what looks like pink snow. No, you're not seeing things; the snow really is pink, particularly in late summer, and is often called watermelon snow. The color is due to an algae *(Chlamydomonas nivalis)*, which turns red as it thrives in the warm summer sun. You may find that hiking through these snowfields discolors your boot soles, socks, and pant cuffs, but don't worry, it's only temporary.

GETTING THERE

From Red Lodge, take US 212 southwest for 12 miles to Forest Service Road 421. Turn right and go 1 mile southwest to the campground.

HALFMOON CAMPGROUND

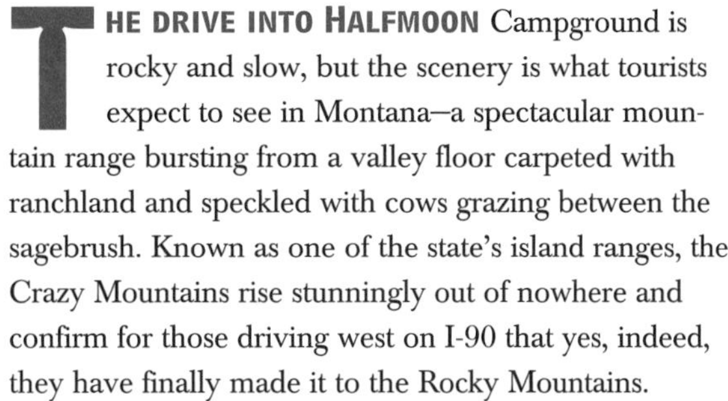

Big Timber and Crazy Peaks loom to the southwest, and 2,000-foot rock-canyon walls rise on either side of the campground.

RATINGS

Beauty: ✩ ✩ ✩ ✩ ✩
Privacy: ✩ ✩ ✩ ✩ ✩
Spaciousness: ✩ ✩ ✩ ✩ ✩
Quiet: ✩ ✩ ✩ ✩ ✩
Security: ✩ ✩ ✩ ✩
Cleanliness: ✩ ✩ ✩ ✩

THE DRIVE INTO HALFMOON Campground is rocky and slow, but the scenery is what tourists expect to see in Montana—a spectacular mountain range bursting from a valley floor carpeted with ranchland and speckled with cows grazing between the sagebrush. Known as one of the state's island ranges, the Crazy Mountains rise stunningly out of nowhere and confirm for those driving west on I-90 that yes, indeed, they have finally made it to the Rocky Mountains.

Called the "Awaxaawippiia" by the Crow Indians, the Crazy Mountains are where Chief Plenty Coups received his leadership vision, and the range remains a sacred, spiritual place for the tribe. As for how the mountains were named, there are a variety of stories, and everyone has their favorite. Be sure to ask locals for their version.

The Crazy Mountains are not a sprawling range but a compact one, extending only about 25 miles; however, what they lack in breadth they make up for in height, with two dozen peaks towering above 10,000 feet. On the western flank is Grasshopper Glacier, a lingering remnant of the glaciers that, like a sculptor's chisel, carved these mountains by etching away mud and stone. Created some 50 million years earlier, the glacier appeared when magma rose from deep within the earth's core to the muddy ocean floor and solidified into igneous rock.

Much of these mountains are in "checkerboard ownership," meaning if you look at an ownership map of the area, the mix of public and private land resembles a checkerboard. Since the approach to Halfmoon passes through private property, respecting private land during your visit is not only important but also simply the right thing to do. When you come to a gate on the campground entrance road, please be sure to close it behind you.

This is a busy place on holidays and weekends, and it is easy to understand why. Your first thought when you arrive at Halfmoon may be much like ours—we don't need to go anywhere else; this is perfection. The setting is amazingly, spectacularly, dramatically breathtaking—Big Timber Peak (10,795 feet) and Crazy Peak (11,214 feet) loom to the southwest, and 2,000-foot rock canyon walls rise on either side of the campground. The stubby Douglas firs are evidence of the short growing season but are more than large enough to provide effective shade and privacy screening. Moss-covered boulders are a subtle indication that melting winter snows last well into summer.

Each of the dozen sites here is somewhat secluded. You're still going to see other people, but each site has plenty of space for a tent and is outfitted with the standard table and fire ring. Everything is in place for a quiet evening spent enjoying dinner and scanning the cliffs with binoculars to spot mountain goats clinging to the edges.

Adjacent to the campground is Big Timber Creek Trailhead #119, where you can take a very short hike to the lower portion of Big Timber Falls (also known as Halfmoon Falls) or continue less than 0.5 miles to the upper falls. Three miles down Trail 119, you'll run into Blue Lake Trail #118, a 1.5-mile spur to Blue Lake, where the fishing is good and the setting for a picnic is superb. A few miles past the Blue Lake Spur, you'll come to Conical Peak.

Even though the trails can get busy on weekends, birds are easy to spot, with eagles and hawks in the sky and an occasional wild turkey rattling the shrubs. Black bears, deer, mountain lions, elk, and mountain goats make hiking an observation adventure. Wildflowers are abundant in some sections and bloom later than those at lower elevations. Since much of the land here is privately owned and is designated as such, please stay on the trails in these areas and note that both Crazy Peak and Moose Lake are on private property and permission is required before climbing.

Yes, it can snow any time of year at Halfmoon, but we're betting that once you're here, it will be hard to tear yourself away.

KEY INFORMATION

ADDRESS: Big Timber Ranger District
P.O. Box 1130
225 Big Timber Loop Road
Big Timber, MT 59011

OPERATED BY: Gallatin National Forest

INFORMATION: (406) 932-5155; www.fs.fed.us/r1/gallatin

OPEN: Memorial Day–September, weather permitting

SITES: 12

EACH SITE HAS: Picnic table, fire grate

ASSIGNMENT: First come, first served; no reservations

REGISTRATION: On-site self-registration

FACILITIES: Hand-pump well, vault toilets

PARKING: At campsites

FEE: $5

ELEVATION: 6,500 feet

RESTRICTIONS: **Pets:** On leash only
Fires: In fire rings only
Alcohol: Permitted
Vehicles: 30-foot length limit
Other: 16-day stay limit; bear country food-storage restrictions; pack-in/pack-out; campground host

MAP

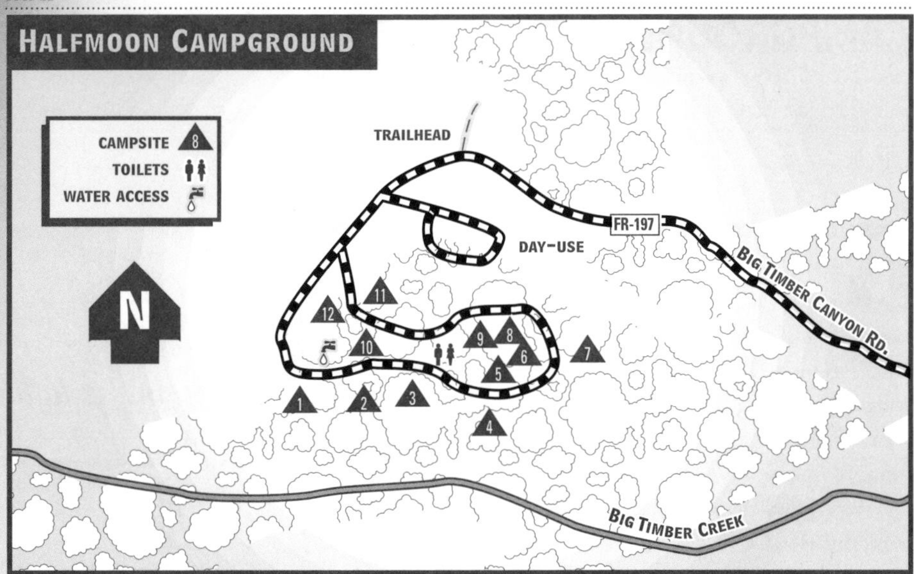

GETTING THERE

From Big Timber, take US 191 north for 11 miles to Big Timber Canyon Road. Turn left and go 12 miles west to the campground.

HOOD CREEK CAMPGROUND

Bozeman

BUILT IN THE 1940S to provide water for area farms and ranches, Hyalite Reservoir is the anchor for a recreation area attracting hikers, campers, anglers, and those just seeking a little time to relax outdoors. Due to its close proximity, it's a prime recreation destination for Bozeman residents and Montana State University students, but there's plenty of room for everyone.

You'll find several Forest Service campgrounds here, but Hood Creek is our choice for tenters. Access is a bit more difficult than at the others, and this cuts down on the number of RVs.

Hood Creek is spread in a narrow band along the reservoir, providing plenty of room between sites as well as a lot of space within the sites themselves. Reservations are accepted for all but seven of the sites here. One of the nonreservable sites is Site 5, the only one set on the opposite side of the road from the reservoir. This is a nicely forested site and isn't a bad choice. Overall, site 17 is the best, even though the road to the boat ramp runs along one side. The boat-ramp traffic is buffered by trees and understory. Site 17 offers plenty of room for a tent, sunlight throughout the day, and spectacular mountain views. Most of the nonreservable sites are the open ones that have great views but lack shade or privacy screening.

The reservoir's setting is pretty remarkable for a man-made body of water. Surrounded by mountains, wildflower meadows, and waterfalls, this area draws a variety of wildlife and birds. There is a no-wake policy on the 1.25-mile-long lake, where canoes and sailboats are plentiful, along with cutthroat trout and arctic grayling. The no-wake policy is enforced and helps keep the noise level down.

The entire canyon is a paradise for hikers, with trails for all skill and stamina levels around every

> *Hood Creek is surrounded by mountains, wildflower meadows, and waterfalls.*

RATINGS

Beauty: ✩ ✩ ✩ ✩ ✩
Privacy: ✩ ✩ ✩ ✩
Spaciousness: ✩ ✩ ✩ ✩ ✩
Quiet: ✩ ✩ ✩
Security: ✩ ✩ ✩ ✩
Cleanliness: ✩ ✩ ✩ ✩

KEY INFORMATION

ADDRESS: Bozeman Ranger District
3710 Fallon Street, Suite C
Bozeman, MT 59715

OPERATED BY: Gallatin National Forest

INFORMATION: (406) 522-2520; www.fs.fed.us/r1/gallatin; reservations (877) 444-6777, www.reserveusa.com

OPEN: Mid-May–mid-September

SITES: 20

EACH SITE HAS: Picnic table, fire ring

ASSIGNMENT: First come, first served; reservations accepted

REGISTRATION: On-site self-registration

FACILITIES: Hand-pump well, vault toilets, boat ramp, picnic area

PARKING: At campsites

FEE: $10 per night, $6 for 2nd vehicle

ELEVATION: 6,700 feet

RESTRICTIONS: Pets: On leash only
Fires: In fire rings only
Alcohol: Permitted
Vehicles: 45-foot length limit
Other: 16-day stay limit; bear country food-storage restrictions; pack-in/pack-out; campground host; firewood for sale

bend. The turnoff for History Rock Trail #424 is on the west side of the road, 1 mile before the reservoir. This fairly steep 1.2-mile trail leads to an outcropping carved with historic graffiti left by early settlers. Unfortunately, more recent (and careless) visitors often leave their marks as well. The trail continues from here for 3 miles to Cottonwood Creek and unless you're prepared to spend the night on the trail, this will be the turnaround point. The trailhead for Blackmore Trail #423 is at the Blackmore Picnic Area before the reservoir bridge. This trail leads to the peak of Mount Blackmore (10,154 feet).

You can hike to Hyalite Peak from the trailhead about 2 miles past Hood Creek. The view from the peak is spectacular, as are the 11 waterfalls along the way. On this 14-mile out-and-back hike, the first half of the trail climbs so gently you probably won't notice you're climbing, although there are a few steep sections. Then the grade gets steeper, and you'll encounter a dozen or so switchbacks. Hyalite Lake sits in a wide, deep basin just past the 5-mile mark; hike the last 2 miles to the top of Hyalite Peak (10,299 feet). Overall, the elevation gain is about 3,300 feet, taking you to a height where snow usually hangs around until July and often returns by Labor Day.

The trailhead for Palisade Falls National Recreation Trail is past Hood Creek and to the left at the Y. This paved 0.6-mile trail snakes through a forest of pine, fir, and spruce to the 98-foot falls.

The trailhead for East Fork Hyalite Trail #434 is about 1 mile farther down East Fork Road. This 11-mile out-and-back trail follows the East Fork of Hyalite Creek, a fast-running home for cutthroat and brook trout and grayling. The climb is gradual for the first few miles with only one steep section as it moves through the forested creek bottoms. Once you pass Horsetail Falls, the grade increases, as does the expansiveness of the views. You'll face a dozen switchbacks before you get to Emerald and Heather Lakes, but this isn't a difficult hike.

In this region you'll find mountainsides dropping steeply down to lakeshores and a wealth of rocky cliffs. On any of these trails you'll be greeted by a wildflower

MAP

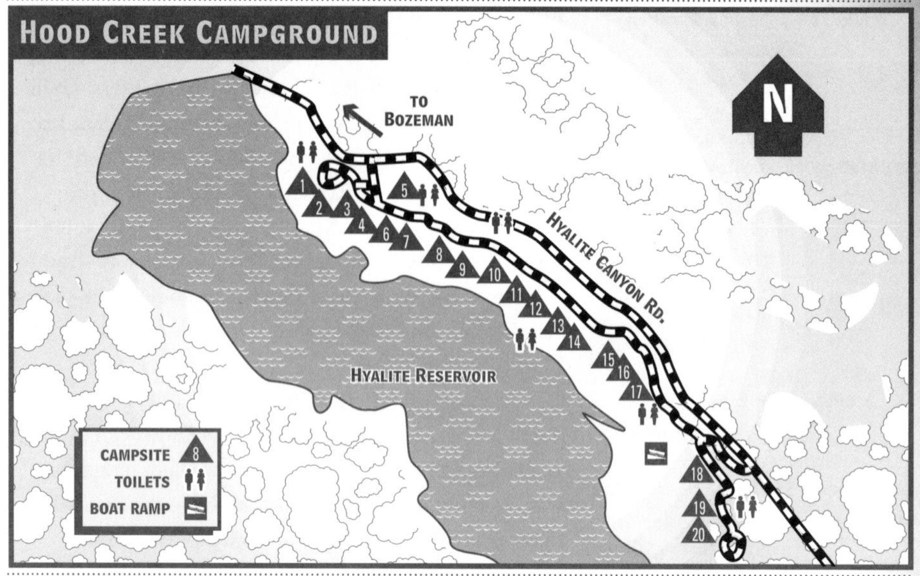

display that evolves all summer, and wildlife viewing is generally good, especially if you're looking for elk, deer, or mountain goats.

GETTING THERE

From Bozeman, Take 19th Street south for 7 miles to Hyalite Canyon Road. Turn left and continue south for 10 miles (crossing over the bridge at the reservoir) to the campground.

POTOSI CAMPGROUND

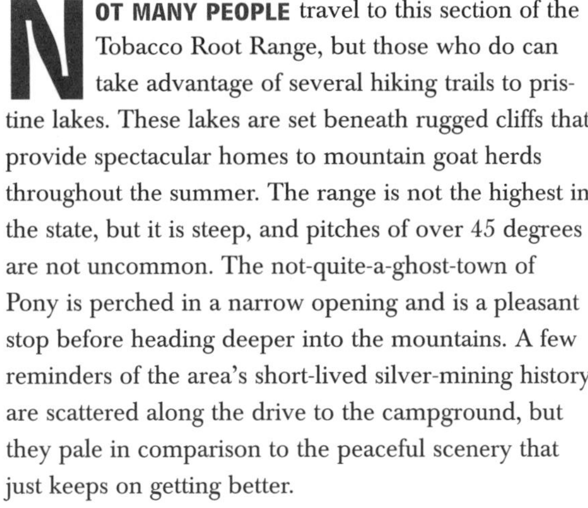

You'll have great trail access at this basic campground in a spectacular setting.

NOT MANY PEOPLE travel to this section of the Tobacco Root Range, but those who do can take advantage of several hiking trails to pristine lakes. These lakes are set beneath rugged cliffs that provide spectacular homes to mountain goat herds throughout the summer. The range is not the highest in the state, but it is steep, and pitches of over 45 degrees are not uncommon. The not-quite-a-ghost-town of Pony is perched in a narrow opening and is a pleasant stop before heading deeper into the mountains. A few reminders of the area's short-lived silver-mining history are scattered along the drive to the campground, but they pale in comparison to the peaceful scenery that just keeps on getting better.

A big plus is the lure of the hot springs. A larger springs is on private property and part of Potosi Hot Springs Resort, but the public upper springs can be reached from the campground trailhead on the east side of the creek. Follow the easy first mile of Trail 308 along South Willow Creek, and when the creek widens, start looking along the creek bed for the log fencing enclosing the hot springs. Climb through the fencing to access the springs. Both are small, and a group of six will fill them to capacity.

Access to the campground can be confusing, since it sits astride South Willow Creek, with five sites on the west bank and the rest on the east bank. Watch for a post with a tent sign at the access roads. A thick forest envelops these compact sites, and even though sites on the west bank are on the creek, sites on the other loop are more private and almost as close to the water. Site 8, on the east loop, is the most spacious and offers the most seclusion; a small stream runs behind it and site 7. If the sites are all filled, several dispersed sites are a good option, since they are still close to the water pump and outhouses.

RATINGS

Beauty: ✩ ✩ ✩ ✩ ✩
Privacy: ✩ ✩ ✩
Spaciousness: ✩ ✩ ✩
Quiet: ✩ ✩ ✩ ✩
Security: ✩ ✩ ✩ ✩
Cleanliness: ✩ ✩ ✩ ✩

Fishing in the creek provides lucky anglers with rainbow, brown, brook, and cutthroat trout, while waders just enjoy the clear, cool water that is a refreshing contrast to the nearby hot springs.

This is a popular place for locals, and you'll encounter a lot of motorized traffic on some trails, especially on the weekends. For those who have ATVs or motorbikes, this is an ideal location. Mountain bikers and hikers shouldn't necessarily shy away however, since many trails have restrictions that help everyone share this corner of the Tobacco Root Range. Wildlife viewing is good for mule deer, elk, moose, and black bears.

Potosi Trail #303 heads west from where the road splits between the campground loops and is solid switchbacks for the first mile to the ridge overlooking the creek that weaves through the campground. The trail runs along the ridge and then climbs another mile before intersecting with primitive Rock Creek Trail #304. Past the intersection, it climbs sharply to another ridge and the Albro Lake– and North Willow Creek–trail systems. Follow Trail #304 down to South Willow Creek Road, and you will be about a mile from the campground. This is a strenuous but manageable 6-mile hike or mountain-bike loop.

Two miles west of Pony is the trailhead for North Willow Creek Trail #301. This trail follows the north side of the creek for 3 miles and then crosses to the south side for the final 2-mile climb to Hollowtop Lake. The last section is rocky, but not too steep. ATVs are only allowed on the first mile of this trail, and motorcycles are not allowed off the trail or around the lake. Another option after the first mile is to take the turnoff to Albro Lake Trail #333, a 5-mile hike to an alpine lake. The trail climbs through mountain meadows with valley views before dropping to the bowl surrounding the lake.

Bell Lake Trail #305 follows the north side of the creek, and for the first 2.5 miles, climbs slowly to a gate where only motorcycles, people, and horses can continue the last mile, a tough climb to the lake. It's hard to believe that at one time, vehicles used this same route to get to Bell Lake.

KEY INFORMATION

ADDRESS: Madison Ranger District
5 Forest Service Road
Ennis, MT 59729

OPERATED BY: Beaverhead-Deerlodge National Forest

INFORMATION: (406) 387-3800; www.fs.fed.us/r1/b-d

OPEN: June–September

SITES: 13

EACH SITE HAS: Picnic table, fire grate

ASSIGNMENT: First come, first served; no 1reservations

REGISTRATION: None required

FACILITIES: Hand-pump water, vault toilets

PARKING: At campsites

FEE: Free

ELEVATION: 6,200 feet

RESTRICTIONS: Pets: On leash only
Fires: In fire rings only
Alcohol: Permitted
Vehicles: 22-foot length limit
Other: 16-day stay limit; bear country food-storage restrictions; pack-in/pack-out

MAP

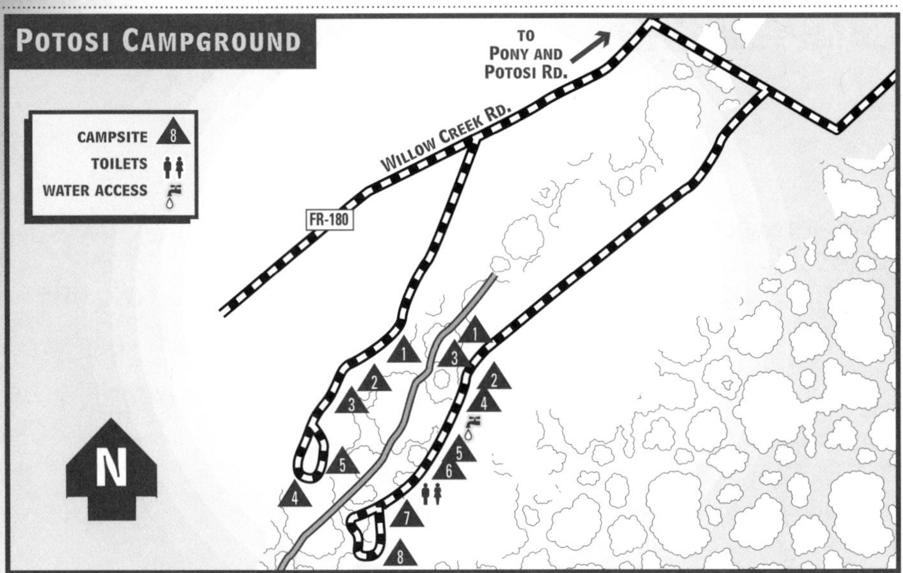

GETTING THERE

From Harrison, take MT 283 for 6.5 miles to Pony. Turn left on Potosi Road. After 4.7 miles, the road becomes Willow Creek Road (Potosi Road will turn to the right). Continue 4.2 miles to a left turnoff for the east campground loop. Or drive another 0.2 miles on Willow Creek Road to the west-loop turnoff and continue to the campground.

SHERIDAN CAMPGROUND

Red Lodge

RED LODGE IS THE gateway to one of the most scenic drives in the United States. The 70-mile-long Beartooth Highway ascends out of Red Lodge through Rock Creek Canyon, serving up spectacular views as it winds to Cooke City and then into Yellowstone National Park. Built between 1931 and 1936 at a cost of $2.5 million, this spectacular highway allows anyone with the nerve to experience what was once only visible to those on foot or horseback: profuse wildflower carpets and a high alpine environment at elevations above 10,000 feet. The sharp switchbacks, unpredictable weather, and remarkable views make each trip on the Beartooth an adventure.

With dramatic, forested peaks surrounding you, it's hard to believe this was once a hotbed of mining activity. Cooke City was home to the New World Mining District, and a railroad transported gold and silver ore to Red Lodge and beyond. But it was the rich coal beds east of Red Lodge that gave rise to the towns of Washoe and Bearcreek, where mines thrived in the first half of the twentieth century, and the valley population peaked at more than 7,000. The mines survived the Depression but were devastated in 1943 when 74 miners died in an explosion at the Smith Mine. This was the state's worst mining disaster and the beginning of the end for large-scale mining in the area.

Six miles south of Red Lodge is Sheridan, the first of several Forest Service campgrounds along the beginning of the Beartooth Highway. A great spot to set up base camp for a few days of exploring this awe-inspiring piece of Montana, Sheridan is small, consisting of just eight campsites. Rock Creek rushes along the western edge of the campground, masking any roadway noise and providing great opportunities for fishing or cooling off in the summer sun. Try to score Site 8 if you can. It's one of the two that aren't reservable (the

Rock Creek rushes along the western edge of this campground.

RATINGS

Beauty: ✩ ✩ ✩ ✩
Privacy: ✩ ✩ ✩ ✩
Spaciousness: ✩ ✩ ✩ ✩ ✩
Quiet: ✩ ✩ ✩ ✩
Security: ✩ ✩ ✩ ✩ ✩
Cleanliness: ✩ ✩ ✩ ✩

KEY INFORMATION

ADDRESS: Beartooth Ranger District
HC 49, Box 3420
Red Lodge, MT 59068

OPERATED BY: Custer National Forest

INFORMATION: (406) 446-2103, www.fs.fed.us/r1/custer; reservations (877) 444-6777, www.reserveusa.com

OPEN: Year-round; full services Memorial Day–Labor Day

SITES: 8

EACH SITE HAS: Picnic table, fire rings

ASSIGNMENT: First come, first served; reservations accepted

REGISTRATION: Self-registration online

FACILITIES: Hand-pump water, vault toilets

PARKING: At campsites

FEE: $10 per night, $6 for 2nd vehicle

ELEVATION: 6,300 feet

RESTRICTIONS: **Pets:** On leash only
Fires: In fire rings only
Alcohol: Permitted
Vehicles: 22-foot length limit
Other: 10-day stay limit; pack-in/pack-out; bear country food-storage restrictions

other is site 4) and is the largest site and has plenty of tent space, dynamite 360-degree views, sun, shade, and access to the creek. Large and shady site 7 is our second pick, with level tent space and beautiful views of the surrounding area. The campground's access to the creek is between sites 7 and 8, but there's enough room that it isn't intrusive. Sheridan is also a good place for a group, since sites 1 and 2 can be reserved together.

Just south of Red Lodge is Forest Service Road 71 (West Fork Road) and access to Basin Lakes National Recreation Trail #6. This is a moderate 4.8-mile hike along the West Fork Rock Creek to a pair of high mountain lakes where the biggest challenges are the last steep mile and how long to spend fishing. On the way to the trailhead at Basin Campground, you'll see plenty of mountain bikers on West Fork Road and the old logging roads that spoke off into the steep and rugged terrain.

Also off US 212 is the Meeteetse Wildife Trail, a 19-mile auto route over undulating hills that winds through a mix of sagebrush-filled flats and lush river bottoms. Sightings of antelope, deer, and moose are frequent, with hawks and golden eagles plentiful as well. Even though there aren't any designated hiking or biking trails, visitors are encouraged to get out of their cars and explore.

Hiking trails generally lead into the Absaroka-Beartooth Wilderness and can be used for day hikes as well as longer backpacking trips. Elevation gains and switchbacks are the norm, and knowing your limits both in terms of time and stamina are important. The ranger-district office in Red Lodge is an important stop for trail maps and current information.

While you're in town, check out Beartooth Nature Center, a wildlife rehabilitation center in Coal Miner's Park, and visit the Carbon County Museum, where you can learn about folks like Calamity Jane, Liver Eating Johnson, Buffalo Bill, John Colter, and Jim Bridger, along with the rainbow of ethnic groups that have called Red Lodge home.

For one of the most unique experiences in the state, stop at the Bear Creek Saloon and Steakhouse on

MAP

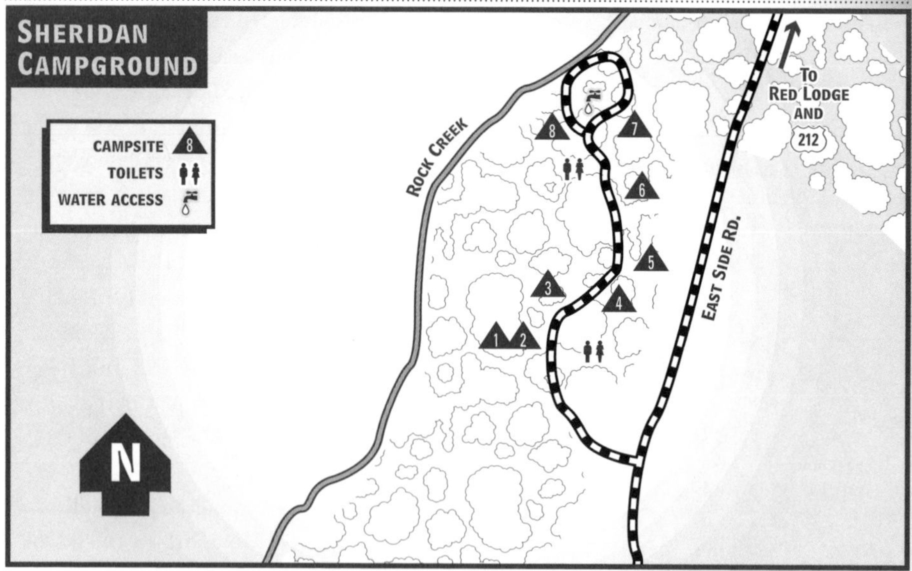

any weekend between Memorial Day and Labor Day to place your bets during the pig races. It's hard to tell who's having more fun—the people or the pigs—but area students are the ultimate winners, since the proceeds fund several scholarships.

GETTING THERE

From Red Lodge, take US 212 south for 6 miles to East Side Road. Turn left and go 2 miles south to the campground.

SWAN CREEK CAMPGROUND

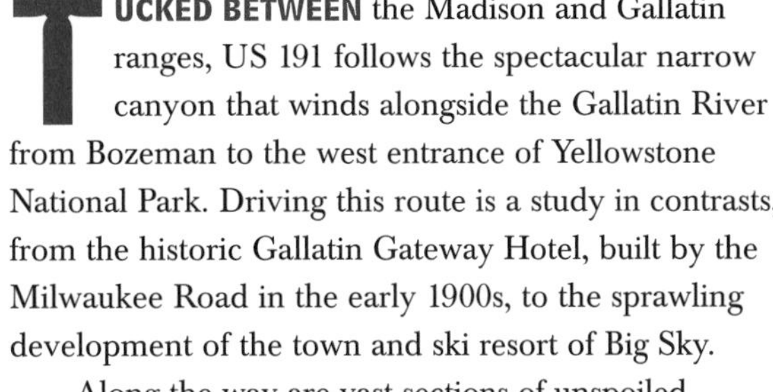

This is a small, densely forested campground in the Gallatin Canyon.

RATINGS

Beauty: ★ ★ ★ ★
Privacy: ★ ★ ★ ★
Spaciousness: ★ ★ ★ ★
Quiet: ★ ★ ★ ★
Security: ★ ★ ★ ★
Cleanliness: ★ ★ ★ ★

TUCKED BETWEEN the Madison and Gallatin ranges, US 191 follows the spectacular narrow canyon that winds alongside the Gallatin River from Bozeman to the west entrance of Yellowstone National Park. Driving this route is a study in contrasts, from the historic Gallatin Gateway Hotel, built by the Milwaukee Road in the early 1900s, to the sprawling development of the town and ski resort of Big Sky.

Along the way are vast sections of unspoiled scenery sprinkled with guest ranches and private cabins. It's tough to take it all in when you're behind the wheel. Drivers must be vigilant of the heavy truck traffic, narrow winding roadway, and blind corners. Truckers may get impatient (since there aren't any passing zones), but take your time anyway. If cars are backed up behind you, stop in one of the pullout spots and let them pass. Remember, you're on vacation. Besides, while you're stopped you can get out of the car and explore the riverbank. There's a good chance you'll see floating parties bobbing by as they take on the river's challenging Class II, III, and IV whitewater. Guided trips are prevalent due to the technical difficulty, and outfitters are available in Big Sky and Bozeman.

Taking some time to fish on this blue-ribbon trout stream is always a good choice. It offers enough mountain whitefish and rainbow, brown, cutthroat, and brook trout to challenge and delight any angler.

Swan Creek is on the east side of the highway, but the turnoff sign for Forest Service Road 481 doesn't give you much warning. Keep an eye on your odometer and the mileage markers and you'll be fine. If you do miss the turn, there are plenty of places to turn around and backtrack. Swan Creek sits a mile off the highway, which makes it the quietest option among the five campgrounds along the canyon. But it is a popular place and nine of the sites here can be reserved. We recommend you take advantage of that option if possible. Sites fill up quickly by Friday afternoon.

Swan Creek is a small, densely forested campground with sites split into two small sections about a half mile apart along the creek. Sites in the first section are a bit farther from the creek than ones in the second, but all are well buffered with thick understory and have better access to the hand pump. Sites 1 and 2 are the nonreservable sites in this section, and they are comparable to the other four in terms of size and privacy.

We prefer the sites in the second section because they all back up to the creek and have a narrow trail leading to the water. The understory here is thick as well, providing privacy and blocking your view of neighboring sites. Sites 7 and 8 are the nonreservable sites, but our favorites are sites 10 and 12. These sites are particularly well suited for tenters, with the picnic table and fire ring up closer to the parking spur and spacious areas near the creek for your tent. No water is available here; you'll have to hike up to the first section.

The creek itself is no more than 10 to 15 feet across, but it offers the same variety of fish as the Gallatin for those looking to hone their skills. If you're seeking other ways to relax, the thick streamside vegetation makes it easy to find a quiet place to set your chair while you lose yourself in a good book or take out a sketchpad and pencils.

Just down the road from the last site is the trailhead for Swan Creek Trail #186. This 2-mile trail is great for families or those who want a stroll instead of a strenuous hike. The route winds along the creek to the base of Hyalite Peak (10,298 feet). Dozens of trails, both to the east and west, are accessible off US 191. A major trailhead lies 6 miles south of the Swan Creek Road turnoff and then 6 miles east on Portal Creek Road (FR 984). From there, you can take an easy hike to Golden Trout Lakes or a steep, challenging hike to Windy Pass. Additional trails interconnect and provide options to please everyone.

KEY INFORMATION

ADDRESS: Bozeman Ranger District
3710 Fallon Street, Suite C
Bozeman, MT 59718

OPERATED BY: Gallatin National Forest

INFORMATION: (406) 522-2520, www.fs.fed.us/r1/gallatin; (877) 444-6777 reservations, www.reserveusa.com

OPEN: Mid-May–September

SITES: 13

EACH SITE HAS: Picnic table, fire grate

ASSIGNMENT: First come, first served; reservations accepted

REGISTRATION: On-site self-registration

FACILITIES: Hand-pump well, vault toilets

PARKING: At campsites

FEE: $10 per night, $6 for 2nd vehicle

ELEVATION: 5,800 feet

RESTRICTIONS: Pets: On leash only
Fires: In fire rings only
Alcohol: Permitted
Vehicles: 45-foot length limit
Other: 16-day stay limit; bear country food-storage restrictions; campground host

MAP

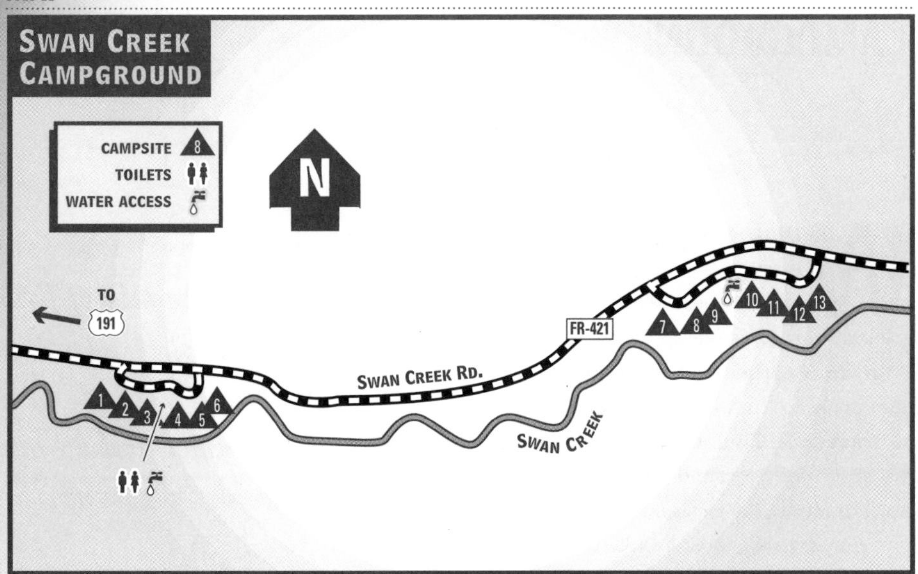

GETTING THERE

From Bozeman, take US 191 south for 32 miles to Swan Creek Road (FR 421). Turn left and go 1 mile east to the campground.

TOM MINER CAMPGROUND

Gardiner

> *A dense mix of firs and aspens provides plenty of shade in summer and vibrant color in autumn.*

WINDING ALONGSIDE THE Yellowstone River through the aptly named Paradise Valley, US 89 from Livingston to this campground's turnoff is one of the most scenic in the state. With the Absaroka Mountains to the east and the Gallatin peaks to the west, even views from the roadway are incredible. Fly-fishing and floating are the draw for this stretch of river, and scores of multimillion-dollar ranches attract the rich and famous.

Access to this area hasn't always been this easy. When Yellowstone National Park first opened, US 89 was merely a trail. Enterprising local rancher James "Yankee Jim" George took advantage of his strategic location and in 1872 began charging a toll to the miners and wagons traversing the narrow pass that crossed his land. Business was good until the Northern Pacific Railroad came to town in 1883 seeking to build a spur into Yellowstone. Despite his protests, Yankee Jim eventually sold his right-of-way to the developing railroad, but his anger remained, and he was often seen violently shaking his fists at passing trains.

There is no toll today on the long road to Tom Miner Campground, but its rough condition gives campers a sense of what travelers in the 1800s faced. The rocky, washboard surface discourages most RVs from making the trek to this high mountain campground, which serves as a jumping-off point for Yellowstone and a base camp for exploring nearby hiking trails.

A dense mix of firs and aspens provides plenty of shade from summer heat and vibrant color in the autumn, while the elevation makes for cool nights and the possibility of snow year-round. Sites are perfect for tents, and a solid understory provides sufficient seclusion from other campers. The Forest Service recently added a concrete vault toilet, a nice improvement from

RATINGS

Beauty: ✩ ✩ ✩ ✩
Privacy: ✩ ✩ ✩ ✩
Spaciousness: ✩ ✩ ✩ ✩
Quiet: ✩ ✩ ✩ ✩
Security: ✩ ✩ ✩
Cleanliness: ✩ ✩ ✩

KEY INFORMATION

ADDRESS: Gardiner Ranger District
P.O. Box 5
US 89 South
Gardiner, MT 59030

OPERATED BY: Gallatin National Forest

INFORMATION: (406) 848-7375; www.fs.fed.us/r1/gallatin

OPEN: June–October, weather permitting

SITES: 12

EACH SITE HAS: Picnic table, fire grate

ASSIGNMENT: First come, first served; no reservations

REGISTRATION: On-site self-registration

FACILITIES: Hand-pump well, vault toilets

PARKING: At campsites

FEE: $7 per night, $3 per additional vehicle

ELEVATION: 7,300 feet

RESTRICTIONS: **Pets:** On leash only
Fires: In fire rings only
Alcohol: Permitted
Vehicles: 42-foot length limit
Other: 16-day stay limit; bear country food-storage restrictions; pack-in/pack-out

the two remaining wood toilets. A hand pump provides fresh drinking water, and a small creek running through the campground enhances mountain views.

Even though Forest Service information indicates there are 16 sites here, currently there are only 12 that are designated, and the best ones are the four (5, 7, 8, and 10) on the left side of the road. These sites are the largest and provide more seclusion since they're backed by a dense stand of trees.

A unique hiking opportunity exists from the campground trailhead. An easy 2-mile hike takes you back thousands of years as you travel the Gallatin Petrified Forest Interpretive Trail #286. This trail loops from the campground and includes signs that describe the volcanic activity that occurred 44 to 53 million years ago, forever preserving this tropical forest. Many of the trees are preserved in an upright position, which raised a debate about whether they were petrified in place or transported and deposited in this position. Recent studies, which included looking at the aftermath of the 1980 eruption of Mount St. Helens, have led researchers to question their previous conclusions. See what conclusions you come to as you explore this prehistoric forest oasis.

Please keep in mind that collecting petrified wood along this trail is prohibited. However, you are allowed to collect one small fragment elsewhere in the 25,000 acres designated as the Gallatin Petrified Forest. Just be sure to obtain a permit from the self-service permit station at the forest entrance or at Gallatin National Forest Ranger District offices.

The trail to Buffalo Horn Pass also starts at this trailhead. This moderately easy 5-mile out-and-back hike follows Trail Creek as it gently climbs to the 8,523-foot summit. Along the way, many additional trails spur off into the Petrified Forest for further exploration.

If you continue on toward Yellowstone from here, be sure to stop at the Boiling River south of Gardiner. A short trail leads down to this spot in the Gardner River, where hot pools and small waterfalls provide a relaxing swimming area.

As you travel throughout Tom Miner Basin, you will be in the company of both grizzly bears and one

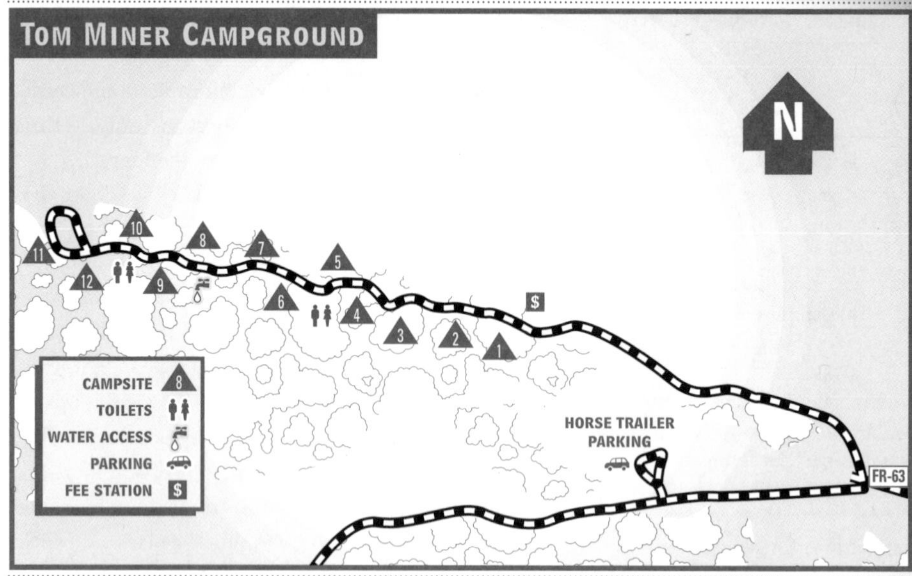

of the West's most controversial canines. Gray wolves inhabit this area after being reintroduced to the Yellowstone ecosystem between 1995 and 1996. This reclusive predator was the center of heated controversy between the ranching community and those interested in restoring this subspecies of the native Northern Rocky Mountain wolf. The wolves in this area have been busy reproducing, and area ranchers have lost livestock and pets due to wolf kills. Efforts to prevent wolf-livestock encounters have been undertaken, to compensate ranchers for their losses.

Additional wildlife-viewing opportunities are abundant, with white-tailed and mule deer, antelope, and elk as frequent visitors to the area, while moose and grizzly bears visit too, but not nearly as often.

GETTING THERE

From Gardiner, take US 89 north for 16 miles to CR 63. Turn left and go 12 miles southwest to FR 63. Turn left and go 4 miles southwest to the campground.

Cameron

WADE LAKE AREA CAMPGROUNDS

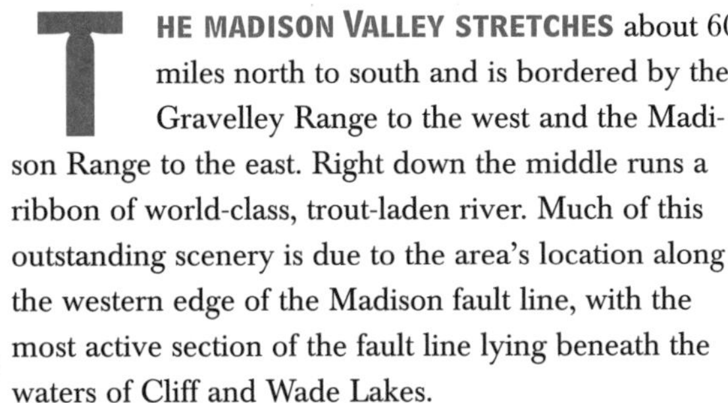

> *The cliffs surrounding these mountain lakes are home to prairie falcons, bald eagles, and osprey.*

THE MADISON VALLEY STRETCHES about 60 miles north to south and is bordered by the Gravelley Range to the west and the Madison Range to the east. Right down the middle runs a ribbon of world-class, trout-laden river. Much of this outstanding scenery is due to the area's location along the western edge of the Madison fault line, with the most active section of the fault line lying beneath the waters of Cliff and Wade Lakes.

Today the lakes' waters are calm and serene, but in 1959, aftershocks from the Hebgen Lake earthquake measured between 5.8 and 6.0 on the Richter scale, and Wade Lake campers awoke thinking bears were shaking their trailers. That is until they and their trailers began to bounce three feet off the ground and they watched the lake slosh like a giant bucket of water, tossing fish and debris up onto its banks.

On the drive in you'd never guess these lakes were here. You leave the highway, cross the Madison River, and drive across seemingly endless views of sagebrush. You pass the ghost town of Cliff Lake and see cabin remnants, but nowhere is there anything resembling a lake. One more hill climb, and suddenly everything changes. The flats begin to roll and the transformation between sagebrush prairie and forest begins. Around the final bend are these mountain lakes, shimmering in the distance.

Part of the Hidden Lakes chain, both Cliff and Wade Lakes are surrounded by cliffs that make shoreline fishing difficult but provide excellent habitat for the prairie falcons, bald eagles, and osprey that call this area home. Once you get offshore, fishing here is a delight. Experts and novices use a variety of styles, from fly-fishing to spin casting to trolling from canoes, drift boats, and float tubes, and the no-wake rules keep noise and activity to a minimum.

RATINGS

Beauty: ✩ ✩ ✩ ✩ ✩
Privacy: ✩ ✩ ✩ ✩
Spaciousness: ✩ ✩ ✩ ✩
Quiet: ✩ ✩ ✩ ✩
Security: ✩ ✩ ✩ ✩ ✩
Cleanliness: ✩ ✩ ✩ ✩ ✩

A spawning channel has been installed to eliminate the need for annual stocking, and it's surprising more anglers don't visit here. The state-record brown trout (29 pounds) was caught at Wade Lake, and Cliff Lake was home to the state-record rainbow trout for over 35 years. Fish are plentiful, and when lake fishing becomes boring, you'll find several blue-ribbon trout streams within a short drive.

The water is a crystal-clear emerald with huge boulders visible beneath the surface. Cliff Lake is more isolated. Its long and narrow shape is a flatwater paddler's dream, with coves to investigate and plenty of places to pull ashore and explore. If you don't have a boat, don't worry. Rentals are available from Wade Lake Cabins at the south end of Wade Lake.

There are three separate campgrounds: Wade Lake, Cliff Point, and Hilltop. Our favorite is at Wade Lake, with 30 sites from which to choose, great lake access, and two of the best public campsites in this area. It would be hard to find a better site than one of these walk-in sites without strapping on a backpack and hiking boots. You can access both walk-in sites from the northwest corner of the parking area near the boat launch. Marked with an inconspicuous sign, these treasured sites are about 50 yards from the parking lot. Both spacious sites overlook the lake and are fairly well hidden from the rest of the campground. Another perk for those lucky enough to snag one of these sites is access to a trail leading to the rocky shoreline and a perfect place to park your canoe or just enjoy your surroundings.

If the tent-only sites are not available, there are many other great choices among the remaining 28. Head for the northwest corner of the loop and choose one of the sites on the outer edge of the loop for views of the lake. These sites should be quieter than the others, but they are a bit tight. With a little ingenuity you'll be set up and enjoying the serenity in no time.

The smallest campground of the trio is Cliff Point, with six campsites on Cliff Lake. All sites sit in the open with little shade, and views from each are grand. The road is rougher here, and the sites are loosely defined, but each does have a picnic table and fire

KEY INFORMATION

ADDRESS: Madison Ranger District
5 Forest Service Road
Ennis, MT 59729

OPERATED BY: Beaverhead-Deerlodge National Forest

INFORMATION: (406) 682-4253; www.fs.fed.us/r1/b-d

OPEN: June–Labor Day

SITES: 54 total

EACH SITE HAS: Picnic table, fire grate

ASSIGNMENT: First come, first served; no reservations

REGISTRATION: On-site self-registration

FACILITIES: Water spigots, vault toilets, boat launch

PARKING: At campsites

FEE: $9

ELEVATION: 6,217 feet

RESTRICTIONS: **Pets:** On leash only
Fires: In fire rings only
Alcohol: Permitted
Vehicles: 30-foot length limit
Other: 16-day stay limit; bear country food-storage restrictions; no-wake boating restrictions; campground host

MAP

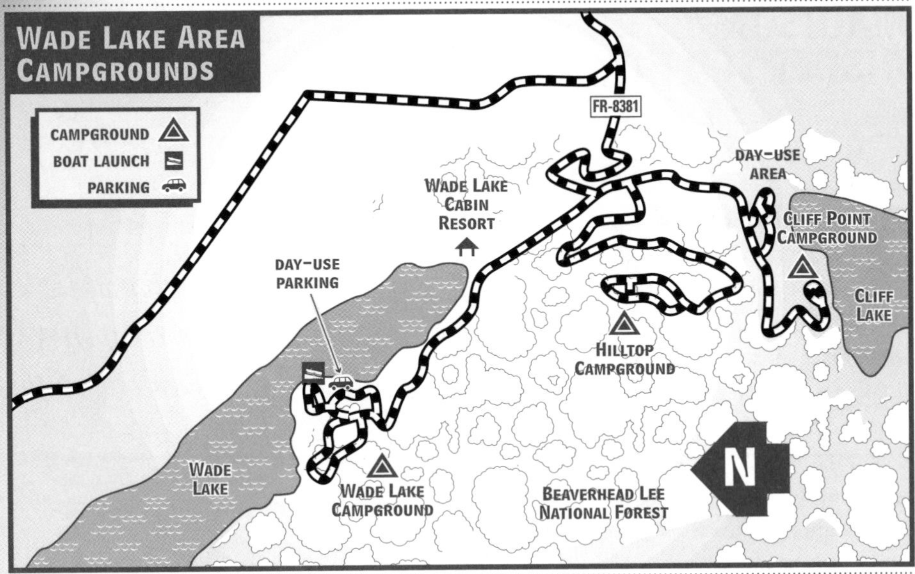

GETTING THERE

From Ennis, take US 287 south for 39.5 miles to FR 8381. Turn right and go 6 miles to the campground.

ring. The campground has a single vault toilet and a water spigot.

Hilltop offers 18 nicely spaced campsites set in a mixture of pines. Sites vary, with some offering great shade cover and others partially open to the sun, wind, and views. From Hilltop, a 0.7-mile interpretive trail winds to Wade Lake Campground. Information about the flora, fauna, and geology of the area is only the beginning, since you'll also see plenty of wildlife. Moose, in particular, are frequently observed along the lakeshores at dusk and in the early morning.

WEST FORK MADISON DISPERSED SITES

Cameron

TUCKED BEHIND A natural rise and isolated from the neoprene-clad anglers on the Madison River is an out-of-the-way road lined with a string of little-known campsites. Just off MT 287, you'll discover this scenic back road where five spacious sites are spread along a 5.5-mile stretch of river frontage. The West Fork Madison River runs cool, clear, and fast, from the Gravelley Range to where it dumps into the Madison River at Lyons Bridge. Brown and rainbow trout are becoming plentiful again, but they're smart—they've had lots of practice outfoxing wily anglers.

Fishing the West Fork or the Madison itself is far different than it was in the late 1980s. Back then counts of over 3,000 rainbow trout per mile were not uncommon, and some days drift boats far outnumbered the cars along the highway. But when whirling disease came to Montana, it hit the Madison and its branches first. The rainbow population was the hardest hit, dwindling to less than 20 percent of its previous number. With strong mitigation efforts, a flood of educational material for anglers and boaters, and impressive research results, the rainbows have come back in many areas.

Campsites here are primitive, and you will need to do more advance planning than you will for the more developed campgrounds. None of the sites has water, metal fire rings, or picnic tables, and not all have vault toilets. What they do have is plenty of space and privacy, beautiful views, and prime fishing access. Each site is marked with a 4-foot-tall, 4-inch-wide fiberglass post with a tent-camping symbol and number near the top. These designate the turnoffs for the individual sites. If you're heading to one of these sites, be familiar with low-impact camping practices to reduce your footprint on the land. In addition, most of these sites have deeply rutted access roads that can make

> *This string of little-known campsites sits along an out-of-the-way road.*

RATINGS

Beauty: ✩ ✩ ✩ ✩ ✩
Privacy: ✩ ✩ ✩ ✩
Spaciousness: ✩ ✩ ✩ ✩ ✩
Quiet: ✩ ✩ ✩ ✩
Security: ✩ ✩ ✩ ✩
Cleanliness: ✩ ✩ ✩

KEY INFORMATION

ADDRESS: Madison Ranger District
5 Forest Service Road
Ennis, MT 59729

OPERATED BY: Beaverhead-Deerlodge National Forest

INFORMATION: (406) 682-4253; www.fs.fed.us/r1/b-d

OPEN: June–mid-September

SITES: 5

EACH SITE HAS: Rock fire ring

ASSIGNMENT: First come, first served; no reservations

REGISTRATION: None

FACILITIES: No water, other facilities vary

PARKING: At campsites

FEE: Free

ELEVATION: 6,000 feet

RESTRICTIONS: **Pets:** On leash only
Fires: In fire rings only
Alcohol: Permitted
Vehicles: RVs prohibited
Other: 16-day stay limit; bear country food-storage restrictions; pack-in/pack-out

things tricky in wet weather. Stay in the ruts as best you can and avoid making the problem worse by driving off the established track.

Site 1 is on the east side of the road and requires four-wheel drive to handle the steep drop down to the site and the crawl back up. This site is bordered by cottonwoods and lies very near the water, with beautiful views of several 9,000-foot peaks to the west and the Madison range to the east. The only improvement provided is a rock fire ring. Bring your own water, and if you're not prepared to dig your own latrine, pass up this site and try one farther south.

Site 2 sits along the West Fork in a serene and peaceful spot. There is a rock fire ring here and plenty of space to spread out. Don't let the high weeds around the concrete latrine fool you—it's cleaned and supplied on a regular basis. The road into the site is rough, and the site has been well used over the years, but it's worth the jaunt. Think of it as bouncing your way to a little piece of heaven.

Site 3 is a beautiful site with all (okay, one) of the conveniences of home. High weeds surround the concrete vault toilet here, but, like at site 2, it was stocked with the essentials when we visited. This is a delightful setting in a shady grove secluded from the road. Two rock fire rings are already established here, and you'll help maintain the site by not adding a third. Be prepared with a fly rod or a good book to make the most of a stay at this site.

Site 4 is another gem, at the end of a rough spur road. It has great river access, plenty of shade, and enough flat ground to make finding a place to rest your head under a star-soaked Montana sky a cinch. The trade-off? No vault toilet; sorry.

Site 5 sits on the west side of the road in a large open area, but you'll find shade along the edge of the tree line. You'll cross a rickety bridge to get here, but the access just enhances the privacy. A concrete vault toilet and large rock fire ring have been added for your convenience.

If these sites are full, head back toward the highway and try one of the seven sites at West Fork Campground. You'll still have great access to the river but

MAP

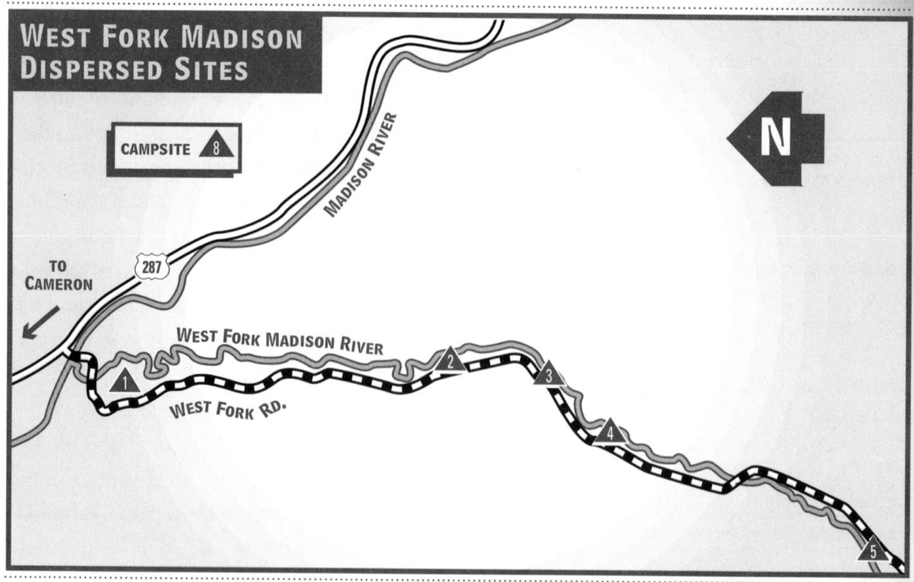

will sacrifice the privacy offered by one of the dispersed sites.

GETTING THERE

From Ennis, take US 287 south for 34 miles. Turn right on West Fork Road and go west. Cross the river and watch for campsite markers.

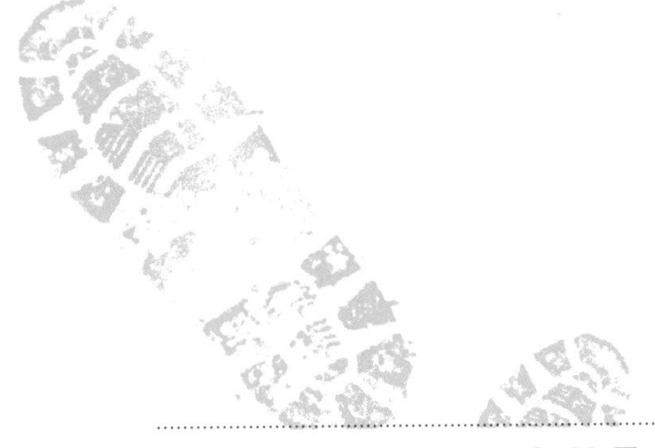

SOUTHWEST MONTANA

BANNACK STATE PARK CAMPGROUND

Dillon

A NONDESCRIPT GUIDEBOARD with letters scratched into it was nailed to a post along a rutted road. It read "tu grasshopper digns 30 myle keep the trale nex the bluffe." This simple message led hundreds of hopeful gold prospectors to Grasshopper Creek, where they expected to find gold just like John White did in July of 1862. Within ten months the population swelled to over 5,000, and like a typical boomtown, by 1865 there were only a few hundred people left.

Claim your site in this ghost town once called 'the toughest town in the West.'

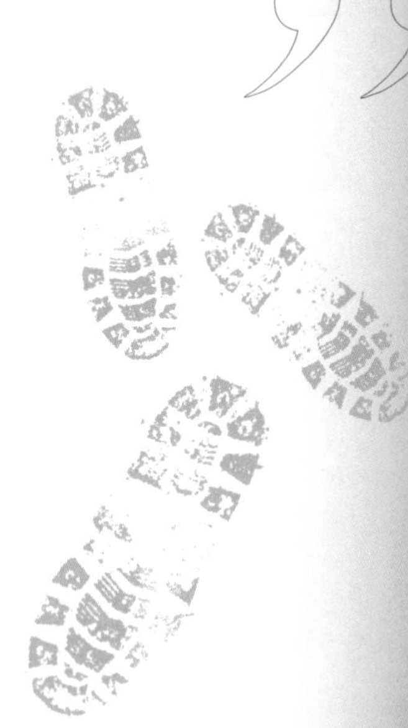

The town was named Bannack, a misspelling of the name for the local Bannock tribe. This was Montana's first territorial capital, its gold bringing more than miners, as others saw potential to make their "pile" offering goods and services to those seeking their fortunes with a pick and a pan.

Men like Sidney Edgerton, Granville Stuart, and Wilber Fisk Sanders arrived here and left their mark on Montana history in ways far beyond the riches of gold. Others, like Henry Plummer, left their mark due to greed and lawlessness. Their stories and those of countless others are recounted here by the interpretive staff, informational and interactive programs, signs, and brochures.

If you love history, you will love Bannack. This town has it all—gold mining, politics, lawlessness, romance, vigilantes, boom, and bust—and presents it in an atmospheric package that retains its dusty streets and weathered buildings. It hasn't been developed and commercialized but remains in a state of arrested decay, allowing visitors to explore the abandoned buildings in ghostly silence and create for themselves a picture of what life in the "toughest town in the West" must have been like.

Most buildings are open to the public. Some of the most well preserved are the Meade Hotel (formerly the

RATINGS

Beauty: ✩ ✩ ✩ ✩
Privacy: ✩ ✩ ✩ ✩
Spaciousness: ✩ ✩ ✩ ✩
Quiet: ✩ ✩ ✩ ✩ ✩
Security: ✩ ✩ ✩ ✩ ✩
Cleanliness: ✩ ✩ ✩ ✩ ✩

KEY INFORMATION

ADDRESS:	Bannack State Park 4200 Bannack Road Dillon, MT 59725
OPERATED BY:	Montana Fish, Wildlife & Parks
INFORMATION:	(406) 834-3413; fwp.state.mt.us/parks
OPEN:	Year-round, full services Memorial Day–Labor Day
SITES:	28
EACH SITE HAS:	Picnic table, fire grate
ASSIGNMENT:	First come, first served; no reservations
REGISTRATION:	On-site self-registration
FACILITIES:	Water, vault toilets
PARKING:	At campsites
FEE:	$12
ELEVATION:	5,790 feet
RESTRICTIONS:	**Pets:** On leash only **Fires:** In fire rings only **Alcohol:** Permitted **Vehicles:** No length limit **Other:** 14-day stay limit; visitor center; campground host; firewood for sale

Beaverhead County Courthouse), the Methodist Church, the Masonic Lodge with its first-floor schoolhouse, and the home of Fielding L. Graves (developer of the first electric gold dredge). Investigating the nooks and crannies can take hours, and a short hike along the gravel road up past the mill to Yankee Flats provides an unspoiled view of Main Street, which has barely changed in over a century. For a more structured experience, stop at the visitor center and see the video on Henry Plummer's stash of gold that has never been found. Interpretive programs are provided throughout the summer, and the third weekend in July brings the park alive with a full-scale living-history event.

The campground at Bannack sits along a creek originally named Willard by the Lewis and Clark expedition in 1805. In 1862, the creek was nicknamed Grasshopper due to the healthy population of grasshoppers along its banks, and the name stuck. The creek's clear water contains cagey brown trout that may prove elusive unless tempted with the smooth cast of a carefully matched fly.

Tent sites have been installed along the creek, giving tenters an opportunity at the choicest sites in the campground. There are actually two separate areas—Vigilante and Road Agent. The former, named after an impromptu group of folks who took the law into their own hands to control the latter, a lawless group who scammed, robbed, and murdered unsuspecting miners for their gold dust.

Our preference is Vigilante, which hugs the creek and offers sites well separated from one another. Mature cottonwoods provide shade from the same high-noon heat that must have made creek-side prospecting a welcome occupation compared to the subsequent hard-rock mining efforts on the surrounding hillsides, especially when the easy pickings from the creek played out. These sites provide a great place for a night of stargazing, with the ghosts of Bannack adding an interesting twist to your evening campfire stories.

Like so many other places in the state, the weather here can be extreme. The elevation is deceiving, since there aren't lofty mountain peaks (or many trees) nearby, but as a family that has awakened here

MAP

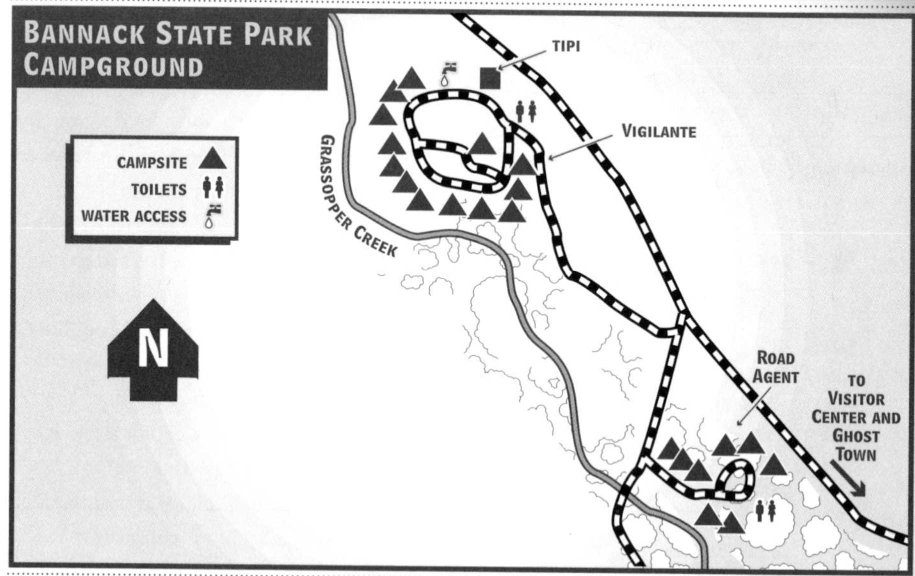

to snow in the middle of July, our advice is be prepared for scorching heat or sub-freezing temperatures no matter what the weather report says.

If you're looking for something a little different, consider leaving your tent in the trunk and trying the tipi that is available for rent at the campground. It's large enough to fit six comfortably and will take you on a journey to the days before gold was discovered and the riches of the area were found in the distant call of a coyote or ghostly hoot of an owl.

GETTING THERE

From Dillon, take I-15 south to exit 59. Go 17 miles west on MT 278. Turn left at the park sign and go 4 miles south to the campground.

Stevensville

CHARLES WATERS CAMPGROUND

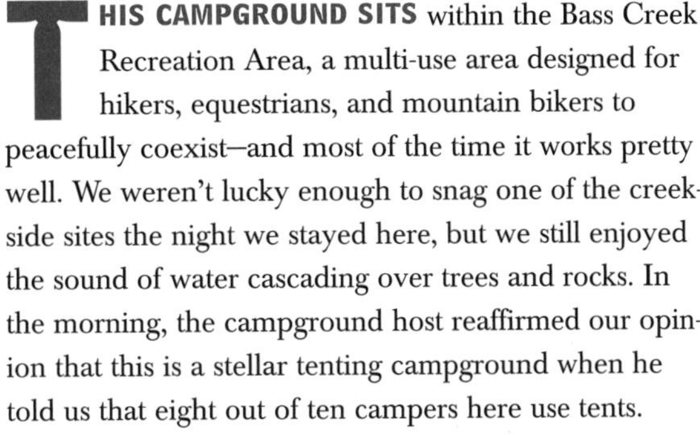

Even if you don't snag a creek-side site, you'll still be able to enjoy the sound of water cascading over trees and rocks.

RATINGS

Beauty: ☆☆☆☆
Privacy: ☆☆☆☆
Spaciousness: ☆☆☆☆
Quiet: ☆☆☆☆
Security: ☆☆☆☆☆
Cleanliness: ☆☆☆☆☆

THIS CAMPGROUND SITS within the Bass Creek Recreation Area, a multi-use area designed for hikers, equestrians, and mountain bikers to peacefully coexist—and most of the time it works pretty well. We weren't lucky enough to snag one of the creek-side sites the night we stayed here, but we still enjoyed the sound of water cascading over trees and rocks. In the morning, the campground host reaffirmed our opinion that this is a stellar tenting campground when he told us that eight out of ten campers here use tents.

Sites 12, 18, 20, 22, or 25 are the best, providing you with a creek-side stay and a spur trail leading to the water. Bass Creek is narrow here, and the water is clear, enabling you to see the cutthroat trout even though there are a lot of trees lying in the creek bed to provide cover for them. It may be wise to steer clear of sites 13 and 15, at the end of the loop road, unless you have a large group or don't mind being close to one. The sign in front of site 14 indicates its capacity is between 12 and 20, and a large open field in front is perfect for throwing Frisbees or a noisy game of softball.

A second campground, Larry Creek, is 1 mile down the road and part of the Bass Creek Recreation Area. This is a group-only area set in a stand of mature trees and may be the nicest Forest Service group site we've found in our travels. If you're still looking for a site, this might be your answer. On the road into Larry Creek, before you get to the campground, on the right are a couple of secret sites tucked on a short spur road. It's easy to miss them, but they're well maintained and provide fire rings and tables. And if you don't mind a short trek to Charles Waters to get water and use the restrooms, you'll be in great shape.

An extensive network of trails lies within the recreation area, and many trails lead into the adjacent Selway-Bitterroot Wilderness. A short spur leads from the campground to Bass Creek Scenic Overlook and is a great way to start the day. From here, Trail #392 is a 3-mile ridge trail. For those seeking to get in better shape, a quarter-mile fitness trail offers workout stations. Those seeking education can choose the half-mile nature trail. Another interpretive trail, the 2.5-mile fire-ecology loop, provides information about the initial impact and long-term effects of fires in the forest. The fire-ecology trail extends into the 6.5-mile day-use trail that offers a gentle hike and several spurs, so you create an individualized route. Hawks, deer, and great horned owls are frequently seen here, as are mountain bluebirds.

The day-use and fire-ecology trails are open to horses and mountain bikes as well as hikers, so if you're looking for a more serious hike, try Bass Creek Trail #4, a 16.8-mile round-trip along the creek to Bass Lake. Mountain bikes may share the trail for the first 2.5 miles, but at that point the trail enters the Selway-Bitterroot Wilderness, where bicycles are prohibited. From this point you will still see horses but probably not as many. Along this segment, the canyon begins to gradually narrow as you are treated to meadow views, rare in the Bitterroot forest, and several gentle waterfalls. The lake itself nestles in a deep canyon, and anglers can try their luck at catching rainbow and cutthroat trout.

Four miles south on US 93 is Kootenai Creek Road. Drive 2 miles west to find the trailhead for Kootenai Creek Trail #53. This well-used trail parallels the route of Trail 4 but follows Kootenai Creek to North and South Kootenai Lakes. Another option is the 4.5-mile hike to St. Mary Peak Lookout #116, which begins south of Stevensville off St. Mary's Peak Road.

To the east of Stevensville is Lee Metcalf National Wildlife Refuge. Named for a long-time Montana senator who grew up in the area, the refuge provides nearly 3 miles of nature trails that wind through river bottoms and meadows. A short, paved path leads through the wildlife-viewing area to a scenic spot on the Bitterroot River, and there is also a scenic drive along Wildfowl Lane that runs the length of the refuge. Bald eagles and osprey nest here, and more than 100 other species are on the confirmed nester list.

KEY INFORMATION

ADDRESS: Stevensville Ranger District
88 Main Street
Stevensville, MT 59870

OPERATED BY: Bitterroot National Forest

INFORMATION: (406) 777-5461; www.fs.fed.us/r1/bitterroot

OPEN: May–September

SITES: 26

EACH SITE HAS: Picnic table, fire grate

ASSIGNMENT: First come, first served; no reservations

REGISTRATION: On-site self-registration

FACILITIES: Water spigots, vault toilets

PARKING: At campsites

FEE: $10

ELEVATION: 3,690 feet

RESTRICTIONS: **Pets:** On leash only
Fires: In fire rings only
Alcohol: Permitted
Vehicles: 35-foot length limit
Other: 14-day stay limit; bear country food-storage restrictions; pack-in/pack-out; campground host

MAP

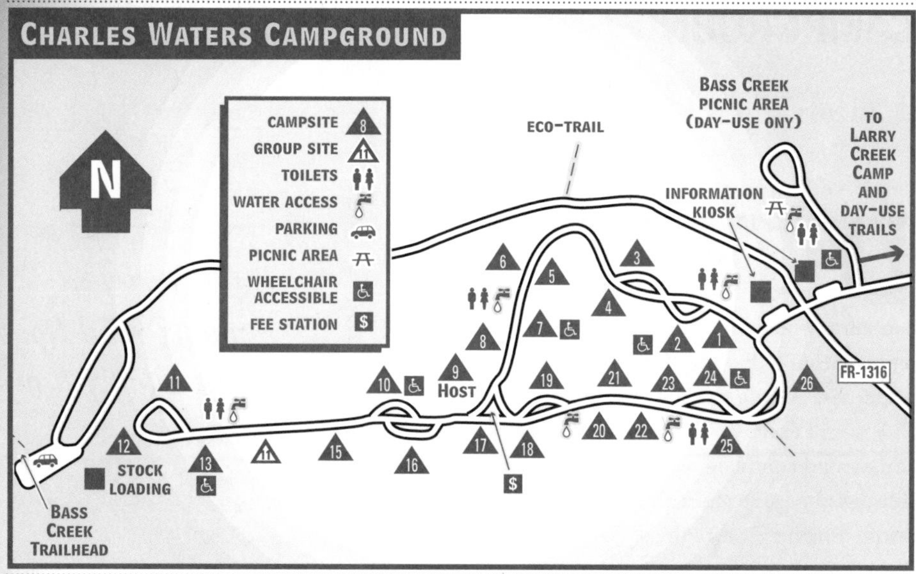

GETTING THERE

From Missoula, take US 93 south for 25 miles. Turn left (west) on Bass Creek Road (CR 20) and go 2 miles to the campground. Parking is at the parking area on Forest Service Road 1316.

From Stevensville, take US 93 north for 5 miles. Turn right (west) on Bass Creek Road (CR 20) and go 2 miles to the campground. Parking is at the parking area on FR 1316.

In the middle of it all is the state's oldest town, Stevensville (population 8,645). It was here in 1841 that Father Pierre DeSmet established St. Mary's Mission. The mission's early years were fruitful; however, by 1850 the missionaries decided to close the mission temporarily. At the same time, Philadelphia native John Owen arrived in the area and took over the mission site, building a trading post and fort. It would be 16 years before the missionaries returned to build a new mission. The "new" mission complex still stands and is open for tours during spring and summer, while the remains of John Owen's trading post are now owned by the state and preserved as Fort Owen State Park.

DALLES CAMPGROUND

Clinton

DALLES IS TO TENT CAMPING what Rock Creek is to fly-fishing—paradise. Set along the creek between steep cliffs, with views of the Sapphire Mountains, this campground may be small, but its location and access to world-class fishing and wilderness areas make it worth the trip. And the trip to Dalles isn't easy; you'll travel down a narrow, rough access road complete with hairpin turns and one-lane sections alongside sheer drop-offs. July and August are prime time here, since the somewhat marshy conditions caused by spring snowmelt dry up and the mosquitoes move on.

Dalles is to tent camping what Rock Creek is to fly-fishing—paradise.

With only ten sites, Dalles is often full, but if you arrive early in the afternoon, especially on a weekday, you'll have a good chance of getting a site. The setting is perfect—steep cliffs rising from the forest floor, views of rugged peaks waiting to be scaled, and the rushing waters of Rock Creek calling below. Each site overlooks the creek, and while some are better situated than others, all have unique features that make them a grand choice for tenting.

Campsites sit on both sides of the road, but the most desirable sites are the three with direct access to Rock Creek. These sites—4, 6, and 8—are definitely the prime ones, since they lie along the steep bank that can be negotiated for some early-morning or after-dinner casting. Parking for site 1 is right along the road. Pull off as far as you can and walk the hillside into this secluded little site, which offers a table, fire ring, and an area to set up a small tent. Restrooms are right behind it. Sites on the opposite side of the road have the advantage of sitting on a slight rise above the road, giving them an added bit of privacy. And it still isn't too far or difficult to access the creek.

Camping along Rock Creek and Forest Service Road 102 is limited to established campgrounds and a

RATINGS

Beauty: ✩ ✩ ✩ ✩
Privacy: ✩ ✩ ✩ ✩
Spaciousness: ✩ ✩ ✩ ✩
Quiet: ✩ ✩ ✩ ✩ ✩
Security: ✩ ✩ ✩
Cleanliness: ✩ ✩ ✩ ✩

KEY INFORMATION

ADDRESS: Missoula Ranger District
Building 24-A
Fort Missoula
Missoula, MT 59804
OPERATED BY: Lolo National Forest
INFORMATION: (406) 329-3814; www.fs.fed.us/r1/lolo
OPEN: Mid-May–September
SITES: 10
EACH SITE HAS: Picnic table, fire grate
ASSIGNMENT: First come, first served; no reservations
REGISTRATION: On-site self-registration
FACILITIES: Water, vault toilets
PARKING: At campsites
FEE: $6
ELEVATION: 4,200 feet
RESTRICTIONS: **Pets:** On leash only
Fires: In fire rings only
Alcohol: Permitted
Vehicles: 32-foot length limit
Other: 14-day stay limit; bear country food-storage restrictions; pack-in/pack-out

series of designated dispersed sites. Dalles is our pick as the best of the established spots, and we've included information about the 15 dispersed sites at Rock Creek in a separate listing (see page 151) to encourage you to try one, especially if there are no sites available here.

The fish in Rock Creek are cagey. They are fished frequently and have become mischievous. A catch here takes skill, patience, and plenty of plain old luck. But who could ask for a better competition arena? Abundant streamside undergrowth fills with wildflowers throughout the summer, and the scenery is spectacular.

Throughout the Rock Creek Corridor and elsewhere west of the Continental Divide, you may see small plastic items stapled 10 to 12 feet high on the tree trunks. Designed to be as unobtrusive as possible, they house repellents, as part of the Forest Service's response to bark-beetle infestations that have impacted hundreds of thousands of acres across the state. Ordinarily, the beetles feed on dead trees, but with the number of recent forest fires, much of the deadfall and undergrowth has been burnt out, so they've turned to live trees for food, taking a devastating toll on remaining forests. Trees under severe stress due to years of drought are unable to produce sap and natural repellents, so they easily fall prey.

A mile and a half north of Dalles is the Welcome Creek Wilderness Trailhead. Trail 225 starts by crossing a suspension bridge over the creek and then follows the creek before climbing to the top of Cleveland Mountain. Additional trails cross the dramatic canyons, heavily forested slopes, and rocky ridges of this 29,000-acre designated wilderness area, but this is the most popular trailhead.

Gold was discovered in Welcome Creek in 1888, and placer mines quickly evolved and almost as quickly played out, but not before one of the largest gold nuggets ever found in the state—close to 1.5 pounds—was discovered. Following the miners were fugitives who took refuge in the steep terrain, establishing hideouts and disappearing into the wilderness. It has been over a century since the miners left, but the weathered remains of several cabins can still be found in unexpected spots across the landscape.

MAP

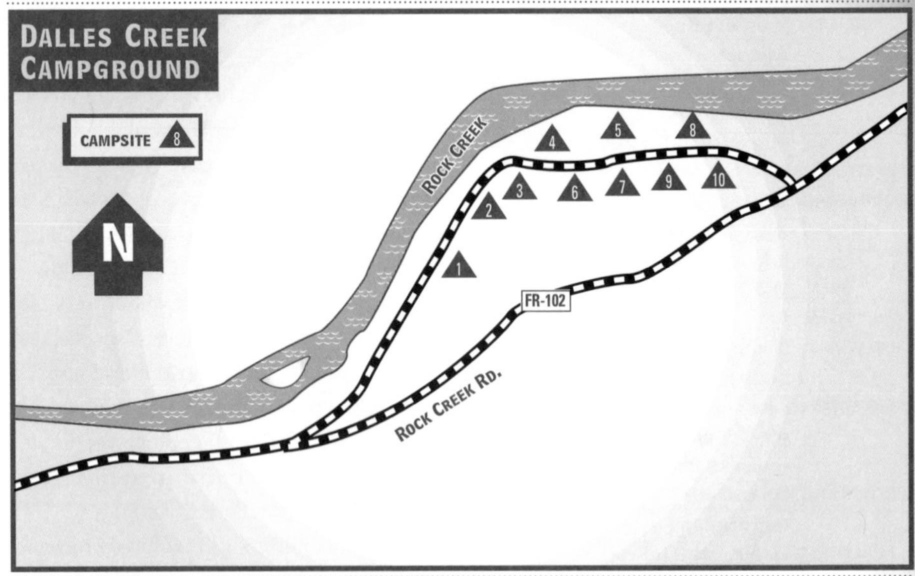

Two miles south of I-90 is the trailhead for Valley of the Moon Nature Trail, a half-mile level path that winds through a creek-side grove of cottonwood trees, habitat for elk, deer, and a wealth of birds like red-naped sapsuckers and yellow warblers. Interpretative signs along the trail explain the geological and natural history of the Rock Creek corridor, aiding amateur geologists in their exploration of this visual wonderland of sedimentary and volcanic rocks.

A few miles farther south is Babcock Mountain, an excellent spot to view the bighorn sheep that come here during their April to mid-June lambing seasons. An interpretive sign at the trailhead describes what makes good bighorn sheep habitat.

GETTING THERE

From Clinton, take I-90 east for 5 miles to exit 126 (Rock Creek). Go south on Forest Service Road 102 for 14.5 miles to the campground.

GRASSHOPPER CAMPGROUND

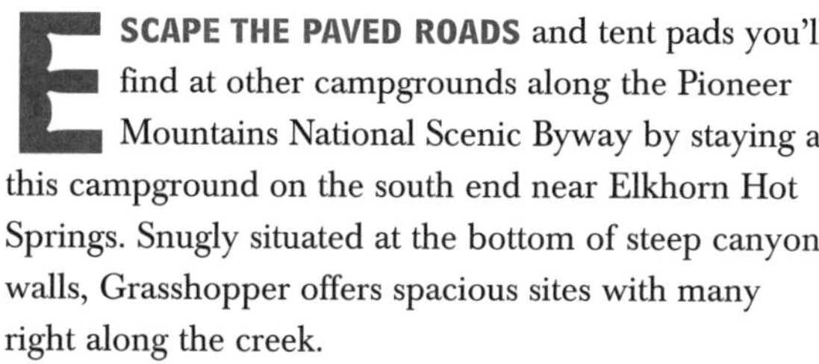

Spacious creek-side sites tucked at the bottom of steep canyon walls beckon campers.

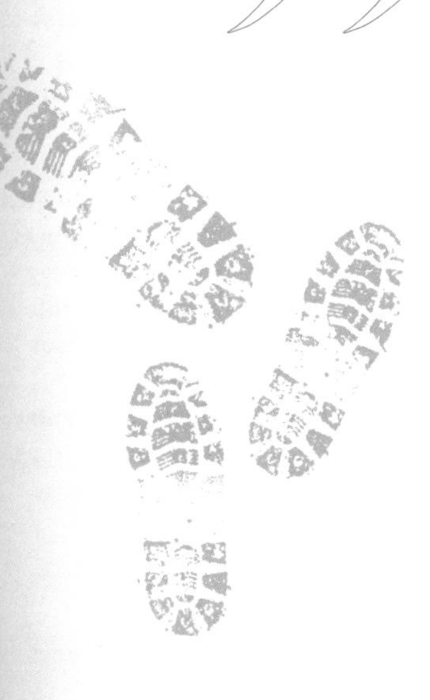

RATINGS

Beauty: ✩ ✩ ✩ ✩ ✩
Privacy: ✩ ✩ ✩ ✩
Spaciousness: ✩ ✩ ✩ ✩
Quiet: ✩ ✩ ✩ ✩
Security: ✩ ✩ ✩ ✩
Cleanliness: ✩ ✩ ✩ ✩

ESCAPE THE PAVED ROADS and tent pads you'll find at other campgrounds along the Pioneer Mountains National Scenic Byway by staying at this campground on the south end near Elkhorn Hot Springs. Snugly situated at the bottom of steep canyon walls, Grasshopper offers spacious sites with many right along the creek.

Pioneer Mountains National Scenic Byway, designated in 1989, is a picturesque ribbon of road winding between the 10,000-foot-plus peaks of the East Pioneers and the lower forested slopes of the West Pioneers. Fifty peaks exceed 10,000 feet, topping out with Mt. Tweedy, at 11,154 feet in the eastern range. As close as these ranges are to one another, they bear little resemblance, with one gently rounded and the other sharply peaked. The difference lies in the amount of sandstone that has been eroded away from the granite surface below. Overall, the Pioneers are a rugged range dotted with lakes, laced with hiking trails, and well worth exploring.

Both Wise River and Grasshopper Creek weave from side to side along the highway, split by a 7,800-foot divide about halfway down the highway. The Wise River runs north, draining into Big Hole River near its namesake town, while Grasshopper Creek originates high in the mountains and runs south for 50 miles, passing through nearby Bannack State Park before emptying into the Beaverhead River. Fishing here focuses on brook, rainbow, and cutthroat trout.

The setting is peaceful, with the gentle sound of Grasshopper Creek, lack of road noise, and scent of pines providing idyllic surroundings. Sites 9 through 17 hug the creek bank and provide a great place to rest after a day of exploring all the area has to offer. Our favorite sites are 9, 10, 11, and 12. Each is situated along the creek and offers a feeling of seclusion. If these sites are already taken, try sites 15, 16, or 17, and you will still be along the creek. Even if the creek-side sites aren't available, any of the sites here will work; they're all spacious and suitable for tents.

A short walk from the campground to the northeast (you could take the car but . . .) leads you to Elkhorn Hot Springs. The pools, built in 1918, offer hot waters to sooth tired, aching hiking muscles, and while facilities are rustic and basic, it's a charming step back to the 1920s, when wealthy tourists first discovered the region.

If you want to do some hiking, there is a trailhead 2 miles east of Elkhorn Hot Springs on Willman Creek Road (Forest Service Road 7441). Sawtooth Lake Trail #195 is an 8-mile out-and-back hike to a mountain lake where the unusual golden trout is the main draw. Some sections of this trail are a bit steep, but the switchbacks help.

The trailhead for Blue Creek Trail #425 is just north of Grasshopper. This 7-mile hike is fairly level and interesting enough to keep kids entertained (especially with all of the lovely creek crossings). For those seeking something more strenuous, Brown's Lake Trail #2 begins at Mono Creek Campground (just north of the hot springs). It will take you 6 miles up to Tahepia Lake. The key word here is *up,* with two sections containing most of the 2,500-foot elevation gain.

Riding the backbone of the West Pioneers is Pioneer Loop National Recreation Trail #750. This 35-mile loop can be accessed from various spur trails and is well worth the time and preparation needed for a few days of backpacking.

Eleven miles north of the campground is Crystal Park, one of the most unusual public-access sites operated by the U.S. Forest Service. Visitors are actually encouraged to dig for treasures beneath the soil, and every day throughout summer you'll see visitors of all ages on their hands and knees, armed with hand trowels, searching for a cache of six-sided quartz crystals and amethyst.

An alternative to Grasshopper is a secluded site at Boulder Creek, located in about the center of the Byway. Drive to the end of the main campground road

KEY INFORMATION

ADDRESS: Dillon Ranger District
420 Barrett Street
Dillon, MT 59725

OPERATED BY: Beaverhead-Deerlodge National Forest

INFORMATION: (406) 683-3900; www.fs.fed.us/r1/b-d

OPEN: Mid-June–mid-September

SITES: 24

EACH SITE HAS: Picnic table, fire ring

ASSIGNMENT: First come, first served; no reservations

REGISTRATION: On-site self-registration

FACILITIES: Water spigots, vault toilets

PARKING: At campsites

FEE: $8

ELEVATION: 6,900 feet

RESTRICTIONS: **Pets:** On leash only
Fires: In fire rings only
Alcohol: Permitted
Vehicles: 25-foot length limit
Other: 14-day stay limit; pack-in/pack-out

MAP

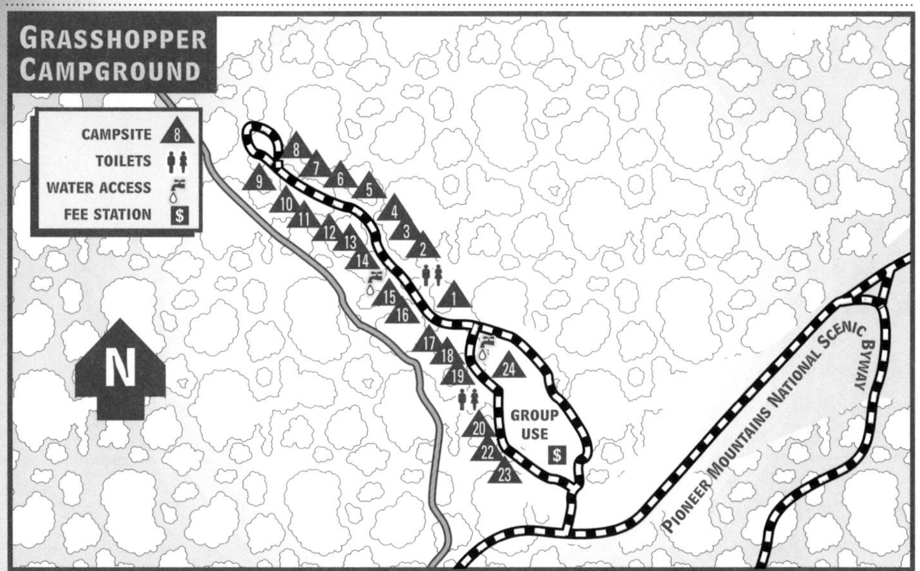

GETTING THERE

From Wise River, from MT 43, go south for 37.5 miles on the Pioneer Mountains National Scenic Byway to the campground.

From Dillon, take I-15 south for 3 miles to exit 59. Go 27 miles west on MT 278 to the Pioneer Mountains National Scenic Byway. Turn right and go 11.5 miles north through Polaris to the campground.

at the end of the loop. Look for the primitive road sign and bump your way about 1,500 feet along deep ruts. Just before the road turns to the right and starts to head uphill, you will find the site nestled among a stand of pines to your left, on the creek bank. This is a primitive site with no picnic table. Use Leave No Trace practices and take the time to walk to the main campground to use the restroom facilities.

LOST CREEK STATE PARK CAMPGROUND

Anaconda

A CRYSTALLINE CREEK flows through this narrow canyon creating an unexpected oasis in a landscape scarred by the mining fury of the past. Dwarfing the creek bed on either side are 1,200-foot limestone and granite walls, which provide habitat for mountain goats and bighorn sheep. Interpretive signs are strategically placed to educate visitors about the area's unique geology, which dates back 1.3 billion years. Colorful bands of gray and pink granite, originated as molten magma, forced its way into fissures and deposited a wealth of mineral resources.

> *A crystalline creek in this narrow canyon creates an unexpected oasis.*

This quiet place adjacent to the Beaverhead-Deerlodge National Forest and the town of Anaconda includes a 25-site campground that is split between sites on the upper and lower portions of the park road. The upper sites sit on an "island" at the end loop of the entrance road. The sites here are very tight, and only a few have a level spot on which to comfortably pitch a tent. Set on the inside of this loop, site 1 is roomy, with the tent and picnic area set slightly below the parking area. Site 6 is protected by large boulders and has plenty of level tent space but does sit very close to the road. Lost Creek Falls is visible from these sites, and a paved walking trail leads to the base of limestone cliffs below the 50-foot waterfall.

Sites 10, 11, and 12 run along the creek. Each is well shaded, has enough space to pitch a tent, and provides dramatic views of the towering rock walls. Mule deer and black bears frequent the area, particularly in spring, but it is the possibility of seeing bighorn sheep or mountain goats on the ledges or moose along the creek at dawn and dusk that is the main draw.

Mountain goats may also be visible from the designated pullout area where you enter the park. You might be fortunate enough to witness a pair of bighorn rams going at it like linebackers, but you'll probably

RATINGS

Beauty: ✩ ✩ ✩ ✩
Privacy: ✩ ✩ ✩ ✩
Spaciousness: ✩ ✩ ✩
Quiet: ✩ ✩ ✩ ✩
Security: ✩ ✩ ✩ ✩
Cleanliness: ✩ ✩ ✩ ✩ ✩

KEY INFORMATION

ADDRESS: Region 2
3201 Spurgin Road
Missoula, MT 59804

OPERATED BY: Montana Fish, Wildlife & Parks

INFORMATION: (406) 542-5500; fwp.state.mt.us

OPEN: May–November

SITES: 25

EACH SITE HAS: Picnic table, fire grate

ASSIGNMENT: First come, first served; no reservations

REGISTRATION: None required

FACILITIES: Hand-pump well, vault toilets

PARKING: At campsites

FEE: Free

ELEVATION: 6,000 feet

RESTRICTIONS: **Pets:** On leash only
Fires: In fire rings only
Alcohol: Permitted
Vehicles: 23-foot length limit
Other: 14-day stay limit; bear country food-storage restrictions; pack-in/pack-out; campground host

hear the crashing of their horns long before you see them slamming into each other at full speed. Rocky Mountain bighorn sheep are well suited for the Lost Creek area. Their specially shaped hooves cling to the rock faces in ways that many rock climbers can only dream of, and their superior eyesight insures that they'll see you well before you focus your binoculars. The best viewing times are in winter and spring, although occasional summer sightings do occur.

The lower sites are well designed for tents, with extremely level and spacious layouts. These sites lack the views available from the upper campground, but they compensate with a creek-side location. There are no designated parking pads here, so you may find vehicles parked somewhat haphazardly.

All campsites are located near the narrow park road; however, the thick understory and winding road help alleviate both noise and speeders. The temperature here is often cooler than in nearby Anaconda, since the window of direct sun during the day is severely limited by the shadows cast by the canyon walls.

Hiking is limited to an abandoned roadway near the end of the park road. This path meanders along the creek for 6 miles, making it a good out-and-back hike.

Mining is what brought this area to the world's attention back in the late 1800s. Anaconda, like Butte, began as a company town for copper magnate Marcus Daly, where he built the "Old Works" smelter to process ore from the Butte mines. Daly spent vast amounts of his own money enticing Montana voters to establish Anaconda as the state capitol in 1894, but it wasn't enough. The city of Helena, backed by Daly's rival copper baron William Clark, won the title by 2,000 votes.

All that remains of the "Lower Works," built in 1889, is the smelter stack. At 585 feet, it is one of the world's tallest brick structures and is protected as a state park. With the mines came pollution of both the land and the water. A century later, Anaconda is one of many communities continuing to deal with the aftermath, but they've put an unusual twist on the reclamation process. Corporate, state, and federal cooperation enabled this site to become the Old Works Golf

MAP

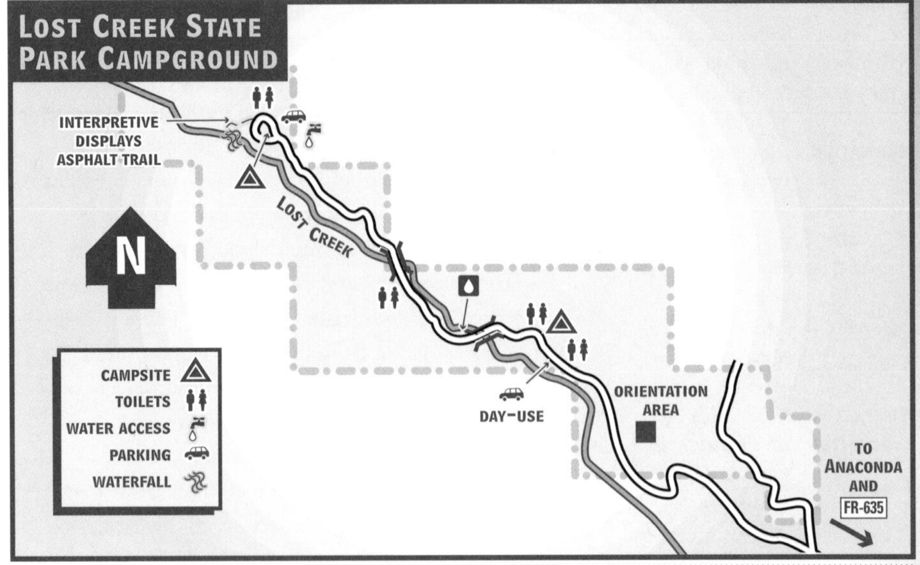

Course, a Jack Nicklaus signature course, where many of the remaining structures have been incorporated as an integral part of the world-class design.

A 1.5-mile, paved interpretive trail in Anaconda climbs above the town to provide an eagle's-eye view of the landscape's mining legacy. Also to the south is Fairmont Hot Springs, a year-round resort with Olympic-size hot pools and soaking pools both indoors and out, along with an outdoor water slide. Day passes are available, and it makes a great alternative for rainy, cold days.

GETTING THERE

From I-90, exit 208, go 5.6 miles west on MT 1 to MT 48. Turn right and go 0.25 miles to MT 273. Turn left and go north 2 miles to Forest Service Road 635. Turn left and go northwest for 7 miles to the campground. (The last 3 miles of FR 635 are gravel.)

From Anaconda, go 2 miles east on MT 1 to MT 48. Turn left and go 0.25 miles to MT 273. Turn left and go north 2 miles to FR 635. Turn left and go northwest for 7 miles to the campground. (The last 3 miles of FR 635 are gravel.)

MARTIN CREEK CAMPGROUND

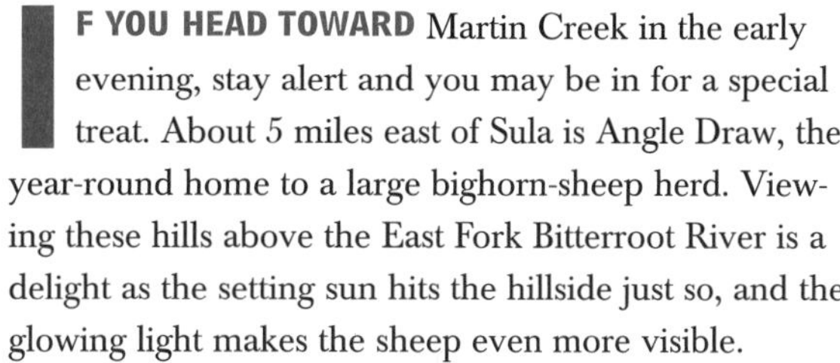

As you drive toward the campground, watch for the bighorn sheep herd at Angle Draw.

RATINGS

Beauty: ☆ ☆ ☆ ☆
Privacy: ☆ ☆ ☆
Spaciousness: ☆ ☆ ☆ ☆
Quiet: ☆ ☆ ☆
Security: ☆ ☆ ☆
Cleanliness: ☆ ☆ ☆ ☆ ☆

IF YOU HEAD TOWARD Martin Creek in the early evening, stay alert and you may be in for a special treat. About 5 miles east of Sula is Angle Draw, the year-round home to a large bighorn-sheep herd. Viewing these hills above the East Fork Bitterroot River is a delight as the setting sun hits the hillside just so, and the glowing light makes the sheep even more visible.

You'll find the BroadAxe Restaurant nearby. Initially, you might not be too impressed by the prospect of a restaurant in the middle of nowhere, but don't make the mistake of passing it up. The BroadAxe serves hearty western fare, and every table comes with a pair of binoculars. These come in handy, since the expansive window-wall overlooks Angle Draw, and diners can watch sheep, deer, and elk and maybe glimpse an occasional bear.

The landscape around you may seem familiar. This valley is the setting for Charlie Russell's impressive 25-by-12-foot painting "Lewis and Clark Meeting Indians at Ross' Hole" which hangs in the Montana State Capitol.

We rolled into Martin Creek late on a Saturday in mid-August and still had our pick of several sites. That's the beauty of Montana's southwestern corner: there are many campgrounds and dispersed sites from which to choose. Bordered by both Martin and Moose Creeks, the campground offers plenty of water frontage for everyone. We spent the night in site 5, our favorite. It's on the back of the loop for privacy, and the sound of Moose Creek ten yards away was quite inviting.

Sites 1 through 4 also border the cold-running creek, where anglers catch brook trout and waders cool off on hot afternoons. The remaining sites, 6 and 7, are well separated from each other and everyone else. Every site here is good, with plenty of room to pitch a tent and spread out. Early Sunday morning we walked a short pioneered trial just behind our camp to a small grove of massive ponderosa pines. Having already visited Big Pine fishing-access site the day before to see Montana's largest ponderosa pine, we agreed that these old brutes were not too far behind in age.

Other base camp options here include the dispersed campsite on the left just before you get to the campground and Crazy Creek Campground (off the East Fork Road west of Sula), where we also spent some time. Crazy Creek does have more of a wilderness feel than Martin Creek, but it's adjacent to an equestrian trailhead, and you may have trouble finding a level spot to pitch a tent. Overall, it's a good alternative and still close to hiking opportunities.

Forest Service Road 5765 leads to the McCart Lookout Trail. The 5.5-mile drive to the trailhead is on a rough but beautiful mountain road that is easily passable in dry conditions. Be cautious if it is wet, since the road may be slick, especially on the downhill trip. From the trailhead, it is a 1.5-mile hike to a lookout that has been retired from active fire use and is now available for rent. McCart has been restored to reflect a 1940s lookout, giving visitors a chance to experience what the original structure looked like. It is listed on the National Register of Historic Places and sits on the edge of the Anaconda-Pintlar Wilderness, offering beautiful views of the Pintlar Mountains to the east and the Bitterroot Mountains to the west.

The Chain-of-Lakes Trailhead lies past the Ranger Station, about 2.5 miles up FR 726. From here you can take a fairly strenuous, 13-mile out-and-back trail that leads to Hope, Faith, and Charity Lakes. The trailhead for Moose Creek Trail #168 is about 2 miles past the campground on FR 432. The first few miles of this trail follow the creek as it winds along the canyon.

The importance of fires within the forests is often misunderstood. Fires are a significant component of the system that keeps forests healthy, but many people see them only as a destructive force that displaces and destroys people and homes while creating a blight on the landscape. Either way, fire plays an important part in the Forest Service's rich history. In the 1930s the Forest Service began exploring alternative ways to fight

KEY INFORMATION

ADDRESS: Sula Ranger District
7338 US 93 South
Sula, MT 59871

OPERATED BY: Bitterroot National Forest

INFORMATION: (406) 821-3201; www.fs.fed.us/r1/bitterroot

OPEN: Memorial Day–Labor Day

SITES: 7

EACH SITE HAS: Picnic table, fire grate

ASSIGNMENT: First come, first served; no reservations

REGISTRATION: On-site self-registration

FACILITIES: Hand-pump well, vault toilets

PARKING: At campsites

FEE: $7

ELEVATION: 5,260 feet

RESTRICTIONS: **Pets:** On leash only
Fires: In fire rings only
Alcohol: Permitted
Vehicles: 35-foot length limit
Other: 14-day stay limit; bear country food-storage restrictions; pack-in/pack-out

MAP

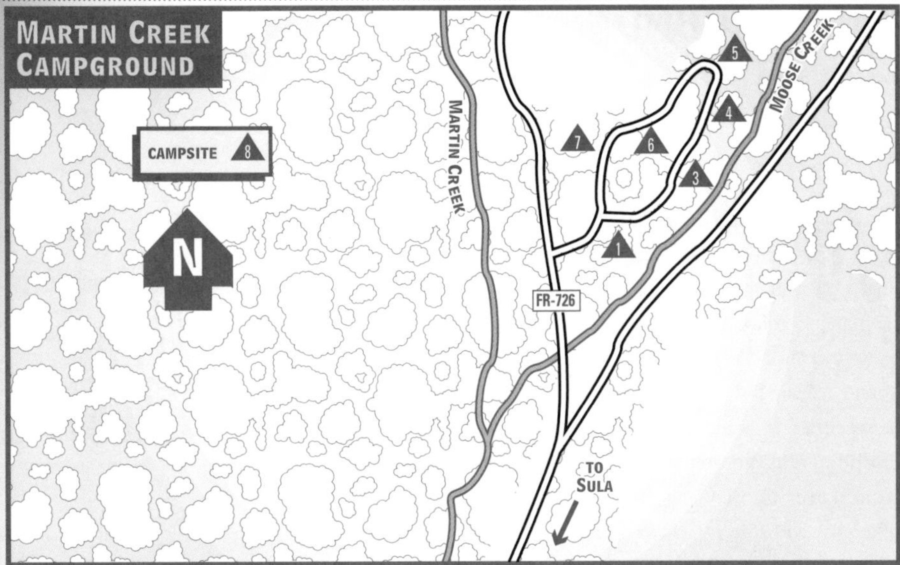

GETTING THERE

From Sula, take CR 101 east 16 miles to FR 726. Turn left to the campground.

fire to avoid another catastrophe like the Great Burn of 1910. The idea of sending firefighters in by parachute began to take shape, and by the spring of 1939, the Aerial Fire Control Experimental Project was directing all of its efforts into parachute jumping. On July 12, 1940, Rufus Robinson and Earl Cooley made the first fire jump for the Forest Service during a fire along Martin Creek.

MINER LAKE CAMPGROUND

Jackson

> *A pair of mountain lakes offers a peaceful place to relax and set up a hiking base camp.*

WITH A SCENIC DRIVE IN and access to numerous hiking trails, this pair of mountain lakes is an ideal choice if you seek a peaceful place to relax and set up a hiking base camp. The heavily wooded campground sits on the larger of the Lower Miner Lakes and offers views of the surrounding Beaverhead Mountains. There are two choices for camping, and the better one is the designated campground area on the main body of the lake. Sites are spacious, with plenty of trees, but there are enough openings that they are sunlit at least part of the day. Sites 12, 14, and 15 are the best overall, with lake views and plenty of room to spread out. Located next to the day-use area, site 11 is just as roomy with good views, but depending on the group, daytime noise may be too much for those who stay close to camp.

Campsites along the entrance road, especially sites 1 through 5, overlook a lily pad–filled section of the lakes. These sites are smaller and less private, but the bugs aren't as bad as you might expect. Nighttime temperatures at this altitude, even in the middle of summer, can get mighty cold. You could awaken to snow and then face temperatures in the 80s by midafternoon; be sure to pack accordingly.

A restriction on gas-powered motors makes Miner Lake a perfect place for canoeing. The clear green water is chillier than it looks, so your swimming time may be limited. Fishing for rainbow and Yellowstone cutthroat trout or Arctic grayling can be an excellent way of beginning or ending the day.

Since designated travel routes in the immediate area are open to motorized use, you may encounter four-wheelers or motorcycles. Travel restrictions begin 2 miles down the road, where a gate marks the trailhead and the end of the road for vehicles. The road from the campground to the trailhead is rough.

RATINGS

Beauty: ✩ ✩ ✩ ✩
Privacy: ✩ ✩ ✩ ✩
Spaciousness: ✩ ✩ ✩ ✩
Quiet: ✩ ✩ ✩
Security: ✩ ✩ ✩
Cleanliness: ✩ ✩ ✩ ✩

KEY INFORMATION

ADDRESS: Wisdom Ranger District
P.O. Box 238
Wisdom, MT 59761

OPERATED BY: Beaverhead-Deerlodge National Forest

INFORMATION: (406) 689-3243; www.fs.fed.us/r1/b-d

OPEN: July and August, full services; generally accessible June–September, depending on snow conditions

SITES: 18

EACH SITE HAS: Picnic table, fire grate

ASSIGNMENT: First come, first served; no reservations

REGISTRATION: On-site self-registration

FACILITIES: Hand-pump well, vault toilets, boat ramp

PARKING: At campsites

FEE: $7

ELEVATION: 7,000 feet

RESTRICTIONS: **Pets:** On leash only
Fires: In fire rings only
Alcohol: Permitted
Vehicles: 20-foot length limit
Other: 14-day stay limit; pack-in/pack-out; nonmotorized boats only; campground host

Hikes from this trailhead run along the eastern slope of the Continental Divide and are considered part of the Continental Divide Trail. The first mile or so is a slow uphill to a fork where you can go left and hike another 2 miles to Upper Miner Lake. Otherwise, 2 miles on the right fork take you to Rock Island Lakes Trail #54, followed by a short, steep climb to Little Lake Trail #87. If you're not dizzy from the altitude, take another steep climb to the top of the Divide and a view to the east of Homer Youngs Peak. At 10,621 feet, it's one of the tallest peaks in the West Big Hole Mountains.

This is also Nez Perce (Ne-Me-Poo) Trail country. During the summer of 1877, Chief Joseph trekked 1,100 miles over three and a half months with a group made up mainly of women, children, the sick, and the elderly. This hearty band of 750 fought over 20 battles against 2,000 troops on their doomed flight toward Canada and freedom. On August 9, the group was ambushed in a battle where both sides suffered severe casualties. The Big Hole National Battlefield outside Wisdom provides interpretive programs and access to the battlefield itself. The Nez Perce National Historic Trail runs along MT 278 in this area, and additional information is available at the Battlefield visitor center.

It's only 10 miles to the tiny town of Jackson (population 50), where everyone's water comes preheated to about 135 degrees from its hot-springs source. In 1806, William Clark dutifully recorded the facts: "This Spring contains a very considerable quantity of water, and actually blubbers with heat for 20 paces below where it rises. It has every appearance of boiling, too hot for a man to endure his hand in it 3 seconds." He then moved on to experimentation by using the springs to cook wild game. "The [piece of meat] about the Size of my 2 fingers Cooked dun in 25 minutes the other much thicker was 32 minits before it became Sufficiently dun." Today's visitors use the water for soaking and relaxing at Jackson Hot Springs and have their meals at the restaurant cooked on the stove.

As you drive throughout the Big Hole Valley, you may see large wooden contraptions that look a little like catapults sitting in the middle of fields. These are called beaver slides and were invented by two local

MAP

ranchers in 1910 to help them stack hay. Not much has changed over the past century in this "Land of 10,000 Haystacks," and you'll still see the slides being used during haying season.

GETTING THERE

From Jackson, take MT 278 south for 0.5 miles to CR 182 (Miner Lake Road). Turn right and go 10 miles west to the campground. (After 7 miles, the road becomes Forest Service Road 182 and narrows to one lane.)

PHILIPSBURG BAY CAMPGROUND

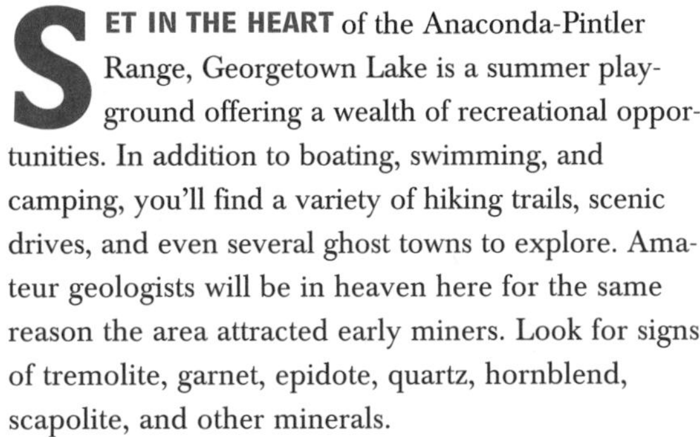

"In the heart of the Anaconda–Pintler Range, Georgetown Lake offers many recreational opportunities."

SET IN THE HEART of the Anaconda-Pintler Range, Georgetown Lake is a summer playground offering a wealth of recreational opportunities. In addition to boating, swimming, and camping, you'll find a variety of hiking trails, scenic drives, and even several ghost towns to explore. Amateur geologists will be in heaven here for the same reason the area attracted early miners. Look for signs of tremolite, garnet, epidote, quartz, hornblend, scapolite, and other minerals.

Formed in 1900 when a dam was built across Flint Creek, the lake is named for the mining town of Georgetown Flats, which was born, boomed, and died in less than 20 years during the late 1800s. Today its placer-mining remnants lie buried below the reservoir.

For tents, Philipsburg Bay is our pick over Lodgepole or Piney Campgrounds due to its thicker tree stand of conifers, wide range of campsites, and proximity to the lake. There are three loops at Philipsburg Bay, and in each of them you will be near the activity around the lake while sacrificing a fair amount of peace and quiet. Sites fill up quickly on sunny weekends, so try to set up camp early. The range of choices here offsets the minor inconveniences. Generators are allowed, but restrictions are enforced, so don't be afraid to let the campground host know if someone is violating quiet hours.

Although Loop C is the most desirable, it's also the only one that takes reservations, so the odds of getting a site without one are slim, and your neighbors will probably be large and metallic.

Loop B is the smallest of the three loops, and sites along the back end of the loop are best. Site B9 has space for two cars and there's a nice tent pad, but it is near the restroom, which can be either positive or disruptive, depending on your point of view. Site B6 also

RATINGS

Beauty: ✩ ✩ ✩ ✩
Privacy: ✩ ✩ ✩
Spaciousness: ✩ ✩ ✩ ✩
Quiet: ✩ ✩ ✩
Security: ✩ ✩ ✩ ✩ ✩
Cleanliness: ✩ ✩ ✩ ✩ ✩

has space for two cars and a nice tent pad and is more private. Sites on the inner loop are quite large, but you'll be very conscious of your neighbors. Another advantage to B6, B7, and B9 is that they put you on the back side of the loop instead of adjacent to sites from loop A.

In Loop A you'll find more RVs, since there's more room to maneuver, but for the most privacy, head for sites A7 through A10, A12, A14, or A16, where you won't have another camper right in your backyard.

You'll see many boats on the lake, especially on weekends, and fishing for kokanee salmon and rainbow trout draws anglers to the shores and secluded coves. The day-use area is very popular, especially in July and August, but during the week the crowd thins out.

At the southwest corner of the lake you can access a leisurely hiking trail going either east or west, and two major trailheads for several trails leading into the Anaconda-Pintler Wilderness are also within about an hour's drive. You can reach both by traveling west on MT 38 (Skalkaho Highway), past mile marker 46, and turning left at Moose Lake Road. From there it's 10 miles to the Moose Bridge Trailhead or 15 miles to the Middle Fork Trailhead.

On days when you're looking to expend a little less energy, drive 11 miles north on MT 1 to Philipsburg, a historic mining town named after mining mill manager Philip Deidescheimer. (Thankfully they used his first name and not his last.) Today, the entire town is a national historic district and retains much of its late-1800s architecture. It's a good destination for a dreary day, particularly for those in the mood to shop. Several antique stores are supplemented by a dynamite candy store and a nationally renown sapphire gallery (both closed on Saturdays). In deference to the 20 ghost towns within a 50-mile radius, the county museum is also home to the Ghost Town Hall of Fame.

If you find the surroundings a bit too crowded at Philipsburg Bay, consider Springhill Campground, 10 miles south on MT 1. While it's not on Georgetown Lake, it is a nice alternative and is close enough to easily get to the lake during the day. Springhill is set in a mixture of ponderosa pine, willows, and thick brush

KEY INFORMATION

ADDRESS: Pintler Ranger District, 88 10-A Business Loop, Philipsburg, MT 59858

OPERATED BY: Beaverhead-Deerlodge National Forest

INFORMATION: (406) 859-3211, www.fs.fed.us/r1/b-d; reservations (877) 444-6777, www.reserveamerica.com

OPEN: Mid-May–September

SITES: 69

EACH SITE HAS: Picnic table, fire grate

ASSIGNMENT: First come, first served; reservations accepted

REGISTRATION: On-site self-registration

FACILITIES: Hand-pump well, vault toilets, beach, boat ramp

PARKING: At campsites

FEE: $12t, $5 per additional vehicle

ELEVATION: 6,416 feet

RESTRICTIONS: **Pets:** On leash only
Fires: In fire rings only
Alcohol: Permitted
Vehicles: 32-foot length limit
Other: 14-day stay limit; bear country food-storage restrictions; campground host

MAP

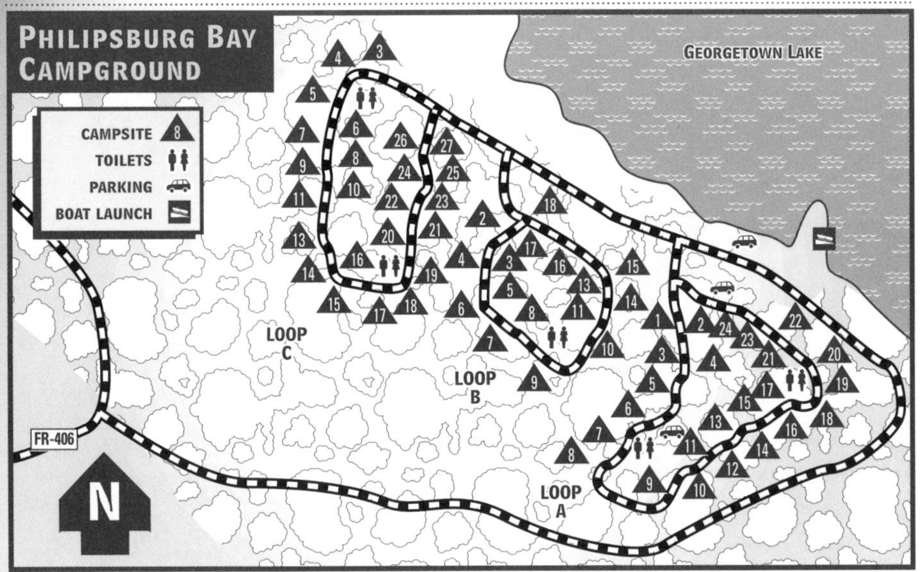

GETTING THERE

From Philipsburg, take MT 1 south for 11 miles to Georgetown Lake Road (Forest Service Road 406). Go west for 1.7 miles to the campground.

along a creek. Site 10, the pick of the campground, is set off from others on the outside of the loop. Site 12 also sits on the outside, with a spacious tent area and views of the surrounding area, which makes for a nice morning wakeup. A loop trail starts behind site 3 and ends behind the campground host's site, offering early risers a chance to enjoy a short hike with their first cup of coffee.

RESERVOIR LAKE CAMPGROUND

Dillon

SET ON A 45-ACRE LAKE in a narrow slice of the Beaverhead-Deerlodge forest, this campground is a quiet respite after a beautiful, albeit bumpy, 60-mile drive from Dillon. On the drive, you'll pass through sagebrush plains and grasslands and may begin to doubt that there is a forest at the end of the road, but the Beaverhead Mountains loom ahead of you, and your campsite will be only 3 miles as the crow flies from the Idaho-Montana border and the Continental Divide Trail. The access road is part of the designated Nez Perce National Historic Trail and follows a portion of the route used by Chief Joseph as he valiantly attempted to lead the Nez Perce across the Canadian border to safety.

"Your campsite will be only 3 miles as the crow flies from the Idaho–Montana border and the Continental Divide Trail."

The Beaverhead portion of the forest and the mountain range are named after a rock near Dillon that the Shoshone called Beavershead, because it resembled the head of a swimming beaver. It was a significant landmark recognized by Sacajawea when she accompanied the Lewis and Clark Expedition and has been preserved as a state park 13 miles north of Dillon, on MT 41.

Another explorer, Canadian Alexander Ross, was in charge of Fort Walla Walla for the North West Company until it merged with the Hudson's Bay Company, and he was sent on an expedition to provide more detail about the Snake River country. During April, October, and November of 1824, he traveled and camped in this area until crossing Gibbon's Pass and reaching the Bitterroot Valley, which would eventually be named Ross' Hole.

Most sites at Reservoir Lake are well spaced. Only sites 8 and 11, on the inside of one of the loop roads, feel crowded. Our favorites are sites 9 and 10, since each is large and has a nice view of the lake through the trees. Site 15 is roomy as well and set on a high

RATINGS

Beauty: ✩ ✩ ✩ ✩ ✩
Privacy: ✩ ✩ ✩ ✩
Spaciousness: ✩ ✩ ✩ ✩ ✩
Quiet: ✩ ✩ ✩
Security: ✩ ✩ ✩ ✩
Cleanliness: ✩ ✩ ✩ ✩ ✩

KEY INFORMATION

ADDRESS: Dillon Ranger District
420 Barrett Street
Dillon, MT 59725

OPERATED BY: Beaverhead-Deerlodge National Forest

INFORMATION: (406) 683-3900; www.fs.fed.us/r1/b-d

OPEN: Mid-June–mid-September

SITES: 16

EACH SITE HAS: Picnic table, fire ring

ASSIGNMENT: First come, first served; no reservations

REGISTRATION: On-site self-registration

FACILITIES: Hand-pump water, vault toilets, boat launch

PARKING: At campsites

FEE: $8

ELEVATION: 7,065 feet

RESTRICTIONS: **Pets:** On leash only
Fires: In fire rings only
Alcohol: Permitted
Vehicles: 16-foot length limit
Other: 16-day stay limit; pack-in/pack-out

spot overlooking the lily pads on the southwestern end of the lake. This site is in the open and perfect for those seeking the early morning sun and clear views of the night sky. Sites 16 and 17 sit by themselves on a short spur road. There is ample space between these and sites 12 and 13, on the inside of the second loop road. Shy away from site 7; it has a good view but is near the outhouse and day-use parking lot.

Don't leave the canoe behind when visiting this campground. You will probably want to paddle the lake's shimmering, clear water. Swimming sessions may be short, as the water remains cold well into summer, but the day we were here the chilly temperature was not much of a deterrent for swimmers young and old. Fishing is for brook trout and can be just as successful from the shore as from a boat.

A motor restriction on the lake helps keep things quiet, but you will encounter motorized vehicles like ATVs and motorbikes in the surrounding area, since some forest roads are open to motorized use. Notices requesting riders to push their machines out of the campground before starting them up are posted, but this rarely happens. However, most drivers are respectful and travel at slow speeds. We found that the vehicles didn't intrude too much on the quiet, and we still think the setting and general serenity outweigh the occasional distraction.

Bloody Dick Creek runs to the west of the lake and offers fishing for mountain whitefish and brook and rainbow trout. Both the creek and nearby Bloody Dick Peak (9,817 feet) were named for an early English settler named Richards who liberally sprinkled his conversation with the very British adjective "bloody." About a half mile from the campground is another namesake for Mr. Richards, Bloody Dick Cabin. This one-room cabin is available for rent from the Forest Service for those who might opt for a bunk bed and a roof.

A variety of trails beckon hikers and bikers alike. Eunice Creek Trail #157 provides access to the Continental Divide Trail, and Trail #77 runs north on a ridge above the creek. A shorter but still steep trail heads northeast from the campground to Selway Mountain, where the views across the Divide are dramatic.

MAP

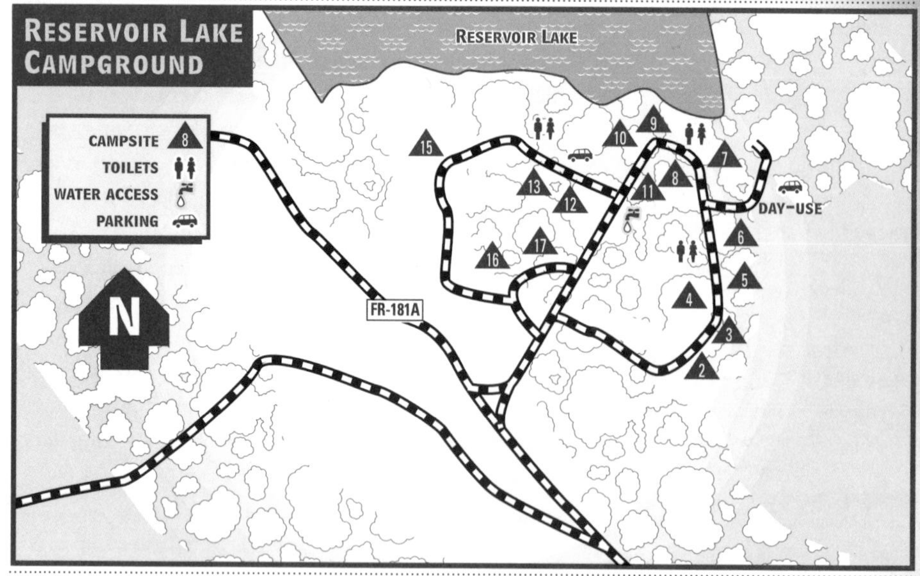

GETTING THERE

From Dillon, take I-15 south for 19 miles to exit 44. Take MT 324 west for 17 miles to Forest Service Road 181. Turn right and go 18 miles to the campground.

Clinton

ROCK CREEK DISPERSED SITES

This is a primitive fly-fishing paradise.

RATINGS

Beauty: ✩ ✩ ✩ ✩ ✩
Privacy: ✩ ✩ ✩
Spaciousness: ✩ ✩ ✩ ✩ ✩
Quiet: ✩ ✩ ✩ ✩
Security: ✩ ✩ ✩ ✩
Cleanliness: ✩ ✩ ✩ ✩

Rock Creek is fly-fishing heaven—full of cold, fast-moving water and deep pools broken by enormous boulders. A wealth of sly rainbows, browns, cutthroats, and whitefish dodge among the shallow riffles, undercut banks, and submerged vegetation. Caddis and mayfly hatches challenge anglers to peruse their fly box for the best match to present "tastefully" across the water's surface.

Rock Creek Canyon is a 50-mile corridor running south from I-90 near Clinton. This road cannot be traveled quickly, but in such a breathtaking setting, why would you want to rush? The road is narrow and rough with some hairpin turns, and RVs are strongly discouraged from traveling it. In many places it's one-lane travel close to the water's edge or another edge you may prefer to avoid. Using the many pullouts along the way as a courtesy to other drivers is a must and gives you a chance to check and see if fish are rising.

Try to arrive here well before nightfall. You'll be able to negotiate the road, enjoy the scenery, find a site, and set up camp before dark and enjoy a serene evening under the stars. Camping is allowed only in designated campsites along the corridor, and these range from the dispersed sites detailed here to more traditional, established sites (see Dalles). Using a dispersed site takes a bit more preparation, since these sites have no tables, water, or restrooms. You'll have to know the proper way to improvise your own latrine without negatively impacting the land or water, but don't let that stop you from trying it for at least a couple of nights. If you get desperate, you can always access the water and restrooms at the established campgrounds along the corridor.

If you choose to stay at one of these sites, please respect the vehicle barriers that protect fragile ground and be sure to take everything, including all garbage, with you when you leave. All mileage numbers indicated below are the distance south from I-90.

Dispersed site 1 (mile 12.6) sits within a lush mixture of firs, pines, and birch willows with thick undergrowth. The creek hugs the right-hand side of the road, with the campsite and skree slopes to the left.

Dispersed site 2 (mile 13.2) sits on a natural bench overlooking Rock Creek, and you'll find great access for fishing or wading.

Dispersed site 3 (mile 15.7) appears to be more of a parking area for anglers than a campsite. It will work in a pinch, but there are better alternatives.

Dispersed site 4 (mile 17.8) is a short pulloff along the road with a fire ring and plenty of space for a tent. A short trail from the main site leads to a tent site further from the road; you can choose either one.

Dispersed site 5 (mile 18.7) has plenty of space to spread out and get comfortable. Here you'll be close to the water and nicely sheltered from the road.

Dispersed site 6 (mile 20.9) is a roadside pulloff with good access to the creek, but it's very close to the road and offers little privacy.

Dispersed site 7 (mile 23.3) is a cozy walk-in site perfect for a small group.

Dispersed site 8 (mile 23.8) has a pull-out area for parking, and there's a short walk down to the creek-side tent site.

Dispersed site 9 (mile 24.0) is actually along Cougar Creek and on the opposite side of the road from Rock Creek. This is one of the best sites, with plenty of space and privacy and the added perks of a rock fire ring and a large bench where you can sit to enjoy your dinner.

Dispersed site 10 (mile 24.5) has a parking pulloff along the road with walk-in access to a great creek-side site.

Dispersed site 11 (mile 26.8) is a nice wide site, but access is deeply rutted and quite muddy in wet weather.

At mile 27 is the Rock Creek Microburst/Snag Viewing site. It was a pleasant day in 1989 when a sudden microburst, or tornado-like windstorm, ripped down hundreds of trees in this canyon. A roadside

KEY INFORMATION

ADDRESS: Missoula Ranger District
Building 24-A, Fort Missoula
Missoula, MT 59804

OPERATED BY: Lolo National Forest

INFORMATION: (406) 329-3814; www.fs.fed.us/r1/lolo

OPEN: Mid-May–September

SITES: Dispersed

EACH SITE HAS: Stone fire ring

ASSIGNMENT: First come, first served; no reservations

REGISTRATION: On-site self-registration

FACILITIES: None at sites

PARKING: At campsites

FEE: Free

ELEVATION: Varies

RESTRICTIONS: **Pets:** On leash only
Fires: In fire rings only
Alcohol: Permitted
Vehicles: No restrictions, but RVs are discouraged
Other: 14-day stay limit; bear country food-storage restrictions; pack-in/pack-out

MAP

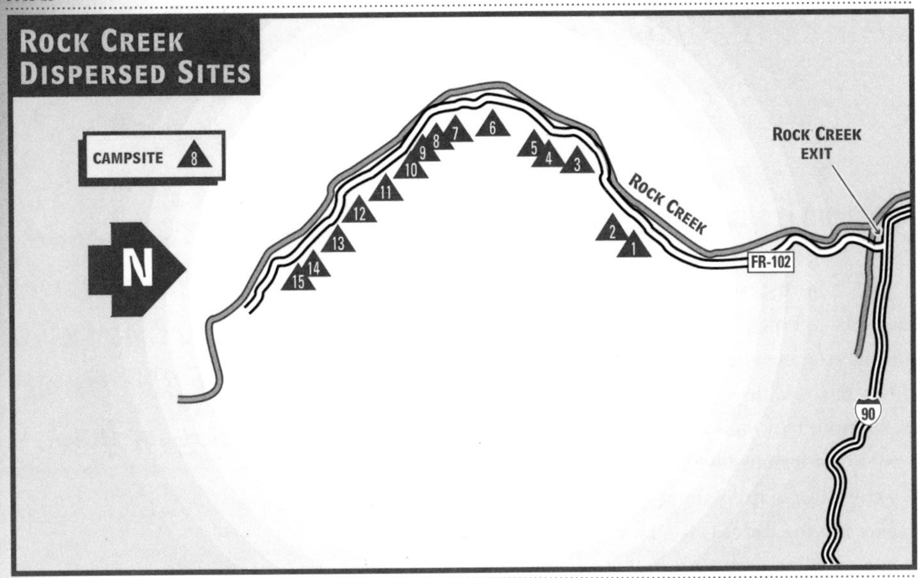

GETTING THERE

From Clinton, take I-90 east for 5 miles to exit 126 (Rock Creek). Go south on Forest Service Road 102.

interpretive sign describes how the creation of the dead trees you see here produced habitat for wildlife, especially cavity nesters such as woodpeckers.

Dispersed site 12 (mile 28.5) has a short drive-in, is farther from the creek than many of the others, and is messy in wet weather.

Dispersed site 13 (mile 30.6) is spacious, includes a fire ring, and lies just off the road on the creek side.

Dispersed sites 14 and 15 (mile 32.4) are across the road from the creek and tucked well off the road. The first is a wide but open site, while the second is tucked back in the trees for more privacy.

TWIN LAKES CAMPGROUND

Wisdom

THIS IS THE BIG HOLE river valley, famous as the land of 10,000 haystacks, where the setting sun casts its glow on endless stretches of ranchland broken only by cottonwoods lining the riverbanks and haystacks set against a glorious mountain backdrop. Early settlers used the term "Big Hole" for any wide mountain valley, and here the name stuck. It's easy to understand why the people who make this valley their home are willing to put in the long hours to make a living here. It is a land of cattle and sagebrush, a history filled with stories of gold, and fishing on one of the nation's most famous trout streams in a landscape that played an integral part in the Nez Perce tribe's 1877 flight to Canada.

Chief Joseph and the Nez Perce tribe broke camp after the Battle of the Big Hole and headed south on August 10, 1877. This hearty group would travel the length of the Bitterroot Mountains, across Bannack Pass, and well into Idaho over the next five days. Think about it: this wasn't just a group of young warriors; there were plenty of women and children, too. They had been traveling for weeks, had just fought one battle, and would walk nearly 150 miles as the crow flies across the steep mountains you see around you to the site of the Birch Creek Affair on August 15. Makes any hiking we do seem pretty simple, doesn't it?

We learned on our drive to Twin Lakes that this is a journey where you should take your time, not only because the road is rough but also because there is no reason to rush. The scenery is just too beautiful, and when we slowed down, we encountered all kinds of delights. Watch for deer—you're sure to see some. Keep an eye out for hawks and golden eagles perched in snags or soaring high above, and if you're lucky, creek crossings may reveal a Great Blue Heron looking for lunch.

If you're lucky, creek crossings may reveal a Great Blue Heron looking for lunch.

RATINGS

Beauty: ☆☆☆☆☆
Privacy: ☆☆☆☆
Spaciousness: ☆☆☆☆
Quiet: ☆☆☆☆
Security: ☆☆☆☆
Cleanliness: ☆☆☆☆

KEY INFORMATION

ADDRESS: Wisdom Ranger District
P.O. Box 238
Wisdom, MT 59761

OPERATED BY: Beaverhead-Deerlodge National Forest

INFORMATION: (406) 689-3243; www.fs.fed.us/r1/b-d

OPEN: Late June–Labor Day

SITES: 21

EACH SITE HAS: Picnic table, fire ring

ASSIGNMENT: First come, first served; no reservations

REGISTRATION: On-site self-registration

FACILITIES: Hand-pump well, vault toilets, boat launch

PARKING: At campsites

FEE: $7

ELEVATION: 7,200 feet

RESTRICTIONS: Pets: On leash only
Fires: In fire rings only
Alcohol: Permitted
Vehicles: 25-foot length limit
Other: 16-day stay limit; pack-in/pack-out

Sites at Twin Lakes are nicely spaced; the first three are located just beyond the turnoff from Forest Service Road 183. Our favorites are sites 4 through 10, with their great locations near the lakeshore allowing unimpeded access and their thick cover of pines for shade. Sites 12 through 17 are on the inside of the loop created by the main road and the campground road, and while they are great sites with good views of the lake, they are not as private as the others, and road noise and dust may be bothersome.

Twin Lakes is actually a single body of water along Big Lake Creek, and this 84-acre lake is an excellent place to use a canoe or kayak to explore or to fish from your boat for grayling and brook, rainbow, or lake trout. Those without boats can easily spend an entire day wading, skipping rocks, fishing from shore, and even swimming in the heat of the day.

Another option for anglers is to head for the west end of the lake. The creek here is particularly good with a fly rod, lightweight tippet, and a size-22 Griffith's Gnat presented upstream of a pool or along a bank undercut.

This is also an excellent location if you want to try a section of the Continental Divide Trail. Twin Lakes Trail #467 begins at the entrance to the campground and can be used as an easy 4-mile out-and-back hike, or you can keep going another 0.75 mile along pioneered routes to the Divide. To the south is Slag a Melt Creek and to the north is Jumbo Mountain.

Originally called Crossings and then Noyes, the town of Wisdom is still little more than a crossroads, but it's the closest town to Twin Lakes. A stop for a cold drink and a burger will introduce you to some of the finest and friendliest folks around, and the conversation will range from the weather to politics to local gossip. The night we stopped for dinner, they were having a community potluck. We were enthusiastically invited to join and weren't allowed to contribute either food or funds; it was a special evening of stories and laughter surrounded by great food.

MAP

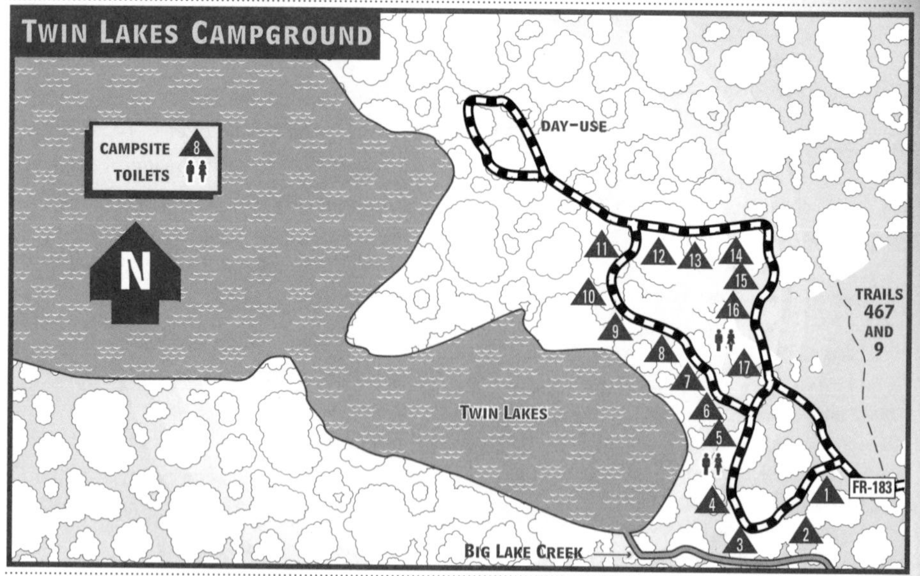

GETTING THERE

From Wisdom, take MT 278 south for 7 miles to CR 1290. Turn right and go 8 miles west to FR 945. Turn left and go 5 miles south to FR 183. Turn right and go 5 miles southwest to the campground.

UPPER LAKE COMO CAMPGROUND

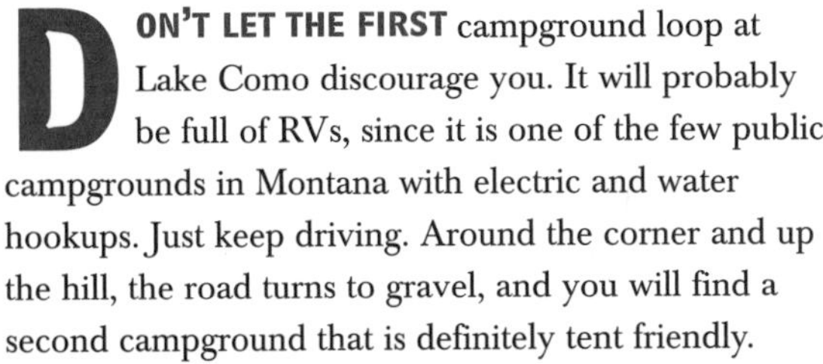

> *This camp is set within thick stands of fir and hemlock trees with views of El Capitan and Como peaks.*

DON'T LET THE FIRST campground loop at Lake Como discourage you. It will probably be full of RVs, since it is one of the few public campgrounds in Montana with electric and water hookups. Just keep driving. Around the corner and up the hill, the road turns to gravel, and you will find a second campground that is definitely tent friendly.

With the 9,000-foot-plus El Capitan and Como Peaks reflecting in the water and access to the recreational facilities on Lake Como all within walking distance, this is a busy location. Arriving here midweek may be your best bet for securing a choice spot. Set among thick stands of fir and hemlock, sites here are spacious and level, even though the campground road climbs a bit as you make your way along the one-way loop road.

Site 3 is well separated from the others but small, while site 4, farther up the road, also provides a lot of privacy along with plenty of space to spread out. Sites 6 and 7 were our least favorite, since 7 is tight on space and 6 is adjacent to the concrete vault toilet. Parking for site 8 is a little below the tent area, and this slight elevation allows a nice view and provides additional privacy. Site 10 offers a great overlook of the pond below. There's no water within the interior of the campground, so be sure to look for the available spigots off to the right just before the fee sign at the trailhead near site 1, or you can fill up in the lower campground. Even though bear-country food restrictions are strictly enforced and there is a lot of activity, you may still encounter a bear in the area. Precautionary and safety information is posted at the fee station, and the campground host will know about the latest sightings.

Cooling off in the lake is a popular pastime, and the beach and roped-off swimming area can get crowded on warm summer weekends, so stake out

RATINGS

Beauty: ✩ ✩ ✩ ✩
Privacy: ✩ ✩ ✩
Spaciousness: ✩ ✩ ✩ ✩
Quiet: ✩ ✩ ✩
Security: ✩ ✩ ✩ ✩ ✩
Cleanliness: ✩ ✩ ✩ ✩ ✩

your spot early. Motorboats and water-skiers dominate on weekends, but even then there are still quiet spots for canoes. Fishing the lake is also popular, and many try their luck at landing a rainbow trout, kokanee, Westslope cutthroat trout, or mountain whitefish.

This campground offers two great trails to explore if you're looking for a short morning hike before everyone else gets up. One is above the campground, and the other circles the pond below site 10. For a longer hike, the 7-mile Lake Como National Recreational Loop Trail starts from the trailhead near site 1 and begins with a 0.25-mile disabled-accessible surface. The section along the north shore (Trail 502) is for foot and bicycle travel only and offers wildflower meadows and views of the Como Peaks, while the southern half of the loop (Trail 580) is also open to horses, is not as scenic, and ends near the beach area. Both trails stay close to the water and provide plenty of bird-watching opportunities.

From the campground it's about 3.5 miles to the west end of the lake and the waterfall. There you can take Trail 580 to the west, instead of continuing around the lake, and travel a route along Rock Creek through a densely forested, steep canyon. The mile from the waterfall and pack bridge traverses an area in recovery from the 1988 fire, but once hikers enter the Selway–Bitterroot Wilderness, the forest becomes green again. This trail is heavily used by pack horses, but for those up to a challenge, offshoots from the rushing Rock Creek waters offer crossings that range from easy to treacherous. Plan to head back to the campground when you reach one that is beyond your skill level. Successfully crossing it once may provide an adrenaline rush, but remember you'll have to approach it again, and you'll be more tired and prone to injury. Always err on the side of caution; it doesn't make you a wimp, and it just might keep you in one piece instead of ruining a great vacation.

The entire Lake Como area has always been a significant wildlife corridor, and all hiking trails provide opportunities to observe a variety of species. Large populations of elk, moose, and white-tailed deer exist, but when there is heavy trail use, they'll be scarce.

KEY INFORMATION

ADDRESS: Darby Ranger District, P.O. Box 388, Darby, MT 59829

OPERATED BY: Bitterroot National Forest

INFORMATION: (406) 821-3913; www.fs.fed.us/r1/bitterroot

OPEN: Memorial Day–Labor Day

SITES: 10

EACH SITE HAS: Picnic table, fire grate

ASSIGNMENT: First come, first served; no reservations

REGISTRATION: On-site self-registration

FACILITIES: Water spigots, vault toilets, beach, boat launch

PARKING: At campsites

FEE: $8

ELEVATION: 4,500 feet

RESTRICTIONS: Pets: On leash only
Fires: In fire rings only
Alcohol: Permitted
Vehicles: 16-foot length limit
Other: 14-day stay limit; bear country food-storage restrictions; campground host

MAP

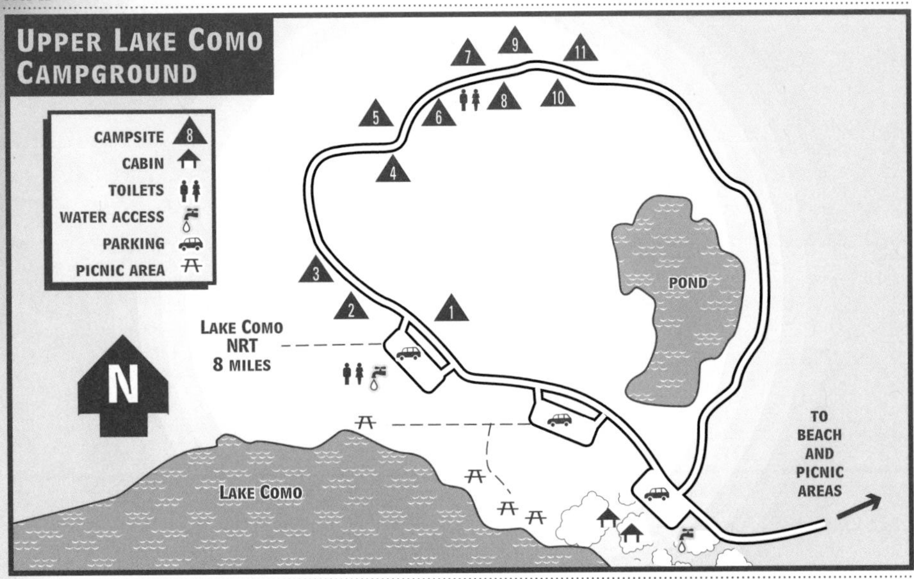

GETTING THERE

From Darby, take US 93 north for 4 miles. Turn left on CR 82 and go 4 miles west to the campground.

From Hamilton, take US 93 south for 12 miles. Turn right on CR 82 and go 4 miles west to the campground.

South on US 93 in Darby is the historic Darby/Alta Ranger Station. Open seven days a week from 8 a.m. to 5 p.m., it provides informative displays about the Depression-era Civilian Conservation Corps and Forest Service history. The helpful staff is ready and willing to answer questions and distribute information about hiking trails, recreation, and road conditions.

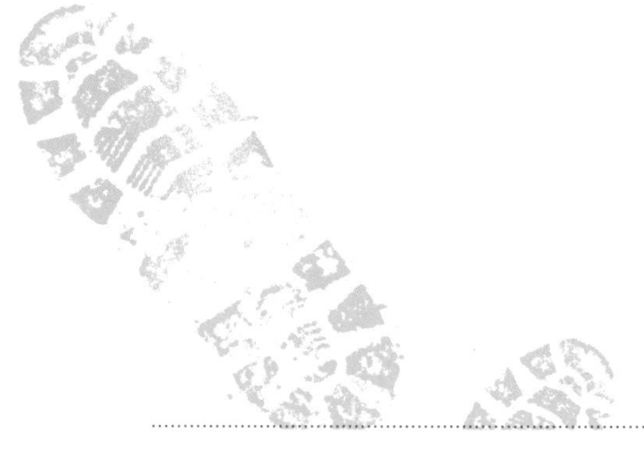

APPENDIXES **AND INDEX**

APPENDIX A
CAMPING TIPS

CAR CAMPING IS A GREAT WAY to see Montana. It offers the flexibility to stay places where others may not tread without forcing you to strap on a backpack. As you explore, please use camping techniques that will minimize your impact on the sites you use. Like the efforts of a careful backcountry camper, using these techniques will leave the site in good condition for the next person to enjoy.

Here are a few things to consider as you plan your trip:

Try to keep your group size small. If you are traveling in a large group, consider splitting up so that no more than eight people are at a campsite. Wear and tear on a site with a large group of people can be significant even if you only stay a short time.

Use care when traveling. Stay on designated roadways. Be respectful of private property and travel restrictions. Familiarize yourself with the area you will be traveling by picking up a map that shows land ownership. These maps are typically available from Forest Service offices for a small fee.

When selecting a site, consider your space requirements and match the site to your needs. Overcrowding a site increases the impact.

Avoid hanging or tying clotheslines, hammocks, and equipment on or to trees. In many developed campgrounds you may see this being commonly practiced, but be responsible and do your part to reduce damage to trees and shrubs.

Keep a clean kitchen area and avoid leaving food scraps on the ground both during and after your visit. Maintain a group trash bag and be sure to secure it in your vehicle at night. Many sites will have a pack-in/pack-out rule, and that means everything: no cheating by tossing orange peels, eggshells, or apple cores in the shrubs. Someone will find them later.

Use established fire rings and always inquire about current fire restrictions in the area. Bring your own firewood or use bundled firewood. Collect downed or dead wood only where allowed. Avoid burning garbage in your campfire, since trash often does not burn completely and, over time, fire rings will fill with burnt litter. Be sure your fire is totally extinguished when you leave the area. If you use a dutch oven, be sure to use a fire pan and elevate it to avoid scorching or burning the ground.

Grizzly and black bears are part of Montana's rich natural heritage, and by making wise choices, campers can help prevent bears from becoming conditioned to seeking human food. The constant search for food influences every aspect of a bear's life, so while camping in bear country, regulations require storage of food items in a vehicle or in site-provided bear-proof boxes. Keep food and garbage secured (including canned goods, soft drinks, and beer) and resist the temptation to take food into your tent. You also need to stow scented or flavored toiletries such as toothpaste and lip balm, as well as cooking

APPENDIX A CAMPING TIPS

(continued)

grease and pet food. Common sense and adherence to the simple rules posted in the campgrounds will help keep you and the bears safe and healthy.

If you are planning to try a dispersed site, the lack of toilet facilities and water are the biggest challenges, but bringing large, filled water jugs and a portable toilet are the easiest and most environmentally friendly solutions. A variety of toilets are available from outdoor-supply catalogs, or in a pinch, a five-gallon bucket fixed with a toilet seat and lined with a heavy-duty plastic trash bag will work just as well. (Be sure to pack out the trash bag.)

A second, less desirable method is to dig eight-inch deep "cat holes." These holes should be located at least 200 yards from campsites, trails, and water and in an inconspicuous location with as much undergrowth as possible. Be creative and find spots with a great view for you, just make sure you aren't providing the view for others! Cover the hole with a thin layer of soil after each use and do not burn or bury your toilet paper; pack it out in resealable plastic bags. If you will be in the campsite for several days, dig a new hole each day, being careful to replace the topsoil over the hole from the day before. In addition to the plastic bags, your outdoor toilet cache should consist of a garden trowel, toilet paper, and pre-moistened towelettes. Select a trowel with a well-designed handle that can also double as a toilet paper dispenser.

Avoid doing dishes and laundry or bathing in streams and lakes. Food scraps are unsightly and can be potentially harmful to fish. Even biodegradable soap can be harmful to fragile aquatic environments.

Be courteous of other campers. Observe quiet hours and keep noise to a minimum.

Most of all, leave your camp cleaner than you found it. Pick up all trash and "micro litter" in your site, including in your fire ring. Disperse leftover brush used for firewood.

APPENDIX B CAMPING EQUIPMENT CHECKLIST

Camping is more fun when you can enjoy it at a moment's notice. You never know when the opportunity may arise to head for the hills, and when it does, wouldn't it be nice to be able to pack your car with all the essentials drawn from prepacked boxes carefully cleaned, resupplied, and stored after your last trip? It's a nice fantasy isn't it? Unfortunately, it's one we've never actually experienced, but we do keep trying.

COOKING/KITCHEN

(Packed in a plastic box)
Bowls
Can opener
Cook pots with lids
Cooler
Dishcloth and towel
Dishpan
Dry-food box
Dutch oven and fire pan
Five-gallon water jug
Flatwear
Frying pan
Insulated plastic mugs
Large serving spoon
Lighter or matches
Paper towels
Plates
Pocketknife
Rain tarp or dining fly
Sharp knife
Spatula
Spices, salt, pepper
Stove and fuel
Strainer
Tablecloth
Tinfoil
Trash bags
Wooden spoon

SLEEPING QUARTERS

Ground cloth
Pillow
Sleeping bag
Sleeping pad
Tent and rain fly

MISCELLANEOUS

Candles
Day pack
Extra batteries
Firewood
First-aid kit
Flashlight
Folding camp chair
Lantern
Maps
Phone card
Premoistened towels
Reclosable plastic bags
Saw/ax
Toilet paper
Water bottles

OPTIONAL

Binoculars
Books
Camera
Cards and games
Field guides
Fishing rod
Frisbee

APPENDIX C SOURCES OF INFORMATION

ARMY CORPS OF ENGINEERS
P.O. Box 208
Fort Peck, MT 59923
(406) 526-3411
www.usace.army.mil

BEAVERHEAD–DEERLODGE NATIONAL FOREST
420 Barrett Street
Dillon, MT 59725-3572
(406) 683-3900
(406) 683-3913
(24-hour recorded information line)
www.fs.fed.us/r1/b-d

BITTERROOT NATIONAL FOREST
1801 North First Street
Hamilton, MT 59840-3114
(406) 363-7100
www.fs.fed.us/r1/bitterroot

BUREAU OF LAND MANAGEMENT
Montana State Office
P.O. Box 36800
Billings, MT 59107-6800
(406) 896-5500
www.mt.blm.gov

BUREAU OF RECLAMATION
Montana Area Office
P.O. Box 30137
Billings, MT 59107-0137
(406) 247-7295
www.gp.usbr.gov

CUSTER NATIONAL FOREST
1310 Main Street
Billings, MT 59105
(406) 657-6200
www.fs.fed.us/r1/custer

FLATHEAD NATIONAL FOREST
1935 3rd Avenue East
Kalispell, MT 59901
(406) 758-5200
(406) 758-5367 (TDD)
www.fs.fed.us/r1/flathead

GALLATIN NATIONAL FOREST
P.O. Box 130
Bozeman, MT 59771
(406) 587-6701
www.fs.fed.us/r1/gallatin

GLACIER NATIONAL PARK
West Glacier, MT 59936
(406) 888-7800
www.nps.gov/glac

HELENA NATIONAL FOREST
2880 Skyway Drive
Helena, MT 59602
(406) 449-5201
www.fs.fed.us/r1/helena

KOOTENAI NATIONAL FOREST
1101 US 2 West
Libby, MT 59923
(406) 293-6211
www.fs.fed.gov/r1/kootenai

APPENDIX C SOURCES OF INFORMATION

(continued)

LEWIS AND CLARK NATIONAL FOREST
1101 15th Street North
Great Falls, MT 59405
(406) 791-7700
www.fs.fed.us/r1/lewisclark

LOLO NATIONAL FOREST
Fort Missoula, Building 24
Missoula, MT 59804
(406) 329-3750
www.fs.fed.us/r1/lolo

MONTANA DEPARTMENT OF FISH, WILDLIFE & PARKS
1420 East Sixth Avenue
Helena, MT 59620
(406) 444-2535
(406) 444-1200 (TDD)
www.fwp.state.mt.us

MONTANA DEPARTMENT OF NATURAL RESOURCES AND CONSERVATION
P.O. Box 201601
Helena, MT 59620-1601
(406) 444-2074
www.dnrc.state.mt.us

MONTANA WILDERNESS ASSOCIATION
P.O. Box 635
Helena, MT 59624
(406) 443-7350
www.wildmontana.org

NATIONAL FOREST SERVICE
Northern Region
Federal Building
P.O. Box 7669
200 East Broadway
Missoula, MT 59807
(406) 329-3511
(406) 329-3510 (TDD)
www.fs.fed.us/r1

TRAVEL MONTANA
301 South Park Avenue
Helena, MT 59620-0533
(406) 841-2702
(800) 847-4868
www.visitmt.com

YELLOWSTONE NATIONAL PARK
Yellowstone National Park, WY 82190-0168
(307) 344-7381
www.nps.gov/yell

INDEX

C

D

E

F

I

J

K

L

M

N

O

P

R

ABOUT THE AUTHORS

KEN SODERBERG WAS BORN an avid outdoor enthusiast and has been working in the outdoor-recreation profession for nearly 25 years. Since moving to Montana in 1992, he has learned how to fly-fish and successfully guide a raft through whitewater. He has backpacked with toddlers and teenagers, and continues to seek new routes for hiking and canoeing throughout the state.

Vicky Soderberg has traveled extensively in the U.S. and Europe working as a travel writer. She enjoys wandering off the well-traveled routes. Since their move to Montana, Vicky has encountered bears in campgrounds and come up close and personal with a moose while cross-country skiing. She is the author of the "Montana Family Outdoor Guide," and co-author of "Along the Trail with Lewis and Clark."

The couple lives in East Helena, Montana, and along with their three children—Betsy, Ellen, and Tyler—have covered thousands of miles while camping across Big Sky Country.